THE DAWNING

THE DAWNING

MILKA BAJIĆ-PODEREGIN
Translated by Nadja Poderegin

A Novel

INTERLINK BOOKS
An imprint of Interlink Publishing Group, Inc.
NEW YORK

First American edition published in 1995 by

INTERLINK BOOKS
An imprint of Interlink Publishing Group, Inc.

99 Seventh Avenue
Brooklyn, New York 11215

Copyright © Honeyglen Publishing 1987, 1995

Originally published in Serbo-Croatian in Belgrade by Jugoslavijapublik, 1987
First published in English in the U.K. by Honeyglen Publishing, 1988

Library of Congress Cataloging-in-Publication Data

Bajić Poderegin, Milka, 1904–1971.
[Svitanje. English]
The dawning / Milka Bajić Poderegin: translated by Nadja
Poderegin. — 1st American ed.
p. cm. — ([Emerging voices. New international fiction])
Originally published: London: Honeyglen Publishing, c1987, 1995.
ISBN 1-56656-198-1—ISBN 1-56656-188-4 (pbk.)
1. Serbia—History—1456-1804—Fiction. I. Title. II. Series.
PG1418.B235S8613   1995
891.8'235—dc20   94-48736
                                                    CIP

Cover illustration: The Fugitives from Herzegovina by Uros Predic
Courtesy of the National Museum of Belgrade

Printed and bound in the United States of America

10 9 8 7 6 5 4 3 2 1

Contents

Foreword   vi

The Dawning   1

Glossary   328

Notes   331

Foreword

The Dawning is one of those rare novels in Serbian literature which succeed in describing the life of the population under the Turkish Empire without being burdened by religious and nationalistic prejudices and ancient conflicts.

Before 1918, the whole of Serbian literature, regardless of genre, was either explicitly or implicitly inspired by the struggle for liberation and unification. The literature expressed the Serbian peoples' view of their distant past as part of the present reality—in which they interpret the period from the defeat at the battle of Kosovo in 1389, to final victory over the Turks in 1912—as a long purification through national martyrdom under Islam. (According to folk mythology, the collapse of the medieval Serbian State was the result of the sins of the rulers and aristocracy: Prince Lazar, who led the Serbs into the battle of Kosovo, was faced with a choice between victory and the earthly kingdom on the one hand, and the Kingdom of Heaven on the other. The latter was only to be obtained through defeat, suffering, and the relentless struggle for freedom. He chose the Kingdom of Heaven, and thus determined the course of Serbian history after 1389.)

This concept of martyrdom and the struggle for freedom was deeply embedded in the literature of the centuries preceding the First World War, and a great deal of the prose that concerned itself with this past exaggerated the divide between the Christian and non-Christian populations. It usually overlooked the fact that a large part of the Muslims in Yugoslavia were Serbs who had adopted Islam, and that their old family ties were maintained for decades and sometimes centuries in those regions where there was little migration. As a celebrated example, Mehmed Pasha Sokolovic can be quoted. He was the Grand Vizier of the Sultan Suleiman the Magnificent. He was taken to Turkey as a child, converted to Islam there, and later rose to be one of the most powerful men in the Ottoman Empire. (The Nobel prizewinner Ivo Andric wrote about him in his novel, *The Bridge Over the Drina*.) It was he who renewed the Orthodox patriarchy of the Serbs in Pec and appointed his relative, Maxim, as the first Patriarch. Because the Muslim population conducted many of its legal affairs through its religious establishments, the renewal of patriarchy offered a similar outlet to the Serbs, and was of immeasurable benefit in preserving national integrity and homogeneity.

The action of *The Dawning* begins toward the end of the first half of the nineteenth century and takes place in Sandzak, a region whose geopolitical significance grew with the emergence of two Serbian States— the principalities of Serbia and Montenegro—which strove to reclaim this region and to establish their common frontier through it. There was at the time a distinct trend which favored the Austrian Empire as the successor to the Turks in the Balkans. Russia, on the other hand, tended to intervene on behalf of the Slav people. After the Berlin Congress of 1878, which acknowledged the sovereignty of Serbia and Montenegro but gave Austria the right to Bosnia and Herzegovina, Plevlje, the town where the story takes place, found itself under the dual rule of a Turkish civilian presence as well as an Austrian military one.

The Balkan War of 1912, which ended the Turkish domination over Greece, Bulgaria, Macedonia, and Southern Serbia, finally brought freedom to Plevlje. Although in the wake of that war, a brief armed conflict took place in 1913 between Bulgaria and Serbia over the Macedonian frontier.

The First World War marks the collapse of the Austro-Hungarian Empire and completes the historical framework of *The Dawning*. Milka Bajić-Poderegin has woven a masterly description of the customs and everyday life of a Serbian family. The story is written with lightness and clarity, and the character outlines are sharp and compelling, especially in their portrayal of the Serbian women who, like some Roman matrons, confront the hardships of their condition with stoical strength, destined to outlive not only their husbands and brothers, but their sons and grandsons too.

Djordje Janic

1

They brought her from the house of Borisavlejevic in New Town to the house of Zarkovic. The whole of Golubinja was at the roadside, some to see the bride, others her dowry, for it was rumored that she came from a wealthy home.

Loose cobblestones splintered under the hoofs of the festive wedding horses as they pranced up the steep lane, tossing their heads. Behind them the train of packhorses moved heavily, their necks low under the load that hid them so that only their legs were visible. The drivers walked alongside them, pausing from time to time to slap their flanks with a birch.

The first of the horses carried two large, leather-covered trunks with decorated metal corners. On top of these lay a patterned woven carpet, rolled up and tied with cord. The other horses were laden with bundles of bedding, oriental rugs, silver and copper dishes.

The procession stopped at the oldest of the Zarkovic houses, and the first to dismount was the bride.

Savka was barely fifteen, slight and slim-waisted, with a fair complexion, chestnut hair, and dark eyes. A long china-blue dress with a design of yellow flowers fell in thick folds to her small feet in their black kidskin shoes, and from her head the airy white veil floated down her back to the ground.

Timid and bewildered, Savka approached the main gate and took hold of the chubby two-year-old boy who was put into her arms. According to custom she raised him three times above her head, kissed him three times, and gave him back into the care of the nearest bridesmaid. Then she was handed a sieve of wheat-grain which she threw in handfuls over her head, a symbol of happiness and good fortune in the new home. Giving the empty sieve to one of her brothers-in-law, she crossed herself and moved nervously towards the gate.

The bridegroom, who had arrived earlier with the best man and the heralds, was waiting for her there. He took her hand and led her across the courtyard to the house. Walking beside him, she realized for the first time how tall he was, for she scarcely reached to his shoulder. At their betrothal, and later at the church, either from confusion or shyness, she had not had the courage to look at him, and throughout the journey they had been separated.

Tane was in his early thirties, robust and dark, with strong, clear-cut features. His suit looked as if it had been molded on him and was in the traditional Herzegovina fashion: a red *koporan* embroidered and braided in gold, and over it a jerkin so thickly trimmed with black silk braid that the petrol-blue cloth was barely visible. Round his waist he wore a multicolored cummerbund of pure Constantinople silk, the long tassels at one end falling over his dark blue *shalvare* trousers. From below the knee to the black shoes, his legs were encased in white leggings fastened at the side with golden hooks.

The crowd cheered their congratulations—"Mashallah, what a beautiful bride!"—as Tane crossed the courtyard leading Savka to the foot of the broad stone steps. There he left her with her sisters-in-law, who embraced her and took her indoors to eat and to refresh herself. Then they arranged her veil, smoothed the folds of her dress, and led her into the spacious refectory to wait upon her guests.

There at the far end of the room she remained standing the whole day long, her hands folded below her breast, dazed with fatigue and tobacco smoke and the strong aroma of the heavily spiced dishes, the spirits and wine. She felt as if she was still swaying on horseback, and her knees shook with the endless standing. The sound of cymbals and drums echoed in her ears, and pounded her into a longing to curl up in a corner and sleep.

The round tables were kept supplied with a constant variety of fresh dishes, and the feast, which was accompanied by music and song, lasted well into the night. After midnight the first to leave were the guests, then the relatives, and finally the musicians. Telling Joka, the old servant, to pay the cooks and send them away as soon as their work was finished, Tane led his bride upstairs.

The best room had been chosen for the wedding night, and some of the things from Savka's dowry were already laid out there. In the middle of the carpeted floor lay a mattress on which was a fine cotton sheet, some frilly embroidered pillows, and a lilac silk eiderdown turned up at one corner. A silver ewer, a glass, and a dish of Turkish delight stood on a low bench beside the mattress.

They stopped at the door to take off their shoes, then Tane removed her veil and, kissing her hair, carried Savka to the *secija*, or low sofa, and placed her gently on his knee. He caressed her and began to unfasten the clasps of her collar.

"No!" Savka cried tearfully, and begged him to let her undress alone. She ran across the room and hid behind the big trunk, where she crouched, slipping off her *fistan*, petticoat, and stockings. Then, in her chemise and long pantalettes, she made a dash to the mattress and slid under the eiderdown.

Tane unwound his cummerbund and feverishly pulled off the *koporan* and *fermen*. As he fumbled with the waistband of his *shalvare*, Savka whispered, "Blow out the lamp, please!" She was cowering in fear.

Wearing only his shirt, Tane came and lay beside her. He propped her head on his arm and, raising her face, began to unbutton her chemise. She tried to pull away, pressing her hands to her breast.

"You mustn't be shy, you are my wife now," he said softly. "Let me find those hidden white doves!" and tearing open her chemise he began to kiss the small round breasts. She pushed his head away, then realizing it was in vain she gave in. But when Tane tried to untie the knot of her long pantalettes, Savka struggled in terror.

Savka's pillow was wet with tears. She lay awake, staring at Tane who slept beside her, his forehead bathed in sweat, his broad, hairy chest rising and falling evenly under the crumpled shirt. This was not what, in her secret dreams, she had imagined such a night would be. Dispirited and disillusioned, her face still wet with tears, she sank into a numb and heavy sleep.

When the first blush of dawn touched the sky, Tane woke and looked at his young wife. With flushed cheeks and lips softly parted, she was breathing silently like a child. He was about to wake her and make love to her again, but seeing her sleeping so peacefully he held back, moved by an odd feeling of compassion. He lifted the eider-down and studied her thoughtfully, finding her more beautiful than he had imagined. Firm as an apple, he thought, but still green, still innocent.

Savka stirred in her sleep and turned over. One thick tress had come untied and her hair spilled over the pillow; the torn chemise revealed a smooth shoulder. Tane pressed his face into the wavy strands of her hair that smelled of flowers, and, smiling, fell happily asleep.

After they had washed and dressed, Tane showed Savka round the house, then took her to the kitchen, which was a separate building on the other side of the courtyard. He reminded her to bring some money for Joka, the present that custom demanded. Savka took her embroidered velvet purse from the trunk and put it in her pocket.

Everything in Tane's home was in the Turkish style. As the eldest son he had taken care of things after his father's death, and when the time came, had built a house for each of his brothers, opened new shops for them, and kept this house and the old shop for himself, as was the custom. By the time he had married off his brothers, his own marriage had come rather late. Now he asked Savka whether she thought him too old for her. She shook her head as she walked obediently behind him.

The house was built spaciously on two floors. At the front, on the first floor, was the *doksat*, a projecting extension of the room with large windows. All the rooms were carpeted, as was the covered out-side staircase. There were rugs on the sofas that matched the designs on each carpet, and cushions embroidered in colored wools. White-tiled stoves and an occasional stool were the only furnishings. The walls were bare except for a frieze of somber, ancient icons painted on wood. The large windows were hung with curtains of white, loosely-woven silk.

After inspecting the rooms, Tane and Savka went down to the store-rooms in the basement. Tane opened the low, heavy doors backed with iron, and proudly pointed to a quantity of barrels, earthenware pots, wooden cases, tubs, and sacks of provisions. "You can keep anything here," he said, "ham, smoked meats, cheeses, lard, pickles, peppers—anything you like! These rooms are as dry as tinder."

Savka was silent, quite unaware of her surroundings. Tane, her husband, was not the man of her dreams and this made her insensible to everything else.

They crossed the courtyard with its square, white flagstones, and entered the kitchen. Joka was there, waiting for them.

Joka had come to the house when Tane was a small boy. She had looked after him and his brothers, and after the death of their mother had taken charge of the whole household. When the brothers separated, she had been included in Tane's share, together with the house.

Now, as Savka approached, Joka bent to kiss her hand, but Savka drew back.

"No, not her hand," Tane said to Joka, "even though she is your mistress. She is too young!"

Savka went over to the hearth, crossed herself and stirred the embers with the poker, symbolizing her acceptance of her new home, and placed a large silver coin on the mantelpiece for Joka. Then, knowing what was expected of her, she looked round the kitchen.

Here the cooking was still done in a cauldron, and the baking under a *sach*, an iron lid that served as a primitive sort of oven. On the wall hung gleaming cooking pots, frying pans, coffee pots, kettles, and ladles. Under them a row of large copper dishes with covers stood on the earthen floor next to decorated water jars and earthenware jugs. On some shelves were rows of silver plates and mugs.

"You keep everything clean and in very good order," Savka said.

She followed Tane to the garden gate. As they entered she caught her breath at the beautiful sight that stretched before her far into the distance. Jasmine grew along the white wooden fence, with lilacs and mulberry trees and a row of plum trees. At the far end the ground rose in gentle waves to an old ash tree that spread its branches beside a well and spilled shadows over the velvety grass. Like a necklace of colored beads, a long flower bed cut through the middle of the lawn, while under the windows of the house carnations glowed in narrow wooden boxes, spreading their sweet scent on the fresh morning air.

Tane, cheered by seeing Savka's sadness lift, took her hand and led her to the ash tree. From there the whole of Plevlje and its outskirts could be seen. He pointed to the stables at the end of the next field. "That's where I keep Dorat, my horse. There's not another to touch him in the whole district! Every morning I walk him through the town and along the main road to the Cotina River, but once past the bridge and in the fields, we gallop all the way to Ilino Hill. He takes me like a flash of lightning! Can you see it there, in the distance, the small hill with the church on top?"

Savka nodded, but sadness had touched her face again. She turned away and went over to the carnations, picking one and putting it in her hair. Tane watched her with pleasure. Then he went and laid his hand on her shoulder, leaning close. "I'm glad you like it here," he said. "When the garden was laid out, I wouldn't let them plant anything but trees and flowers. Joka wanted onions and potatoes grown there at the bottom. She said nothing productive came out of all this land, but to me the sheer beauty of it is produce enough!"

"It's very, very beautiful," Savka said from her heart.

"You won't have much to do in the house," Tane went on. "Nobody to look after. Neither young ones crying, nor old ones coughing, as they say! So you can spend plenty of time out here when the weather is fine. I myself like to pass an hour or two here in the evenings, listening to the call to prayer from the minarets, with the wind bringing the scent of flowers."

They strolled across the garden and stopped by the well. Tane lowered the bucket, filled it, and pulled it up again. He dipped a shallow cup in the water and passed it to Savka. "Drink, and see how good it tastes. Real mountain water, always ice-cold!" He then told her how the well had been constructed, and how the water was filtered through silver-sand.

But Savka was thinking of the times she would spend out here, alone with the flowers, weaving the same dreams, although she had always known she would never again see the young man from Sarajevo. He had sent a carnation in the letter that had arrived a few days before her wedding. Unable to read, and afraid of asking anyone to read it to her, she had burned the letter. The carnation still lay hidden at the bottom of her trunk.

Tane, seeing that Savka was lost in her own thoughts and was no longer listening, took out his watch and sighed. "Breakfast time," he said. "We mustn't keep Joka waiting."

As they left, Savka turned to look once more at the garden.

The house seemed already full to overflowing, yet Tane brought home something new nearly every day. In the first month he had bought Savka a necklace of thirty-five large ducats, a *tepeluk* covered in pearls and small gold coins, and a *libade* embroidered in gold and trimmed with mother-of-pearl. In spite of all this, Savka was sad and endured Tane's caresses with difficulty, especially in the first few months. She wondered why honeymoons were so called, and she longed for her times of solitude when she could dream in peace.

When Tane went to work she would go and sit in the *doksat* and look towards Plevlje, encircled by its bare, rocky hills. She pined for New Town with its plum orchards and dense forests, and for her parents' estate in Zlatar where there were gentle pastures and clear mountain streams. She pined too for the uncles and aunts who had cared for her since she was orphaned in early childhood. The memories of the house in which she had been brought up, its elegance, the frequent trips to Sarajevo—and the young man she had seen there—haunted her loneliness. There they had dressed in Viennese fashion: sophisticated, different, not only on account of their clothes, but because of the manner in which they talked and carried themselves, even the way they smoked their fine, thin cigars. That was how she had imagined her future husband: slightly taller than herself, with chestnut hair and soft almond eyes like those of the young man she had seen. Yet—her uncles had given her to Tane.

Tane, however, never stayed long in the house, and Savka found some comfort in this. She respected him but felt timid in his presence. In the morning, she would keep him company as he dressed and at the breakfast table. At noon she would send him his lunch by one of the servant boys, then spend the rest of the day puttering around the house, helping Joka, or absorbed in her needlework. Savka embroidered shawls in gold thread, inventing her own designs of vine leaves and sprays, and pouring into them all her heartache and longing. She went to church accompanied by her sisters-in-law, and paid visits according to the established rules and traditions of the house of Zarkovic.

Tane worked in his shop and in the new warehouse he had opened after his marriage, assisted by his apprentices and a foreman who also went with him on his business trips out of town.

As soon as the Muslim priest called for afternoon prayer, Tane would close his shop and store-rooms, dismiss the boys, and walk back past the Great Mosque toward Trebovina, and from there to Citluk. He sometimes went as far as Bezdan to watch the Breznica River burst from under the rock, boiling and foaming as it tore down the narrow gulley from the mountains. He would stay there for hours, gazing up at the high crags and the four small watermills that stood in a row, one above the other beside the steep river bank, leaning against the sheer mass of Glavica. Somber with rain and time, they would have been almost invisible but for their roofs of rounded red tiles. Only when shadow covered the hills around him and began to creep towards Citluk would Tane leave for home. Once there, he would linger in the garden a little longer, waiting for dusk to fall. In bad weather he would go straight home from work, and up to his room, where he remained. Sometimes he visited his brothers, or they came to him for a chat in the long winter evenings. He never went to coffee houses or taverns, and seldom to church. Reserved in his approach to people, he was neither rude nor too friendly. He talked little to Savka and left all his tenderness toward her for the night.

In the second year of her marriage Savka gave birth to their first daughter, Jelka. Then two years later another girl, Jula, was born.

Children brought many changes to the house. Savka found in them a fulfilment and purpose in life, and Tane became gentler and more forthcoming and began to alter his routine. He came home earlier and spent all his free time with his daughters, carrying them piggyback round the house, or making them swings and playing with them in the garden. Even Joka seemed livelier. She took as much trouble with them as if they had been her own grandchildren, sharing the care of them with Savka. As time went on, Savka grew more and more fond of Tane. She came to love him as a friend, and as the bread-winner and protector, especially after the girls were born. Grateful for her motherhood, which had given her a quiet happiness, she felt an increasing new bond with Tane as the father of her children, and found pleasure in looking after him.

A steady, patriarchal harmony reigned in their house, without discord but with no exceptional joy.

One morning Tane told Savka not to send his lunch to the shop that day because he would be coming home before noon to get ready for a business trip to Cajnice, where he was meeting some men from Sarajevo. She would have to pack enough food for three days for himself and for Todor, his foreman. As soon as he had left, Savka started to make pies, roast two chickens, and cut ham and smoked pork in thin slices. She took a few hunks of cheese out of a barrel, filled two round wooden containers with a special kind of cheese spread, and put everything, including salt, onions, and peppers, into the *bisage*, a bag for use on horseback.

At noon Tane returned, accompanied by Todor. After they had eaten, and had their coffee, Tane went to rest and Todor to groom and saddle the horses ready for the trip. Savka and Joka cleared up in the kitchen, and the children ran out to play nearby.

The sun had already hidden behind the top of the big ash tree, and shadows were spreading into the courtyard when Savka said to Joka, "Shouldn't we wake him? The shade has reached the big flagstones and it will soon be too late for them to start on such a long journey."

"If they want to leave today, it's high time they were off," said Joka. "Better make some coffee and tell him to hurry."

Savka made the coffee and went upstairs. She quietly entered the room where Tane was sleeping and put the tray on a stool. Taking his hand, she gently woke him.

He opened sleepy eyes and stared at her, then started up as he remembered his trip. "I'm glad you woke me," he said. "I would have overslept."

"How can you ride in this heat?" Savka said as he sipped his coffee. "Why not leave tomorrow before dawn while it is cool?"

"I'm afraid that's impossible. The meeting is arranged for tomorrow morning and the deal is important. We must be off at once."

As Savka left the room he got up, stretched, and began to dress. Taking his money-belt out of the trunk, he tied it firmly round his waist. Over this he wore a broad leather belt with two pistols. Then he put a few coins into a purse, pulled the strings tight, and stuffed it deep down into the pocket of his *shalvare*. The key of the trunk he left on a shelf for Savka in case she should need it, then looked round the room to make sure he had forgotten nothing.

From the stairs he called Todor, who soon appeared leading Dorat already saddled. Taking the bags of food from Joka, he hung them in front of the saddle. In the courtyard, he said goodbye to Savka and Joka, and they both kissed his hand. Todor opened the gates and led the horses out into the street. Tane mounted from the mounting-block and set off, Todor in front, holding the reins.

As they turned into the school lane, Savka whispered to herself, "Safe journey!" She helped Joka to shut the gates, then went indoors. It was terribly hot and she mopped her forehead with her handkerchief, wondering how the travelers would stand it among the barren rocks and cliffs.

"I wish to God the master didn't have to leave today!" Joka exclaimed. "He couldn't have chosen a hotter one if he'd tried." She went back to her kitchen to finish polishing her copper dishes.

Savka threw all the windows open, hoping a draft might stir the stagnant air, but heat seemed to stream in from everywhere. It was impossible to tell whether it came from the earth or from the sun that burned steadily in the low leaden sky. She slipped off her bolero and, taking her sewing basket, went and sat on the narrow sofa in the *doksat*. But as she was about to thread her needle, she remembered that it was considered a bad omen to do any sewing when a member of the family was on the road, so she put her basket aside and folded her hands in her lap.

Soon the children came in. Savka washed their hands and faces in the big copper basin and changed them into fresh nightgowns, while Joka brought up their supper tray.

Suddenly dark clouds covered the sky and everything sank into a dusky blueness as heavy drops of rain began to fall.

"Quick, Joka!" Savka called. "Shut all the windows!"

Even as she spoke, thunder rolled ominously through the clouds. Darkness and torrents of rain fell simultaneously, turbulent, racked by the thunder that echoed endlessly among the mountains. Writhing fiery serpents of lightning tore the sky as Savka, wide awake with fear, crouched by her children, whispering prayer after prayer.

Around midnight, there was a furious banging on the gates of Jovo Zarkovic's house. The entire family was wakened by the noise in spite of the storm. Jovo got up and went to the window. Seeing the rain still pouring down as if the heavens were opened, he muttered to himself, "At least it can't be a fire."

Without bothering to dress, he threw a jacket over his shoulders, slipped his bare feet into the wooden slippers that lay outside the door, and hurried across the courtyard to the gates. "Who is it at this time of night?" he called.

"Todor, Tane's foreman. Please open!"

Jovo threw open one of the gates. Todor stood there, bareheaded without his fez, covered in mud and drenched to the skin. Seeing him in such a state, Jovo was suddenly seized by alarm that something might have happened to his brother. "Where is your master?" he cried.

"On . . . on the road . . . near Boljanic."

"Why there?"

"He's dead."

Jovo stared at him, motionless.

"The Turks killed him," Todor said in a frightened whisper.

Jovo grabbed him by the shoulders and pulled him into the courtyard. "What Turks, damn you?"

"We—we were ambushed and couldn't defend ourselves. They slit the master's throat, seized the gold and his horse, and set me free."

"Liar!" Jovo was shaking with rage. He dragged Todor closer and whispered threateningly—he would have shouted had it not been for

11

the Turkish patrols—"Speak up or I'll throttle you! Where is my brother?"

"Dead, I tell you! Lying on the road with his throat cut."

Glancing quickly round him, Jovo dragged Todor to the storeroom, pushed him inside and locked the door, taking away the key. His wife was waiting for him on the balcony, trembling like a leaf. Realizing that she had heard everything, Jovo led her into their bedroom and shut the door. "Stop crying!" he said. "There's no time for that now." Then he told her to go to all the Zarkovic houses, except Savka's, and tell them about Tane. He warned her to let nobody see her in the streets. The Turkish police were at the Crossroads and it would be disastrous if they heard about this. It seemed clear to Jovo that Todor was guilty, but the Turks would not arrest him alone. They would seize as many Serbs as they could lay hands on and throw them into the dungeons of the Beas Tower in Solun. It was essential to find Tane that night and bring him home before dawn. "Tell Stevo and Spasoje to arm themselves, saddle their horses, and wait for me by the Golubinja valley," he said to his wife. "But Savka must hear nothing of this till we return."

Jovo's wife was still crying, wiping her eyes with the corner of her scarf. "Calm down," he said, "and don't add to our troubles. Wait! Tell them to take an extra horse and tie some rugs over the saddle."

His wife murmured her assent and went to do his bidding. As he dressed, Jovo wondered what to do about Todor. He would have to be left where he was until Tane was brought back. Then they would see. Todor must have killed for money. The story about the Turks did not ring true. But *why* had he come back here, why not just escape? He sighed, pushed the revolvers into their belt, then went to saddle his horses.

On foot, keeping close to the houses, he led the horse until he reached Golubinja. His brothers were waiting for him. They went down to Bezdan, crossed the river, and rode alongside Mount Glavica to the main road. It stopped raining as they approached Boljanic. Unable to find any trail, they left the road again and began to search the rocky ground beside it, scanning every shadow amongst the scanty trees and shrubs.

They found Tane under a large cobnut bush. With his head thrown

12

back, he was lying in a pool of blood. They stood staring, rigid and numb.

Jovo was the first to move. He took off his fez and made the sign of the cross. "God rest his soul," he whispered. Stevo crossed himself and Spasoje began to sob.

They spread a large rug near the body, and in raising Tane's head to lift him on to it, discovered another wound on the back of his skull. The murderer, Todor, must have taken him by surprise and knocked him out while he was resting in the shade of the bush. Grimly Jovo took off his scarf and wrapped it round Tane's neck. Then the three brothers solemnly kissed his forehead and wrapped up his body, lifting it gently on to the horse's back, where they tied it securely.

They arrived at Jovo's house before dawn and carried Tane's body into the big room, locking the door. Jovo told his wife to keep the children upstairs and not to come down until he called, then he took his brothers to the pantry. After bolting the door they sat down to decide Todor's fate. He could not be tried by the Church Council because they were not allowed to deal with murder cases, but the brothers were certainly not going to hand him over to the Turkish judge. "Let us judge him ourselves," said Jovo, and his eyes were bloodshot with hate. The thirst for revenge stirred in the other two and they echoed their agreement.

They went to the store-room and unlocked it, entering silently. Only after Spasoje had lit the lantern did they see that the room was empty. The window that overlooked the garden was wide open, the bars torn away, and lying on the floor was a hatchet.

"For God's sake how did you come to overlook that?" Spasoje muttered through clenched teeth.

Speechless, Jovo stared at the window.

"We can't go after him now," said Stevo, "but if ever I set eyes on that murderer . . ."

"Nobody must know about Tane," said Jovo, pulling himself together. "We'll say he was thrown by his horse and died at once when he hit his head on a rock."

Through friends they secretly obtained everything for the burial. Tane's body was put in a coffin and the lid was nailed down, and only when daylight had settled over the town did they go to break the news to Savka.

When Savka heard how Tane died, she swayed, and without uttering a sound, fell unconscious to the floor. They splashed water over her face and rubbed her temples till she came round. She sat still, numb with grief, looking round dully with dry eyes.

Soon a crowd of people filled the house. Tane's death was mourned quietly, with suppressed sobs. A whisper that he had been killed by the Turks swept through the town, and the whole of Plevlje assembled for the funeral.

The relatives and neighbors returned to the house from the graveyard and settled in the ground-floor rooms for the night of mourning. But Savka was taken straight upstairs, too weak to stay on her feet. Joka quickly spread out the bedding and helped her undress. She lay quite still, white and rigid as a marble statue.

"Let me get you some coffee," Joka said.

Savka shook her head, frowning painfully, and closed her eyes. A stifled moan escaped her, then gradually she relaxed and tears began to run down her temples.

Joka blew out the lamp, waited a little, and quietly left the room.

When the forty days of mourning were over, Savka sent a message to Tane's brothers asking them to come over and advise her on the running of the house and estate.

After all three had arrived and exchanged the customary greetings, Savka began to speak.

"My children and I have nobody but you now our home is without its master and we are without protection." Tears began to run down her face as she continued, "We beg you to take us under your wing and care for us." Here she crossed the room to the trunk and took out two bags of money, a roll of faded papers, and a bunch of keys. Placing these before them, she went on, "Tane's money is in the big bag, and in the small one are the fifty ducats I brought with me as part of my dowry. The roll of papers are the deeds of the estate at Zlatar that was left me by my father. The keys are of Tane's shop and store-rooms. As a woman, I am not equipped to run everything, so I beg you to take it all into your hands and look after us. We will be grateful to obey you as long as we live. May God bless and reward you with happiness and health."

She stood there in front of them, her two daughters at her side, absently stroking the hair of the younger child, while tears still ran down her cheeks.

"You must try to be strong in your grief, Savka," Jovo said. "Put your faith in God. He forsakes no living creatures, from the bird in the tree to the worm in the earth. He will not leave you or your children without his grace. As for us, we will see that none of you will ever want for food or shelter. It isn't easy for you, I know. Without a master the house is empty. But there is no escape from destiny. The sky is too high and the earth too hard."

The children began to cry, and Savka took them out to Joka, gaining a little time in which to calm herself.

When she returned she refilled the men's glasses with raki and withdrew to the door, where she remained standing.

Jovo lifted the larger bag; it was heavy. "There is plenty here," he said. "We must count it." Savka protested that there was no need; she knew he would look after it better than if it were his own. "Money is for counting," he said, and spilled the ducats on the table. Placing one on top of the other, he arranged them in piles of ten. There were exactly one thousand one hundred and fifty ducats. He replaced the money in the big bag and put it next to the keys. The deeds and the smaller bag he handed back to Savka. "These are yours," he said. "Keep them and don't worry about the rest. We'll see you get everything you need."

The brothers stayed a little longer, then left. Savka, relieved of anxiety for the future, felt some comfort from their visit.

As time went on, Savka grew accustomed to her widowhood. Long ago she had learned to accept her fate, however difficult life might be. In the moments of sadness or worry she would find consolation in some kind of work. She seldom left home except to go to the graveyard, or to church on All Souls' Day, and to pay the usual visits to her sisters-in-law, though she did this less often now for fear of being unwelcome.

One day Jovo came to see her unexpectedly. Savka wondered what had made him suddenly remember her and his brother's children, though she tried not to show her surprise.

"Well, Savka," Jovo said. "How is life?"

"As God wills, praise and glory to His name."

"It can't be easy to live as you do."

"If it is my destiny, there is no choice but to endure it."

"It is not your destiny to mourn forever," he said. "You can't remain a widow to the end of your life. It's time for you to marry again."

Savka looked up in amazement, but he continued, "People are asking about you, and I've heard that you have refused offers of marriage. It's natural that you could not think of it for a year or two, but soon, on St. Ilin's Day, it will be three whole years since Tane's death, and time to put an end to your solitude."

"I can bear that," Savka said. "I have the children to care for, and the house. There is a lot of work to do in the courtyard as well."

Jovo hesitated, undecided whether to tell her the true reason for his visit. Then he came directly to the point. "We, that is all three of us, would like you to get married. Please don't think you are a burden to us—God forbid! But an unexpected opportunity has occurred to marry you off, better than anyone could wish, and it would be foolish to miss it. A wealthy businessman from New Town is asking for your hand. He is a good man, honest and respected, they say, a widower and childless." He stopped to wipe the perspiration from his forehead. "There is one thing, though. He does not want your children." He dropped his eyes and continued mechanically, "We advise you to accept. Nobody would ignore a proposal like that, not even an unmarried girl. Don't worry about your children, we will take care of them as if they were our own. It wouldn't be easy to begin with, but God may bless you with more children, and these two will take it in their stride and grow used to us. We will bring them to visit you, and you could also come to us."

Savka stood there, numb, as though struck by lightning. Then she began to twist her hands and the tears rolled down her still face. She spoke with difficulty, "I have promised to obey you, so let it be as you wish. But I beg you to give me a few days in which to calm myself and rest my eyes on my children." Here she broke down completely.

"Listen, girl!" Jovo said. "I don't mean to upset you. We only want what is best for you. You live alone, you're young, and youth has its demands: it is the law of Our Lord. In time this man will grow fond of you and feel sorry for your little ones and take them under his roof for your sake. We are not forcing you into anything. It is for you to decide and let us know."

Savka could not stop her tears, but tried to brush them away with the back of her hand. "I know you wish me well," she said.

"Cry," Jovo told her, "it will do you good. Now I'll leave you in peace to think things over. You are only twenty-five and life is long. Both your children are girls and will marry and leave you one day. Something might happen to the three of us brothers, and then what would become of you?" With these words he left her, clearly offended.

Savka stood there dazed, even forgetting to show Jovo out, then slowly went to the room where Tane's photograph hung on the wall. She took it down and sat on the floor. Swaying to and fro, she moaned a low, sing-song lament, "My Tane . . . my only friend . . . show me the way . . . tell me what to do. How can I live without my children, dearest . . . Oh, why did you leave us . . . why did you have to die by the murderer's knife?"

After a while she grew calmer and wiped her eyes with her scarf, putting the picture back on the wall. She realized that her brothers-in-law were afraid she would be a burden on them one day and wanted to marry her off. Life is short, Jovo had said, and that was true. If her children married there would indeed be nothing left for her but to hang around their homes, or be pushed from one sister-in-law to another. And what was she to them? An outsider, not of their blood. There was no choice but to marry. She stared before her, oblivious of herself and her surroundings.

Then, with a start, she tried to collect the thoughts that were slowly forming at the back of her mind. Jovo said this suitor was a good man and might become fond of her. After all, Tane had grown to love her, and she was still young and easy-natured. She would look after him well and he would begin to be sorry for her children and let them come to her. They must be patient for a while, but they might not have to wait very long.

That evening she sent Joka with a message accepting the proposal.

It was decided to keep the news of Savka's wedding from her children and to hold the ceremony in Jovo's house, since it was the furthest away. The preparations began a whole week beforehand. Savka's brothers-in-law spared no expense: it was as if they were giving away their own sister. Their wives made plenty of pies and other dishes, enough to entertain the whole of New Town.

On the appointed day the groomsmen arrived at Jovo's house and a messenger was dispatched to ask Savka to come there for the traditional receiving of the engagement ring.

She sent the children off to one of Tane's relatives for the night, and as soon as they had left she began to dress.

Arranging her hair around the headdress, she put on a *fistan* trimmed with lace, and draped a shawl of white Venetian lace across her shoulders, fastening it on her breast with a spray of diamonds. Over this she wore the *libade*, and was on the point of choosing some rings from her mother-of-pearl jewel casket when her children's cries reached her ears. Terrified, she rushed to the window and threw it open. The two little girls were running up the steep road, screaming and tearing their hair. She stood frozen, unable to move until they came bursting into the room. Seeing their mother all dressed up, their cries grew even louder and they threw themselves at her feet.

"Don't leave us, Mother, don't!" They clung to the rich folds of her *fistan*, their hair disheveled, cheeks burning, and tears pouring down their faces.

Savka knelt and put her arms around them, weeping with them. She kissed them and stroked their hair, her heart torn by indecision and despair. Then, resolutely, she drew them closer and made her decision. "There, there, calm yourselves," she said. "Don't be afraid, your mother will never leave you, come what may."

She helped them to their feet, then put her jewels back in the casket. Taking off the *libade* and the *fistan*, she dressed herself again in her black clothes. With infinite care she replaced everything in the trunk where it would stay till her death. The jewelry would then go to the two girls and the clothes would dress her for her burial.

She called Joka and asked her to take a message to her brothers-in-law to beg them to forgive her, but she could not come, neither would she ever marry and leave her children.

18

As soon as the Zarkovics received her message, all three hurried over to try to persuade her that it was impossible to back out now. Savka remained silent but unshaken. Infuriated, Jovo began to shout; his eyes burned into Savka's. "Aren't you ashamed, leading us on like this so that we can never look these people in the face again? What about the expense—both theirs and ours? Everything is ready for the ceremony to begin, how can they go back to New Town now?" As Savka remained silent he went on, "And all this trouble because of those two good-for-nothings! Do you think they will bother to ask you how you will manage when *they* get married? How did they find out, damn them?" He turned to them and they pressed closer to their mother in terror. "Speak up, you two!" he shouted. "Who told you about the wedding?"

The younger child hid behind her mother while the elder, still sobbing, told how they had met a group of girls by the fountain at the Crossroads. When they caught sight of the two children, they began to laugh and whisper, and one of them had called out that their mother was to be married. "She will go off to New Town and leave you behind, shame on her!" the girl had cried.

Tane's brothers exchanged looks. After a tense pause they went silently away.

Nobody ever knew how things were put right with the grooms-men. They left the town quietly at dawn to avoid being seen. Savka's brothers-in-law never mentioned the matter again.

From that time on, Savka withdrew into utter solitude. She began to save and cut her household expenses by half. Vegetables were planted in the flower garden, and she started to rear chickens in Dorat's stable. Her life was wholly devoted to her children and she brought them up as well as she knew how.

And time flowed on: the days subtly weaving into months, the months into years. The children grew, gaining in strength, while Savka's youth slowly faded.

2

From an early age Jelka was noted for her beauty. She was tall, like her father, with tawny hair and large dark eyes. From Savka she inherited her slender waist and white, silky-smooth skin. Her joyous nature and high spirits had, from her fifteenth year, caused worries for her mother, who kept her on a tight rein and did not allow her further than the garden gate. Jelka would meet her girl-friends there in the evenings to watch the young men as they strolled along the cobbled street and exchange a few words with them. Seen most frequently hanging around her house were Janko from the Hill and Pavle from Mocevac. They were blood brothers and did everything together, even courting. Both came to Golubinja every evening and stayed to have long conversations with Jelka, and it was difficult to tell which was the most smitten by her, whilst she, little flirt, enjoyed turning the heads of both.

In the beginning she wanted them both to be infatuated, partly to amuse herself, but also to make the other girls envious because two such splendid young men were competing for her attention. For a time it seemed to her that she liked them both equally well, and she felt that if either one of them asked for her hand, she could marry him—both were handsome, wealthy, and well-thought-of—but, as time went on, it was Janko who appealed to her more and more.

Everything about him became dear to her: the way he strode up to Golubinja, his hair, the color of tobacco leaves, the deep look in his blue eyes which made all the blood drain into her heart. On parting, the pressure of his hand bewildered her and she would go back through the garden shaken. To hide this excitement from her mother, she would run to Joka in the kitchen quarters and work at something there until she felt calmer. She lived in a dream. Janko was always in her mind. She could hardly wait until dinner was over to go to her room and give herself up to her dreams.

One evening, the longing for Janko was so overwhelming that she could not fall asleep. She got up, lit the lamp, and began to work on her embroidery, trying to occupy her thoughts, but it was no good. She could not count the rows, the threads became mixed up, tangled and snapped, and the stitches were so uneven that she had to undo it all three times. She gave up and began to stare dreamily at the light of the lamp. Her eyes misted over, anguish gripped her, and everything became oppressive as if the walls of the house imprisoned her. She dismantled the embroidery frame, placed the skeins back in the box, and put it and the embroidery away on the shelf, then quietly tiptoed into the room facing the street and opened the window.

The night was beautiful. A large full moon softly lit the whole of Plevlje. "Where is Janko now?" she thought, looking toward the Hill at the Kojics' houses. Her heart contracted as she remembered that he had once told her how all the other girls would linger long at their front doors and it was only she who locked herself in the house before dark, like the Turkish women. "How can he know how long they stand about there if he does not roam round the streets when he leaves here? They say he has turned the head of many a girl, then left her, and anyhow he does not even think of marrying yet."

Everything was quiet. A fresh breeze cooled her burning forehead, and the scent of lilacs came from the neighboring courtyards, filling her with deep yearning. From the Golubinja hills a song could be heard:

A young rider races across the field
On a black horse, over the level field . . .

The next lines were lost, carried away by the wind, then returned, stronger and clearer, coming from nearby:

Your eyes have wounded me deeply,
Your hair draws me over the field.

Jelka recognized Janko's voice and a flutter of happiness flooded her. When she heard footsteps approach her window, she called softly, "Is that you, Janko?"

"Yes. How did you hear me?"

"Why come here at this late hour?"

"I can't sleep." He paused, then went on, "Thinking of you. Why hide it?"

"How can I believe that when you say the same thing to every girl?"

"You are the only one for me now. From the very first time I saw you, you swept my mind away."

She said nothing, speechless with excitement.

"Come down for a chat."

"I don't dare. Mother would kill me if she knew I was out at night."

"Steal out somehow, so your mother does not see you."

"I can't. My Savka sleeps lightly; she would hear if a fly flew through the house."

"Is there no way we can meet alone?"

Jelka thought for a moment, then said, "When you come with Pavle tomorrow I shall pretend to have a headache and come back to the house early, then you can come back here again as soon as you part from him. I'll wait for you by the gates. If it is still early, even Mother won't be angry."

This cheered Janko and he drew closer to the wall and asked in a whisper, "Do you love me a little?"

"I don't know."

"Am I like everyone else to you?"

"No." It slipped out, and she regretted it.

"That means you love me."

"Don't ask me anything now, but go before someone sees you here so late. Don't you realize that we shall soon hear the call to dawn prayer?"

"I long for you so. I would give the whole word if I could kiss you at least once."

Jelka recoiled. That disturbed her. "Look what he means to do," she thought, "have a good time with me as he has with all the others." She leaned out of the window to make sure no one could hear her and said, "Certainly *not*! Because you are so shameless, I won't meet you tomorrow after all."

"Forgive me. I don't know what made me say that. I shall never again either say or do anything to upset you, I swear it," Janko said, in alarm.

She was silent.

"Please promise you will come out tomorrow."

Jelka did not answer but closed the window.

Janko waited a little while, then started for home in an anxious mood. He feared that he might have been too hasty and had now spoiled everything, after it had begun so wonderfully. It was clear that she also wished to meet him alone. He went over their entire conversation in his mind but could find nothing offensive in what he had said. "She will come tomorrow, I'm sure," he comforted himself. "But how am I to get away secretly from Pavle? I ought to tell him what Jelka and I have arranged, but I'm afraid. He may deliberately try to come between us, because he too is head over heels in love with her. Better keep quiet and when he sees for himself that she has chosen me, he will keep the way clear for us. That's only right, even if we were not blood brothers."

That night he did not fall asleep for a long time. The worry about Pavle stuck in his mind like a bone in his throat, and he could neither endure it nor shake it off. He got up and opened the window. The cool air of early dawn refreshed him. Clouds, white and soft as cotton wool, were drifting over the sky. The wind rustled in the tops of the sweet chestnuts. There was a smell of spring. From the Turkish quarter he could just hear the sweet distant sound of a *sevdalinka*, a melancholy song, accompanied by a mandolin:

"No trouble greater than longing for love . . ."

Janko remained by the window a while longer, listening to the *sevdalinka*, sighed, and murmured, "Someone else is tormented like me." He closed the window and went to lie down, resolved not to reveal to Pavle his love for Jelka just yet.

Pavle had heard that Janko was meeting Jelka on his own and he had recognized the change in them both, but he feigned ignorance although their lingering looks were like a knife in his heart. He began to think and plan how to draw Jelka away, for her beauty had turned his head too and, torn by jealousy, he forgot that Janko was his blood brother and that he had loved him more than himself. Now he hated him as if he were his worst enemy, and it seemed to Pavle that he would sooner tear Janko's throat with his own teeth than allow him to win Jelka.

Janko, dazed by love, neither noticed Pavle's fury nor suspected what he was plotting. It seemed to him that everywhere nothing but his own happiness existed.

One day, just as he had returned from a meeting with Jelka, his father called him unexpectedly to his room and told him that he must go early the next morning to Metaljka and Zlatno Borje to visit the inns that were run for them by their relatives.

Janko tried to postpone the trip, if only by one day, to let Jelka know. "Must I leave tomorrow? Give me at least a day to find someone to replace me in the shop."

"The matter can't wait," Ratko said. "It will cost less to close your shop than if we fail to prepare Risto and Todo for the arrival of the German troops from Bosnia. There is talk in the Charshija that the temporary troops will leave as soon as the others arrive. The road to Bosnia will then be crowded with traffic, to our great profit. I shall immediately send packhorses after you with beer, rum, *mastika*, and bottled wine, whilst both kinds of raki can be bought cheaper over there. Besides, the roof in Metaljka must be repaired. I hear it is leaking. You'll have to stay for two or three days until you find the craftsmen and choose the materials. Also, I want you to order some new tables and benches to be made quickly and placed outside in

24

front of the inns. Pay whatever they ask to have the work completed before the soldiers start arriving. They say a whole garrison is expected."

Janko could find no excuse for further delay, so he took leave of his father and went to lie down with a heavy heart, as he had that very evening arranged with Jelka to wait for her tomorrow in her back garden after her mother and Joka were asleep.

At daybreak he rose, dressed in a hurry, mounted his horse and set off. Night and day were parting. Over the tall peaks of Ljubisnja the last stars were fading, and above the Trlica rose the blue radiance of dawn. Mist was creeping up the folds of the hills, crawling and spreading like strands of wool pulled from a skein by the carding comb, then dissolving slowly and vanishing.

Janko headed through the densely wooded avenue of the barracks, drenched in the sweet smell of flowering acacias. When he passed the last buildings of the Austrian cantonment and emerged on to the white road that shimmered and twisted around the hills, the sun was blazing and the dew sparkled on the leaves of the bushes by the roadside.

Worried and upset, Janko rode slowly. He was as angry with his father for sending him away so suddenly as he was with himself, because he had not yet told Jelka that he was going to ask for her hand as soon as his elder brother was married. Apprehension and restlessness gripped him. He was uncertain whether Jelka's uncles would allow her to marry him, because the Kojics were not yet counted among the town's gentry, whilst the Zarkovics were a wealthy, well-known family of long standing, and their Serbian ancestry considered to be the oldest in Plevlje. He was not even sure whether she knew who his people were or how rich they had become, and decided to mention casually at the first opportunity how well their business was progressing and that they were going to build a row of three-story houses along the entire length of their street, all the way to the highway leading to Jalija. They would then lease them out to the families of Austrian officers, and when he and his two brothers married, divide the property equally.

With thoughts of Jelka, their engagement, and, once he became independent, his plans to organize his own business and model his way of life on that of the merchants in Sarajevo, he hardly noticed how he reached Metaljka.

Without delay he visited both inns and signed new agreements, sharing with his relatives the trade profits of the last three months. But he was forced to stay for two more days to find and engage craftsmen, select the pine planks from which the tiles for the roof were to be cut, and order the tables and benches. Having arranged with the relatives that they were to raise their prices if the Shvabas, the Austrians, started to move in troops from Bosnia, he set off for Plevlje around the time of the call to late afternoon prayer.

He arrived before dark and, as soon as he had settled his horse in the stable then washed and changed, he started for Golubinja. Seized by a strange anxiety, he was in a mad hurry. It seemed to him almost as if it were not he who was walking, but the streets that were gliding under his feet. He was fretting as to whether Jelka would come out at the prearranged signal and whether she was angry because he had not visited for so long; so, when he caught sight of her in front of her house, his whole being glowed with joy. She appeared to him more beautiful than ever, in her crimson *dimije* trousers and black velvet sleeveless jacket, with her plaited hair falling over her breast, but when he approached, he noticed how pale and sad she looked. He took her by the hand, but she pulled away and turned back to the tall gates and, leaning against them, burst into tears.

Janko was suddenly afraid. "What is the matter?" he asked.

Overcome by her sobs, she could not utter a word.

"What's happened? Is one of your family ill?"

"Worse, much worse," she said through her tears.

"What? Tell me, what? Don't torture me any longer."

"My uncles mean to give me to Pavle."

"What!" said Janko, appalled. "Who told you that?"

"They called my mother to Uncle Jovo's yesterday and told her that they had given their word. The proper engagement will be the day after tomorrow. The preparations are in full swing here at home, and my uncles are sending their servants loaded with food baskets and drinks. The whole neighborhood has already heard that I am promised to Pavle."

"And did they ask you?"

"Did they ask me? No! Neither did anyone ask my mother when they married her off. We have to obey our uncles in everything. They are our guardians."

26

Janko, completely distraught, bowed his head and stared at the cobble-stones. "That traitor Pavle," he said through clenched teeth, half to him-self, then looked up at Jelka, who was still sobbing. Only now had the truth dawned on him. He glanced towards Mocevac and fury overcame him at the thought that he might lose Jelka. "Oh no you don't, my scheming friend, not whilst I live! We'll see which of us will outwit the other!"

Jelka stopped crying and looked at him almost with hatred. "And you would know how to outwit anyone, I suppose? It occurs to you now, after everything is done."

"I was sent on a journey, my love. I never dreamed that Pavle might play me such a trick."

"But why did you not ask for my hand sooner? Why did you wait? 'First past the post wins the prize,' the saying goes. It serves you right for taking so long to make up your mind. It is ages since I turned sixteen."

"Don't, Jelka, be reasonable. Who could expect this from a blood brother? We took an oath at the monastery of the Holy Trinity, be-fore the icons and before the priest, to be eternally faithful. If only he had waited until I came back to ask what my intentions were to-wards you. I wanted, this very evening, to tell you that I would ask for your hand as soon as my elder brother marries."

This angered Jelka still more. "You just go on waiting. By then I shall have borne a son to Pavle."

"Really, you're just being stubborn and contrary," Janko said, hurt. "You know very well that I won't wait now. I'll go straight to my father and brothers, and beg them to ask for your hand tomorrow." He suddenly grew worried and added uncertainly, "My only fear is whether my father will agree that I should marry before Stevo. He is obstinate and self-willed. He is a tyrant."

Jelka's eyes blazed with fury. "God help us, what are you waiting for? As if you were not men but girls, Stevo on the shelf and you beneath it. If he were a bachelor, it might be different, but a wid-ower! He married once and took his turn. Now it is your turn and, if you were not so soft, you would not be afraid of your father, but would go and tell him everything this very evening, even if you knew he'd kill you outright. If my father were alive I would not fear anyone under heaven . . ." She burst into tears again.

27

"Stop, I beg you," Janko tenderly reached for her hand. "I can't bear to see you cry. Be patient and listen to what I shall do if Father rejects my plea; I shall steal you away tomorrow evening, we'll elope to Sarajevo and get married there. I have friends, I also have money, and with money everything is possible. Just tell me that you want me, even if your uncles don't."

Unexpected happiness and hope lit Jelka's heart. She could never before have believed that Janko loved her so much that he would run such a risk for her sake. "I do. It's either you or the grave. Had you not come this evening I would have done away with myself. I wanted to jump into the well or hang myself behind the kitchen, and let my uncles prepare for my funeral instead of the engagement."

Janko drew her to him, put his arms around her, and pressed his lips to hers. Jelka succumbed to a sweet forgetfulness. Only when they tore themselves apart to draw breath did she remember that someone might see them, and when Janko tried to embrace her again, she pushed him away and ran into the garden, shutting and bolting the gates, then froze behind them.

When she heard him leave, she ran to the kitchen quarters and leaned against the wall behind the door to calm her heart which seemed ready to burst. She was twanging like a bowstring. When she grew calmer, she smoothed her hair and pulled up the kerchief which had slipped down, then entered the dining area where her mother and Joka were waiting for her. They were both distressed.

Savka was astonished to see her calm, because she had been crying ever since she learned that she had been promised. "Surrendered to her destiny, poor child," she thought. "She saw for herself that she had no choice but to bear what was preordained."

Jelka's dinner was keeping warm, on a trivet on the hearth.

"Will you eat something now?" Joka asked.

"I couldn't touch a thing, my head is aching, so I'm going to lie down till it's better," said Jelka, and left the room.

"I'm so sorry for her, but I cannot help her," Savka said to Joka softly. "It is her kismet. Many a girl has been deprived of what her heart desired, but if Pavle is good to her, as my Tane was, she will come to love him later, when she starts bearing his children."

"God will arrange everything according to His will and mercy.

His ways are mysterious to us." Joka had been in the front room when Jelka was talking to Janko. She had overheard them arguing about something, and then the mention of elopement, and Jelka's talk about taking her own life had frightened her very much. She was relieved that Jelka had calmed down a little and when she heard the door of the room shutting, she said to Savka, "I'm going to bolt the gates and you had better go straight to bed. We ought to start early tomorrow, there is a lot of work waiting for us."

Once in the garden, she went to the store-room and found two padlocks, then fixed one on the gate in the garden fence and the other on the entrance to the kitchen quarters, saying to herself, "Pray God she'll not jump into the well or hang herself, but if she wants to elope with him, let her elope. She would be neither the first nor the last to do it." Hadn't the daughter of Vidric run away with the Turkish, or rather Armenian doctor, then written from Istanbul how happy she was and that he had married her in the real church, not Catholic? She glanced around the garden once more and whispered, "Merciful Lord, help us tonight."

When she had locked the front door, she went to her room and lay down dressed, determined to keep watch throughout the night.

Janko arrived home full of trepidation, ran up the stairs, and quietly opened the door of his mother's room. "Is Father at home?" he asked in a whisper.

His mother was frightened when she saw him so agitated. "What is it, for God's sake? Why are you in such a state?"

"It's nothing. I asked you where Father is."

"He is in there, in his room, angry for some reason."

Janko stepped in, closed the door behind him, and whispered, "Nana, I beg you, go and ask him to let me see him. I have something important to tell him."

"I don't dare. God help me," she said and crossed herself. "You know how he is when he's angry. I am afraid . . . "

Janko did not wait for his mother to finish what she was about to say, but headed straight for his father's room.

Simuna ran after him, grabbed the sleeve of his jacket, and began to plead. "In God's name, don't go! Don't go, wretched child, he'll shatter you."

"Let him shatter, I'm going."

When he reached the door, he paused, then resolutely placed his hand on the handle, whilst his mother fled downstairs and hid in the forecourt. Ratko was sitting on the divan, smoking. When he saw Janko, he put aside his pipe and his heavy brows bristled.

"You dare enter without asking?" he attacked his son as he entered.

Janko made to kiss his hand, but it was withdrawn angrily.

"Adzo, I came to plead with you," Janko began humbly, looking at his feet, but when he raised his head and confronted those eyes, his voice failed. He felt like turning from his father's threatening glare, but remembered Jelka's words and his courage returned. "Adzo, if you don't respond to my plight, I shall have to escape into the wide world."

Ratko was thunderstruck. He was still for a moment, then fury possessed him, and he growled, "*What* did you say? What are you threatening me with, you worm? You were little more than a pound of flesh when I gave you life, and now you dare to speak to me like this!" He pulled hard on his pipe, then went on, "You won't dare make a move, my falcon, or I shall beat the hell out of you to make sure such thoughts never enter you head again. See what's become of today's youth. What will they think of next? They've become loose and wild. Well fed, filled with drink, hands not blistered, backs not broken with work, but running riot with pleasure. I went out into the wild world from necessity, to earn money, and you want to leave for a whim."

Janko interrupted him. "I am not leaving for a whim, but because of great misery from insult and humiliation." He wanted to continue but Ratko shouted:

"Silence, or I'll take this club to you." He grabbed a thick walking stick which lay beside him on the divan. "Let all three of you know that I will rather break your ribs with this stick than let you do as you please."

Janko too was overwhelmed by anger, and began to boil; the veins on his neck swelled, the blood rushed to his face and it grew scarlet. He clenched his teeth, said nothing but started for the door.

When his father saw this, he grew anxious. "Come back and say what's on your mind, but in two words."

Janko turned back and stood firmly in front of his father. "I want you to arrange an engagement for me tomorrow."

"What have you done, you wretched boy, to be in such a hurry?"

"I have done nothing. I only fell in love with her, but her uncles don't approve of me and want to give her to my blood brother because the Jekics are distinguished and we are not." He paused to see what his father would say now.

There was no change of expression on Ratko's face, he just continued to glower at his son. Only his eyes showed that the words had struck a blow.

Encouraged, Janko continued, "There, Adzo, that's why I'm in a hurry. If we don't get engaged tomorrow, she will be given to Pavle. Everything is agreed and the word given."

"Whose daughter is she?"

"She is Jelka, daughter of the late Tane Zarkovic."

"Does she want you?"

"Yes, Adzo, me or the grave."

"Did she tell them that?"

"No, they didn't ask her. Her uncles do as they wish, and she has to obey because they are her guardians. They have told her mother to prepare. The day after tomorrow the official engagement will take place." He stopped for a moment and sighed. "Worst of all, they consider us to be peasants and do not wish to mix their blood with ours."

Only now did Ratko's face cloud. He pointed to the divan by the window and said, "Sit there."

Janko approached and sat down. They both fell silent.

After a lengthy pause, Ratko began, "Look how high they are soaring—I a peasant and they not! My origins are known, whilst who knows where these Jekics come from? They arrived from nowhere, then became wealthy and put on airs, yet it is said that they are not even Serbs, but Bulgarians. How is it that they are now better than we are, from Mrzovic?" He shook his head, then turned to face his son. "One can see that these Zarkovics don't know our history. How, after the battle of Kosovo our kingdom fell, and every true Serbian soul was either slain or fled into distant villages and mountains — all save the weaklings.[1] They and some nobles took the Turkish faith, after which the nobles became emperors' viziers, agas, and begs, and the paupers remained paupers and Turkish serfs. All this was told to me by the architects with whom I worked as a builder in Bosnia. They had read it in books and learned about it in schools. Later, when the Turks cooled their rage and stopped the slaughter, the Serbs began to descend from the villages and mountains into the towns."

Janko pretended to listen, but only Jelka was in his mind.

Ratko settled more comfortably, crossed one leg over the other, relit his pipe which had gone out, and went on, "Shame on them, to insult you like this. Don't they know that Karadjordje was of peasant stock, and so was Prince Milos? When they started the uprisings, which was not long ago, there were no Serbs in towns."

He got up and began to pace the room, his hands crossed behind his back. "And how did Montenegro hold out until now? Nobody asked who is from the villages and who from the towns, but when the Turks attacked, they cried, 'Hey, brothers, whoever has the courage, come to the defense! The Turks are coming!' Then they all rose, from children to elders, even women came along, some with rocks, others with hoes and scythes, some with shotguns, and they fell upon the Turks, and drove them back into their lairs, and thus remained masters of their land."

Janko was on tenterhooks and did not listen to half his father was saying, but tried to look as if he were interested.

Ratko stopped in the middle of the room and turned angrily on him. He had the impression that Janko was more ashamed of his peasant background than he was concerned for Jelka.

"I'm telling you, if it were up to the peasantry, Plevlje too would now be free, and we would not have remained in slavery since Kosovo for all these centuries. All kinds of people have settled here from God knows where, ignorant of the pledge our ancestors have passed on to us. That is to say we have swallowed our pride and are bowing to the Turks or to the Austrians. With the Austrians, the gentry became wealthier and the poor became beggars, but what will happen to these gentry, I ask you, when one day the Austrians are driven out?" He paused, then rumbled on, "To tell the truth, I too have gained wealth in Austrian times, but I can be what I was before, there is always work for a builder."

He sat again on the divan, looked up at Janko and said, "Oh well, I go on too long, as one does when one is growing old. But first let us see what to do about Jelka. You say she wants you?"

Janko's eyes lit with joy. "She does, Adzo."

Ratko grew thoughtful, took several puffs with his pipe, and began slowly and carefully, "Tomorrow I shall select some of my friends to come with us for the engagement. They are all distinguished people and not condescending, but respectful towards me. We shall begin pleasantly, but if those humbugs open their mouths, we'll show our teeth. We won't give up the girl without spilling blood. Don't say a word to anyone now, not even to your mother, but, by heaven, we shall see who will win. They arranged it all in an underhand way, thought you were still in Metaljka. Well then, we'll give them what for! Pass the word on to Jelka somehow, let the child not fear her uncles' tyranny and let her know we shall defend her. Those bullies, forcing a fatherless child into a marriage."

He placed his pipe beside him, stretched and yawned, then took from his breast pocket a flat watch as large as his palm, opened the cover, glanced at its face, and said, "But we are getting too involved. It was time for bed long ago. Now, go and have a good sleep and don't let anything worry you for as long as Ratko's head is on his shoulders."

Janko leapt up, kissed his father's hand, and rushed out of the room. He ran down the stairs and started towards the gates. Simuna ran towards him, asking apprehensively:

"What happened?"

"Nothing, he didn't shatter me, as you see. Go to your room and sleep. Why skulk here in the dark all this time?"

"And where are you going at this hour?"

"I tell you, there's no need to worry."

She began to plead with him. "Don't go anywhere, Janko, for God's sake! It is late and dark, one cannot see a hand before one's eyes. The night can swallow you, without trace."

"Don't be scared, Nana. Fear itself has seized you and you dread everything. Go and sleep in peace. If Adzo asks for me, say you didn't see me, that's all."

Dismayed, she glanced at the lighted windows of Ratko's room, then whispered, "Very well, Janko, may the Lord protect you," and turned and began noiselessly to climb the stairs.

"She won't be able to sleep all night," thought Janko, looking up after his mother. Then he left the courtyard and headed for Mocevac. Through Citluk and the School Lane he arrived at the Crossroads. He stopped there, not wanting to go towards Golubinja because he knew he would not be able to climb over the high wall or the gates of Savka's home, so he went down Dzevair to Zlodol, then by way of the cornfields and pastures, and arrived at her back garden. He was cheered when he saw a light in Jelka's window and, jumping over the fence, he stole through the bushes alongside it, and reached the wall of the house. Taking a small handful of earth, he threw it against the window pane.

Jelka quietly opened one side and whispered anxiously, "Is that you, Janko?"

"Yes, please come down, I've something to tell you."

"I'll come now," she said, and softly closed the window. She tip-toed out of the room and down the stairs, carefully unlocked the front door, then wary as a cat she crossed the courtyard and reached the gate.

"I can't open it, someone has locked it."

Janko leaned across the fence and lifted her over into the garden. They hid under the ash tree to avoid being seen.

"We shall come for you tomorrow," Janko said, elated. "We'll get in before Pavle's people. You must pretend to know nothing, not a word to anyone, not even Jula. Expect us at dusk."

"And if my uncles won't give me to you?"

"They must. Blood will be spilled if they don't."

"Not that, Janko! I'm afraid."

"Don't fret, my dove, you shan't belong to anyone but me."

Whispering this, he took her firmly round the waist, leaned her against the ash and started to kiss her eyes, lips, neck. Love ignited the smoldering fires of youth, and they began to burn together.

Jelka became intoxicated, languid, and yielding, but when she saw how Janko was trembling, how strangely his eyes were glowing, she grew frightened of him, and of the darkness and silence of the night. With great effort she freed herself from his embrace and whispered,

"I heard the door of Mother's room," then ran to the fence, scrambled over it, and fled into the house.

Janko remained still until the light went out in Jelka's room and everything receded into darkness. When he felt a little calmer, he went to the well, groped for the bucket of water on its rim, wetted his hand to cool his forehead and face, then left the way he had come. When he reached the crossing, he headed for the Charshija, as the high street was called, because it was the only street, apart from the Barracks, lit by lanterns. When he reached home, he silently entered the forecourt and went upstairs.

Going along the corridor he saw his mother peering through the half-open door of her room. This annoyed him and he approached her impatiently, whispering, "You hang about here all night to see when I return. Now you see I am alive and well, leave me in peace."

Dejected, Simuna began to close the door. He felt sorry for her. Everyone shouted at her, from Father to the children, although they all loved her. Remorsefully, he added in a kinder voice, "Sleep, Nana, please." He wanted to say something more tender to her, but not knowing what, he only sighed and went to his room.

In the darkness he reached the mattress laid out on the floor and stretched himself on it, fully dressed. He folded his hands under his head and started thinking about his mother, and the eternal worries that had worn her to a shadow. He resolved to become more caring toward her, now that he was so happy. It seemed to him that he had begun to love the whole world through Jelka, even himself, his own strength and youth and feelings, because he had seen how much he mattered to her. He swore he would improve in every way and be good to everyone. He would give to the poor, pardon the debts of the peasants, make peace with Pavle and never rebuke him for wanting to steal Jelka from him, all to thank God somehow for his great happiness. "It is no trifling matter that a girl like Jelka, who could not be matched anywhere else under the sun, has chosen me, me or the grave. God, will it all come true? Will everything happen without bloodshed?"

He was not a coward, but he disliked arguments, fights, or, God forbid, spilling blood. It would weigh heavily on him to be the cause of some misfortune that would be a sorrow to them all, especially to Jelka and her family.

35

He was afraid that Stevo would provoke an argument. He was fierce and could easily flare up. As for Ratko, he would hold back until someone offended him but then he, too, would be furious. About his younger brother, Petko, he did not worry. He was quiet and timid. Should trouble arise, he would slink off somewhere and hide, like that fellow from Mocevac who hid under the table when all hell broke loose between the Serbs and Turks in the Austrian brothel. It was rumored that knives had been drawn and there were people killed, whilst all the time he had been crouching under the table until the Turkish police arrived. Janko chuckled and felt a little calmer. Settling more comfortably, he began to think about Jelka, about the sweet smell of her hair, the curves of her body, her warmth, and fire spread through him. "How quickly she invented that about hearing her mother's door, only to slip out of my hands!"

The first cockerels began to challenge each other, announcing the approach of dawn. Janko got up, found a pitcher of water in the dark, and drank his fill. He was burning like a torch. Undressing, he lay down again. Unable to sleep, he tossed and turned on his mattress. Fear and hope overwhelmed him in succession. Sleep came only with the first pallor of dawn.

On the following day, around the time of evening prayer, Ratko, with his sons and friends, set off for Golubinja, all dressed in festive Hercegovina fashion, Janko resplendent amongst them. Gold braids shimmered on his chest, he had tucked a silver-plated pistol in his cummerbund and wore a ring with a diamond stone on the forefinger of his right hand. To show his rich wavy hair, he had taken off his fez and held it in his hand. Although apprehensive at heart, he walked cheerfully and with confidence.

Next to him came Ratko, on the short side but firm and compact as if cast in bronze, straddling as he walked, still unaccustomed to the wide *shalvare* trousers cut in the new fashion. Poised, freshly shaven, and with sleek hair, he wore his fez at an angle so that its heavy tassel of black silk cord was flapping against his short neck as his shoulders swayed with each step. On Janko's left Stevo, tall and slim like Janko, and next to him Petko, small and podgy. Behind them walked five of Ratko's friends. All of them had loaded their weapons—in case of trouble.

Once they turned from the Crossroads toward Golubinja Lane, the shutters of the houses began to open and women's faces appeared, full of curiosity. Children instantly gathered and started to follow the group, keeping their distance to avoid being chased away. Nothing took place without them. They were always the first to bring the news of everything that happened on the streets. The women would afterwards take over and embellish the story, and only at third hand would the men hear the news as they returned home from the Charshija.

When they reached Savka's gates, Ratko rapped on the door with the heavy iron knocker.

Savka opened the window cautiously and asked, "Who is it?"

"Friends. Do not worry, open without fear."

She asked Joka to go down to the kitchen quarters, then sent her daughters to Jelka's room. Quickly, she took off her apron and threw it into the washroom, smoothed her hair, and went to open the gates. Seeing that they were many, she stepped back into the forecourt to let the guests through.

"Do you welcome visitors?" Ratko asked.

"Certainly, all people of good will. Welcome to my home." Savka replied, and led them to the big room. They sat down on the cushioned seats against the walls and Savka remained by the door, arms folded beneath her breasts.

"You lock up early, as if you were afraid of something?" Ratko said, looking pointedly at Savka.

"We are women alone, and the house is large, therefore it's difficult to hear everything, so we lock up early to make sure that nobody steals in unnoticed."

Ratko pulled the long pipe out of his cummerbund, took out his tobacco pouch, opened it, and slowly began to fill his pipe. It was plain that he wanted time to decide the best way to start the conversation. The others began to smoke too.

Savka waited, her eyes lowered. She guessed why they had come and was worried.

"Perhaps you are surprised that we have come," Ratko began, "but where there is a marriageable girl one should not be surprised by such guests."

She looked at the whole group, leaned forward slightly as if bowing, and said, "The doors of the house of a marriageable girl are open to everyone, but we haven't such a girl. The elder is promised, and the younger is still a child, and not yet eligible."

Ratko took a leisurely puff at his pipe, then continued calmly, "Is your elder daughter engaged, or merely promised?"

"She is not engaged yet, but her uncles have given their word to a young man and to his father, and have accepted a token gift. That's as if she were engaged. Tomorrow the rings will be exchanged and the pre-nuptial ceremony held before the priest and the witnesses."

"Then that means that the matter is not settled."

"Consider it as settled, because I accept every decision my brothers-in-law make, and my daughter has to agree also. Her uncles take the place of a father, and if she does not obey them, whom will she obey?"

Ratko leaned against the cushions, cleared his throat, and began, "That won't do, Tanovica. Times have changed. Now the girl too has to be asked." He wanted to continue but Savka interrupted him pleadingly:

"Truly I see no fault with you or your young man, God forbid, but I neither can, nor would, break the word of my brothers-in-law."

"All right, Savka, send for them to come here too, and we can discuss matters sensibly as honorable people do."

She welcomed this, ran into the lane, and sent one of the neighbor's children to summon the Zarkovics. Stopping in the kitchen, she said to Joka, "The Kojics have come to ask for Jelka's hand and I have called my brothers-in-law. Let them decide as they wish. God knows, I dare not interfere. May it all end peacefully, please God. You can light the fire and put water on to boil for coffee." Saying this, she smoothed the folds of her dress and adjusted the belt at her waist. Then she took from a chest a pair of black patent slippers, dusted them with a woolen cloth, slipped them on, and stayed there to wait until her brothers-in-law appeared before taking in the refreshments.

The Zarkovics had heard that Ratko had gone with his sons and witnesses to ask in Janko's name for Jelka's hand and were waiting to see whether Savka would turn them back. When they received her summons, all three of them set forth, scowling. They entered the room arrogantly, said "Good evening," and, without a glance at the others, sat down to wait for Savka.

Silence and a brooding atmosphere descended. Ratko did not allow this to deter him, but addressed them calmly to explain why he had come, implying all along that the Zarkovics had been summoned only out of courtesy, to be present at the engagement.

The others remained silent during all this, waiting for Savka to come. When she appeared Jovo said, "'Why did you call us when you have given Jelka to . . . ,'" he gestured towards the Kojics, ". . . to them?"

Amazed, she lowered the tray on to the table and crossed herself. "God protect us, I did not want to discuss anything without you and, what's more, I have told them that Jelka is promised and Jula has not yet reached marriageable age."

Jovo now fixed Ratko with an angry glare.

"Keep calm, and stop scowling, you won't frighten us." Ratko faced him, placing his hands on his knees, his bristling eyebrows knotted across his frown. "But I ask you what kind of word have you given? Did you receive the proposal here and ask the girl and her mother for consent, or did you promise her somewhere in the Charshija and arrange things between yourselves and that young man? If she were your own child, all right, but . . . "

Jovo interrupted him indignantly. "What concern is it of yours how we intend to marry off our brother's daughter? Who are you? We don't even know where you come from, nor who you are. You cannot really think that we would give our girl so lightly to someone whose ancestry is not known? You aim too high. Look about you and seek a match that suits you."

Ratko turned to the window and pointed to the mountains behind the Cotina river. "From out there, behind those highlands, we came to Mrzovic, and originally from Hercegovina, where our forefathers and the Turks had been cutting each other's throats for hundreds of years. They did not lick the feet of the agas and begs but revenged their dead with yataghans. Because of that bloodshed, our clan escaped here to avoid being exterminated by the Turks. Therefore, if we are being compared by our ancestries, ours would carry more weight, and if by wealth—then our purses would prove fuller, because you old gentry are finished. Your time is over and a new gentry is emerging. Times have changed. Young girls are no longer anybody's property, to be given without being asked. Even the Turks don't do that any more."

Seeing that it had come to harsh words, Savka intervened, "I am her mother and I have the right to speak for my daughter. She will marry the man for whom we, I and my brothers-in-law, speak—and we have said our say."

"Not so, Tanovice," said Ratko more gently. "Even you have no right to give your daughter to someone she doesn't want."

"That's right!" his companions cried with one voice.

Jovo found it unnecessary to argue with them any further and, certain that Jelka would consent to his wishes, made an imperious gesture to Savka. "Go and bring her here. Let them hear what she will say, and so put an end to this palaver."

Savka went out and found Jelka by the door, listening. She took her by the arm, drew her closer and whispered, "Go in and say that you will marry the man to whom I and your uncles wish to give you. That and nothing else, do you hear?"

"I hear," said Jelka obediently.

They entered together. Savka remained by the door and Jelka bowed to them all, walked over to kiss the hands of the older men and shake hands with the younger, then retreated to stand beside her mother.

Now Jovo began in a solemn voice, looking steadily at Jelka, "You know, my dear, that we have given our word to Pavle and accepted the token gift. Here now are other suitors. You are free to say whom you wish to marry, Janko Kojic or Pavle Jekic, to whom you are promised."

"Janko," said Jelka, and ran out of the room.

Savka rushed after her and began to scold her. "Shame on you for the dishonor you bring on me today. I wished you to obey your uncles. They have taken us under their wing and protected us. How could you offend them like this? What will people say when they hear how you have put their noses out of joint and made them lose face before the Jekics?"

This upset Jelka and she started to cry.

"Be quiet, it is too late now to repent," Savka said. "Go to your room and wait. Who knows what trouble will now befall us?"

As much as the Kojics rejoiced in Jelka's conduct, so were the Zarkovics shattered by it. They grew pale with astonishment and anger.

Silence fell, as if time itself stood still. It was felt that the solution had not yet been reached.

This silence worried Janko and, instead of joy, a strange fear seized him.

The Zarkovics looked to Jovo to say the last word, but he was dumbfounded. He took a handkerchief out of his pocket and began to rub his forehead, a sign that heavy thoughts oppressed him.

Finally, Ratko began, "Well, it was as the girl wanted, so let us not dwell on it now, but perform the exchange of rings and start the festivities. The engagement ceremony is over."

"It is not over!" Jovo cut in, and glared at the Kojics. "This cannot be solved as lightly as you may think, nor shall we allow an under-aged, capricious girl to settle her destiny with a single word, and tie her life to someone who appeals to her only by his looks."

They all listened to him in amazement, even his brothers.

Ratko stopped, as if unable to believe his ears, but managed somehow to keep control of himself. "But, my good sir, what answer is this, after all you said five minutes ago in front of everybody?"

"You heard it—and there can be no other. Although she has declared that she wants Janko, we don't consent and that's that. Now you know where you stand, so pull yourselves together and go back where you came from. We are not giving up the girl."

Stevo leapt to his feet and stopped in the middle of the room, looking at the whole assembly. "In God's name, man, such tyranny and lawlessness toward an orphan are unheard of!"

Jovo contemptuously retorted, "Don't you throw your weight about here but calm down before I thrash you." With the same contempt he turned to the others. "Has the tyranny not been committed by you? Out of the blue you invade the house of a widow. You do not even let her know you are coming, nor ask whether she will receive you, but burst in like savages without any civility and against all custom. She had to call us, poor soul, to protect her. And, had we not arrived, who knows what villainy you would have committed here? You think this is your mountain wilderness and you can snatch girls as you please."

Ratko stood up, approached Jovo, and began in a threatening voice, "And you, don't keep jabbering and distorting things. We are not children. You are too arrogant and insolent even to imagine that we can be treated in this manner. I solemnly say to you: either find a way of keeping the word you gave to your niece in front of all these witnesses, or you won't get out of this lightly! We are not leaving here until we've brought you to a proper recognition of law and order."

Stevo could hold back no longer, but grabbed Jovo's coat and leaned towards him eyeball to eyeball. "Listen, you! Give up the girl or blood will be spilled."

Frightened that it might really come to bloodshed, Janko stepped in front of his brother and called out to Ratko's friends, "Don't let it come to a feud, you men! In God's name help to calm things down!" Seeing that none of them stirred, he turned to Jovo and began quietly, "Squire Jovo, forgive me for having to tell you that neither you nor my father and brother are in the right. You cannot give Jelka to Pavle when she declared in front of us all that she wants me, nor can they force you by threats to give her to me. A feud could only make matters worse, and weapons would create misfortune for both you and us, but especially for Jelka and her family. Think of your family and the families of your brothers. We have no right to bring ruin upon them out of stubbornness and pride."

The whole room was in commotion. The protests of Ratko's friends were heard as they rose to their feet.

Jovo's brother, Steven, also rose and started to pacify the visitors. "Everything will be solved calmly and peacefully. We, too, won't allow any bloodshed." He turned to Jovo and said sternly, "Why, for God's sake, are you insisting so much? Why try to stop something that is finished? You cannot turn back now. Don't feel sorry for her, let her break her neck. Can't you see that she is behind all this? Let her go to the Devil."

Jovo looked at him as if waking from a dream. He realized that he had no choice and had also become afraid, and to hide his fear he decided to vent his anger upon Jelka. "All right," he said, recovering his breath. "It shall be as she wants, but if one day she regrets it, there is no return for her to this house. Tell her to come and take the ring, but let her know that I am disowning her for ever."

Janko went out to call Jelka and found her in the corridor. She was pale and frightened. Tenderly he drew her to him.

"Don't be afraid, all ended well, you are mine. Call your mother and sister and come in to receive the ring."

She burst into tears. "Adzo Jovo has disowned me for ever."

"Don't cry," Janko whispered to her. "He said it in anger. It will pass, once he sees how fond of him you are. Hurry to conclude the engagement as quickly as possible and make it public. I am going back to see that argument does not flare up again."

In the big room everything had calmed down, everyone was seated again and had begun to smoke. Janko entered, glanced cheerfully at Jovo, and sat beside him in an informal way, then taking out his cigar case, he opened it and respectfully offered it to Jovo. The other, although angry, could not refuse, but took a cigar and let Janko light it for him.

At that moment Jelka came in with her mother and sister. When she saw the two had made their peace, her face lit up and the grief left her heart.

Ratko rose and went to meet her, kissed her forehead and put the ring into her hand. "This is from Janko," he said, then took out of his pocket a handful of ducats. "And this is from me, my daughter. May you be happy and honored, God willing."

Speechless with sheer happiness, she accepted the gift and kissed Ratko's hand.

Janko did not wait for the felicitations and the gift-giving to continue, but rushed out of the room, climbed to the *doksat*, opened the window, and began to fire his pistol. This was the sign that the engagement had been concluded.

Petko, his younger brother, from whom not a sound had been heard until then, also came and he too began to shoot, shouting at the top of his voice, "She's ours, she's ours!"

The women and young girls from the neighborhood came running in, opened all the windows of Savka's house and began to sing:

This house is festive today,
A mother is giving her daughter away
And is rejoicing . . .

The whole of Golubinja came out into the street. The house filled with people. Jovo sent for his men and ordered them to light big bonfires in the courtyards and on the street. All the other relatives arrived too, to congratulate and help in serving refreshments. From somewhere gypsies materialized with fiddles, and the music and *kolo* dancing began.

The bonfires blazed, songs reverberated, and gunshots echoed over the surrounding hills—and the whole of Plevlje learned that Jelka Zarkovic was engaged to Janko Kojic.

That same evening, Pavle and his parents also heard what the Kojics had done to them. They found it more difficult to bear the disgrace than the loss, because it was already known that they had asked for Jelka's hand and had sent her the token gift of a golden chain with a medallion.

Their servant girls later spread rumors through the neighborhood how on that evening Pavle had locked himself in his room and did not come out for three days but had allowed only his mother to enter to bring food, which he returned almost untouched. Secretly, she brought him, under her apron, bottles of absinthe and hid the empty ones so that his father would not discover that Pavle was drinking. He was angry enough as it was, and vented his fury with the Zarkovics all over the house. "Those good for nothings, to let us down in such a way! And they call themselves squires and men of their word! I don't mind about the wench, she never was fit for our house, they say she is a flirt, but because this whipper-snapper of ours had fallen for her like a calf and is inconsolable."

But no wonder lasts more than three days, and Pavle somehow withstood the blow. He did not kill Janko, nor Jelka, nor himself—as he swore he would in the first hours of pain and despair—but began to go and mix with people again. He did not go to Golubinja any more and avoided all places where he might come across Janko.

On the eighth day after Jelka's engagement, when the service in the monastery chapel ended, Pavle caught sight of Janko in front of the archway and tried to lose himself in the crowd, but the other called to him:

"Wait, brother, I have done you no injury, why run away?"

"I'm not running away, nor did the thought cross my mind, but I didn't see you."

They approached each other and shook hands.

"Well, I wish you happiness, brother."

"Thanks, I hope you are not angry any more."

"Heavens! I was not really angry. Had I grabbed the chance, Jelka would be mine. You got in first and we are even now."

"That's right, you'll find another, if not better, not worse than she."

"Of course I will. Girls are as plentiful as fish in the sea. You thought it not possible to live without Jelka but it is, brother, nobody is indispensable."

Janko touched him lightly on the shoulder. "Oh well, brother, let's turn troubles into rejoicing. Come, what about a drink?"

They crossed the Grad monastery courtyard, descended the stone steps, and called in at the booth that was erected against the sheer rock of Biserka, with a row of dark brown tables and benches in front of it. A few townspeople and peasants were already sitting there drinking. They chose a table where they often used to sit before.

"Say, friend, what will you have?"

"I'll have a raki," replied Pavle, and took off his fez, then smoothed his coal-black hair, which was parted on one side. He too was handsome; tall and slim, with penetrating black eyes, long and somewhat heavy face, a thin musctache which grew down the sides of his mouth, and a dignified bearing. If a turban were to be wound around his head he would resemble a Turkish nobleman.

Janko turned towards the counter and called, "One beer and a double raki of the finest brew, if you have it."

"Yes, we have, master Janko, of course we have," the owner replied, and quickly brought the drinks. He wiped the dew off the table with his elbow and put before them a tankard of beer and a glass of golden yellow plum brandy. Out of his cummmerbund he took a few thin chillies and a cellar of fine salt, put them also on the table and withdrew.

"Let me settle it now," Janko stopped him, took out his wallet and paid.

They touched glasses and began to drink, observing the people coming out of the monastery. Both were silent. It was difficult to start a conversation.

Janko thought with sadness, "It was not long ago that we became blood brothers and were blissfully drinking together at this very table." He felt sorry that their love for one another had gone, but just as he was about to utter the words already prepared for this occasion, which he hoped would seal their reconcilation, Pavle looked at him and said:

"Well, how is Jelka? When will the wedding be?"

Janko was suddenly gripped by jealousy and almost burst out, "Leave Jelka in peace," but held back. "We have not yet settled the day. My father wants first to complete the house in the courtyard and link it with the kitchen quarters."

Pavle watched him with a provocative and mocking air. "You had better hurry with the wedding. God knows, someone may steal Jelka from you, even though she is engaged, as Stana was last year—remember, the fair-haired girl?—on the day of her wedding, veil, headdress, and all."

Janko felt like jumping up and grabbing him by the throat, but again restrained himself and said sarcastically, "Are you, by chance, intending to steal Jelka from me?"

"No, actually no, fear nothing from me. I wouldn't have her now if the stars shone on her forehead."

"Nor am I afraid of you, or anyone else, be assured of that."

"Come on, don't be angry, I'm only joking."

"I, too, am joking, and I hope that our friendship will go on as before."

"That's how it should be, if we are men enough," said Pavle, and sighed.

The conversation could not be revived again, although they both tried to break the awkward silence, so they got up and left, each preoccupied with his own thoughts.

They parted by the rock of St. Sava. Pavle descended the Skakavac and turned toward Mocevac, and Janko took a short cut between the monastery's buildings and the graveyard, crossed the pasture which climbed the gentle slope of Glavica and reached the stile. There he sat trying to put his thoughts in order and overcome his anger.

Hatred of Pavle was filling him and that sly reference to the kidnapping of the fair Stana stuck in his mind. "He really is insolent, still thinking of Jelka, just when I wanted to make peace and ask him to be my best man and so save our brotherhood. Nothing will come of that, now there is no longer any trust and love between us. Those are like life; once lost, they vanish for ever."

Janko looked around with a sigh. Memories of his friendship with Pavle surged back. All these surroundings reminded him of it. Together, as children, they had wandered round the Biserka, the graveyard, monastery pastures, Glavica. When the teacher brought their class to the service in the monastery, they could not wait for the priest to finish the litany to climb the long balcony of the monk's cells and come out through Pivara on to Biserka. There they would run and chase one another, climb the trees to pick plums, and press their ears to the ground to listen to the murmuring of the stream that ran underground. They imagined that there were hidden castles of precious stones in which fairies lived, guarded by dragons. From there they would go to the graveyard and read the inscriptions on the heavy crosses roughly hewn out of stone, then stand for a long time before two tombs cut out of monolithic rock which bore neither a cross nor any writing, and wonder what secret they covered. In the pastures they wrestled, or competed to see who could run faster, jump higher, or throw further, or rolled down the gentle hillside, and in autumn they would look for blackberries and sloes in the hedgerows. There was not one place on that whole side of Glavica where they had not played. From there they would have fights with the Turkish children, both boys imagining themselves as historical figures. Janko led the children from Brdo, in the role of Bosko Jugovic, and Pavle the Mocevac children, fancying himself as Prince Lazar.[2] When the guard on the tall rock that served them as a watchtower cried, "Here come the Turks crawling up from below the Muratbeg's field," they would take their slings out of their pockets and wait at the ready, the best marksmen in the first rows and the rest bringing up stones in their caps and placing them at their feet. When the Turks had crept halfway up the field, they would suddenly spring up, howling, charge towards Glavica, pelting them with stones until they were repulsed, then push them back into the narrow lanes where the Turkish quarter began.

That too was a kind of game, and it had its seasons. It would stop during Serbian and Turkish holidays, and in winter when the snow covered everything. A long truce would then take place and they would even befriend each other and, together, build an ice track from the Crnojevics' house down the hill and down the Mocevac all the way to the Milet garden.

The sleighs, shod with steel and adorned with bells, rang and flew like sparks. There was laughter then, shrieking and singing—but as soon as spring began, the fighting would start again.

As teenagers, when dreams began to disturb them, their voices to change and fine hair to grow on their faces and above the upper lip, they left the fighting to the younger boys and wandered around those places where there was a chance to catch a glimpse of the young women and girls who had begun to excite them. They would steal close to the Skakavac valley and, peering through the bushes, observe the Turkish *bulas* picnicking. They came in groups and, well screened by the steep slopes of the valley, sat beside the stream on the soft, silky grass. There they lit fires, made coffee and drank it, smoking small, thin cigars. The younger women would remove their veils, pull up the folds of their *dimije* trousers to below their knees, and wade in shallow water to cool off. The whiteness of their skin, the beauty of their rosy faces and large eyes, outlined with kohl, the sheen of their hair enchanced with henna, were resplendent in the sunshine and they appeared to the boys like nymphs. This friendship continued as they grew up: together they embarked on manhood, together they started smoking and drinking and flirting.

In memory Janko traced the entire course of their friendship and was filled with sadness. Climbing down from the stile, he started for home. He knew then that even if he could tear Pavle out of his heart, he could never free himself of these memories.

3

Ratko had sold his land in Mrzovic after the death of his parents and moved with Simuna and his three older children to Metaljka on the outskirts of Plevlje. He continued to work as a builder until he opened an inn, the Zlatno Borje, and later another one on the road to Cajnice. There his three younger children, Janko, Petko, and Petrija were born.

They lived like peasants, modestly and even frugally, and as their business lay on the busy road between Plevlje and Cajnice, they soon prospered. Ratko paid for his sons' schooling, and when they were old enough he took them into the business. In time, they bought land on the Hill in Plevlje, opposite the Barracks, and on it built two three-story houses and moved there, leasing the inns to his relatives to run while Ratko himself provided their supplies, halving the profits with them. They opened a new inn in one of his houses on the Hill, a general store in the other, and a shop in the Charshija.

Janko worked at the inn and learned to speak German from the Austrian officers and men who patronized it. From them too he learned about the European way of life, which impressed him greatly and which later, when he began traveling to Vienna, he introduced into his own home after the family dispersed. Stevo ran the shop, making a success of it because he got on well with the Turks so that they, as well as the Serbs, became his customers. Honest and wise, he soon won growing respect with the Charshija. Petko worked in the general store, where it was mostly peasants who dropped in; they had taken to him because he knew how to trade with them. He sold kerosene, coffee, oil, and household provisions, but also hatchets, scythes, and other tools, and bought from them honey, smoked meats for his home use, hay for the cows which were kept in sheds at the bottom of the garden, and, on feast days, lambs and piglets for roasting. Ratko was boss and controlled everything.

The elder daughters, Mara and Stojana, had married early, both to artisans, and a little later Stevo married a girl from a good background, but she died a year after she had borne him a daughter, little Olga.

As the business branched out and the income rapidly increased, now that the new lodging houses had been built on one side of the entire street facing Krstata Barracks, Ratko started planning to construct a large hotel by the old Turkish inn at the far end of the Dubure area. He did not wish to marry off his sons until all this had been completed and until Petrija was married, so that the two evils, daughters and sisters-in-law, did not meet under one roof. He hoped his sons would take girls of the middle class, because in his opinion the daughters of the gentry were either spendthrifts or of delicate health, like Stevo's late wife.

Janko's engagement spoiled all his plans and he wondered how he had agreed to it so quickly. "That he should take a girl of the Zarkovic house, thereby making them my in-laws, so forcing me to base my way of life on theirs." He had taken the decision partly out of stubbornness and vanity, but mostly because he was afraid of losing Janko, who he had noticed long before was too susceptible to women, so that when he saw how smitten he was by Jelka, he had been afraid that Janko might elope with her out into the wide world. It pleased him that she was beautiful, as he wished for beautiful descendants, and he found it comforting that she was a fatherless girl who had not been spoiled or indulged by anyone. As her mother was quiet and modest, he did not expect Jelka to find fault with his home. "Even if she were a king's daughter, I'll keep her harnessed and she'll obey and respect me."

Janko could hardly wait for Lent to end. The engagement was announced before Shrove Tuesday, and throughout the following fast he could not see Jelka because she, as a bride-to-be, was not allowed to go out during this time and they could only meet secretly in the garden to exchange a few words.

On the day of Palm Sunday, he resolved to visit Savka at her home. Dressed smartly, he flew towards the Hill. That year Easter fell late, somewhere around St. George's Day; everything was in leaf, and the trees laden with blossom, while rays of sunshine poured down in sheaves, golden yellow and tangible.

The gates of Savka's home were open, so he entered without using the knocker. Savka herself met him at the door, still dressed in her festive clothes.

"I heard a man's footsteps and thought it couldn't be anyone but Janko. I am glad you came. Go to the visiting room and wait while I take off my *tepeluk* and *libade*. I've only just come back from church."

Janko went in and sat on the long seat by the open window. Through the starched curtains of fine hand-woven cotton came the scent of lilacs. The pleasantly shaded room exuded cleanliness, everything was covered with expensive carpets in harmonious colors. On the shelves shone silver bowls and ewers; icons and embroidered cloths decorated the walls. His heart sank at the thought of Jelka moving from such splendor into their house, furnished in the peasant manner, but the knowledge that he had money, and that all this could be acquired, reassured him.

Savka entered. From the door she said that she had told Jelka who had just come in and that she would soon be down with Jula to greet him.

Janko felt a little embarrassed, not knowing how to start the conversation. "I came to arrange the day of the wedding."

"We two cannot make such arrangements," Savka said gently. "Your father will have to get together with my brothers-in-law to agree upon it. That is the custom."

Jelka and Jula brought in refreshments, put everything on the table, then came to exchange greetings. They were dressed alike, in blouses and *dimije* trousers of green cotton with small red dots, and on their feet they wore white stockings and red slippers embroidered with gold.

As soon as Janko saw Jelka's joyous face and glowing eyes, he brightened up and addressed Jula in a brotherly way, "You have become quite a young lady and have grown even taller in these few weeks."

"Indeed, she's of age now, and never moves far from the mirror," Jelka added teasingly.

Jula flushed and was about to answer back, but Savka gave her a stern look and she did not dare. Her appearance differed from her sister's. She was much shorter than Jelka, slender, with light brown hair, parted in the middle and combed into two thick plaits which reached down to her narrow hips. Her eyes were deep blue, the color of lapis lazuli, her face oval and glowing with a delicate flush that rose in her cheeks to below the temples.

Janko stayed a while longer, exchanged a few shy words with Savka without taking his eyes off Jelka, then got up and bade them goodbye.

Jelka and Jula accompanied him to the gates and shook hands. He held Jelka's hand long and tenderly, looking into her eyes, and with difficulty brought himself to leave.

Descending Golubinja, he was saying to himself, "Ah, Janko, Janko, she has really turned your head, the sorceress. Once she's in your arms, she'll make you melt like a handful of snow. So be it, no regrets, just die in her embraces." He turned back to look at her once more, waved and waited until the two girls entered the courtyard, then headed for the Charshija.

Only the Turkish shops were open. He stopped at Korjenac's to see what furnishings could be bought for their house, then looked at the woven carpets from Bosnia, the mirrors, silver-plated jugs and bowls, but did not dare to decide on anything without Ratko's approval.

When he arrived home, he first went to his father's room. "May I come in?" he asked from the door.

Ratko beckoned him over. "You are all spruced up, did you go to church?" he teased, knowing that he had gone to Jelka because he had seen him going down to Mocevac.

"No, I didn't, I went to Golubinja to talk to Savka about the wedding, but she said you have to arrange with her brothers-in-law about the day of the ceremony."

"Heavens! They *are* fussy, making me go to them for this too. Never mind, once we've brought Jelka here, they can forget about seeing me at their home ever again. And why wait for the wedding? The ceremony can be on the third Sunday from this, as soon as the banns have been called in church."

This seemed too soon to Janko, as the thought of all that would have to be altered and acquired crossed his mind. "I think, Adzo, that we should put the house in order before the wedding, buy better carpets and some furniture. We cannot leave things as they are, beautiful houses but nothing in them, everything peasant-like. Their home is carpeted from the threshold to the attic."

"Look how quickly he has become genteel. Does he want to fashion our home like the Zarkovics? No, my son, not if you were the light of my eyes."

"Not because of the Zarkovics, Adzo—I don't like them either— but because of Jelka."

"No, not even for her sake will I change my life, not even if she were a fairy princess. I gave enough money at the engagement and I will see the wedding through with the least possible cost. We'll whitewash the houses, outside and in, clean the windows, scrub the floors and cover them with plain runners and our peasant carpets. I shall give this room to you and Jelka, it is the biggest and lightest, with four windows looking on to the street. We shall furnish it with things from Jelka's dowry. What she brings she will keep. I shall order new shoes for all members of the family and have clothes made for them, and I shan't stint on the food and drink, but I won't give a farthing more, and that's that." He took his long pipe and lit it.

This meant that his mind was made up, and Janko did not dare to add another word.

The next day Janko went to the Charshija and, instead of the silver dishes and carpets he had intended to get, he bought a large mirror and a wash basin and jug of white enamel. He knew that even his father wouldn't scold him for that, as the things were factory made, and a rarity in Plevlje.

At the Zarkovics', too, everything was being prepared for the wedding. Already, the day after the engagement, Savka's brothers-in-law called on her to show that they were not angry because Jelka had chosen the man who was not to their liking, and to consult her about the wedding day.

Savka was surprised and frightened when she saw them. She felt guilty and wished to retreat somehow into herself, to hide her daughter's mistake. She began the conversation, "I am sorry the wretched girl would not listen to us, but chose such an ill-suited man!"

Jovo indicated with a gesture that this would no longer be referred to. "What happened—happened. We parents are not consulted any more, youth has taken the bit between its teeth and goes its own way. God knows, one day my daughter too will do the same. Fat Lazo is propping up my gatepost and I hear he is seeing her whenever I am in the Charshija. And I do not approve in the slightest. As far as his family is concerned, I have no objections; although not as ancient as ours, they are townspeople and wealthy, but the two don't suit one another. She is thin and long like a matchstick and he short and tubby like a bumblebee. Yet what can I do but let her go to the one she wants, as we had to let Jelka? Be that as it may, we came to ask how best to help you now with the dowry, and what you would need us to buy. We shall give money as well, so that you may have everything you need for the wedding. She is Tane's daughter and we must give her a beautiful send-off to show what kind of home she is leaving."

Encouraged by this, Savka sat beside them. "I have enough for her trousseau. From the time she was born, I began to prepare for it. I bought jade and gold to embroider the cushions and covers, and had the Turkish *bulas* weave me a large carpet and long runners for the *secijas* of the same design as the carpet. After Tane's death I could not put aside much money to continue the preparations as I wished, but as soon as the girls grew up I bought thread and they embroidered linen and knitted stockings. All this I stored in the chest. I also have things from my trousseau which are new and will be welcome now." She stopped, as if what she was about to say was not quite appropriate, but nevertheless decided to tell them. "From the gold napoleons she received from Ratko and his party, I can obtain all that is still needed and cover the cost of the wedding, however large it may be."

"Good," Jovo said. "Don't buy any chests, mattresses, and bed covers, we intend to contribute those. I shall go to Sarajevo during the next two weeks and buy her something special, things which cannot be found here. We shall immediately send one of our servant girls to help Joka until the wedding is over, and your sisters-in-law will not leave you on your own, they will come to help you. This is the first joyous day since Tane died, it will be a big occasion for us all."

The next day other relatives and Jelka's girlfriends also came to help. The unfinished covers were being completed, stockings knitted and towels embroidered as presents for wedding guests, and dresses made which Jelka was to take with her. Jelka received many gifts, her aunts proving more generous than her uncles, so that the neighbors came to admire the valuable presents and Jelka's trousseau.

The wedding was a grand affair. The Kojics' guests arrived in a procession at Savka's house and spread out into the rooms where the wedding breakfast was laid, whilst the girls dressed Jelka and sang as they arranged her hair. After they had breakfasted, all the guests went out into the courtyard to wait for the bride.

Jelka was led out by her uncles Jovo and Stefan, tall, dignified, and festively dressed so that she looked even more beautiful and distinguished between them, all in white silk with a wreath of white beads twined in her plaits, which were wound round her head like a crown.

When they surrendered her to her brothers-in-law to be, Petko and Stevo, who were waiting outside wearings sprays of rosemary and the customary best man's kerchiefs, the *chajo*, the master of ceremonies, began to beat the drum decorated with flowers, calling, "*Azurele*, you festive guests, let us begin, let us not tarry, they are bringing out the beautiful bride."

The song of Jelka's friends resounded: "Fair Jelka is led out . . ." and the *chajo* started at the head of the procession toward the monastery, cheering and beating the drum with a small stick. Behind him came the bride with her brothers-in-law, after them Janko with Godfather Colovic from Mrzovic and the best man; then the others. Everyone was merry except Savka, who could not hide the sadness of parting with her daughter and could hardly hold back her tears. When the young girls began to sing "Jelka planted a rose by the house, where her mother will rest on summer days, rest on summer days and pine for Jelka . . .," she burst into tears.

The wedding procession returned from the monastery to the Kojics' houses with a song:

All the groom's guests are rejoicing
His mother most of all.
They brought to her the rose of a girl
As fragrant as a rose.

At the gates Simuna welcomed them with her daughters and little Olga, Stevo's daughter. They were all dressed in urban fashion except Simuna, who was wearing a long dress of heavy bleached woven cotton, embroidered round the neck, down the front and along the edge of the wide sleeves. Over the dress she wore a sleeveless tunic of brown wool and, from the waist down, a heavy overskirt, thickly gathered as if it were pleated, and embellished with embroidery at the hem. Round her waist was a woven sash. Peasant shoes and woolen stockings showed below her skirts. Her head was covered by a white scarf folded and pinned up high, its corners falling down her back, thus revealing the embroidery on the collar and shirt front.

Jelka approached her and bowed to kiss her hand, whilst she kissed the bride's forehead.

Simuna waited until the bride and all the guests had entered the house, then went up to her room to collect herself. She was followed by Janko, who had noticed how deeply moved she was.

"What do you say, Mother, isn't your daughter-in-law beautiful?"

"Yes, truly, like a picture, may she live a long and happy life. When she stepped over the threshold it seemed to me the sun had entered the house," she said, wiping away the tears of sheer pride that flooded her eyes.

Janko embraced her and helped to settle her on the cushions. "Rest a little and calm yourself, then come down later," he whispered protectively, because she appeared to him even more confused and awkward amongst Jelka's relatives. The difference between the Zarkovics and their own guests was obvious to him, and not only because of their clothes and manners; their faces, too, seemed more beautiful, gentler. He was anxious what Jelka would think when she saw how their houses were furnished compared with hers, although they had more money. "Now I'm going to Jelka," he said quietly, and left the room.

When he caught sight of her amongst the guests and she smiled at him cheerfully, he felt easier. Taking her aside, he whispered, "Our home is arranged in peasant fashion, that's how Adzo wants it, but when we are on our own, we will have everything Viennese fashion, like the merchants' houses in Sarajevo."

Jelka smiled. "If you want to. To me every house in which you are is beautiful."

Tears of happiness filled his eyes and he would have embraced her in front of everybody had she not slipped away.

Just then the *chajo* called out, "Come, young bride, the guests expect you to wait on them."

They made a space for her at the far end of the room, where she remained standing and waiting on the guests throughout the day, except when she was led to her own room to have lunch. But in her happiness, she did not feel any fatigue.

In the morning, Jelka woke slowly and dreamily. In all her sinews she felt a pleasant languor, intoxicated by the cool mountain air which poured in waves through the wide open windows. From the towers of the nearby mosques came the chant of the muezzins.

"*Saba*," she thought and sleepily opened her eyes. When she saw Janko's broad shoulders beside her, endless joy overwhelmed her. She drew closer and breathed in deeply the fragrance of the nape of his neck, then slipped from under the cover and went to the chest containing her clothes. From it she took *dimije* trousers and a blouse of silky rose-colored cloth, red slippers, white stockings, and a fine transparent kerchief fringed with tiny black beads. She washed and dressed, then went to the mirror to comb her hair. Having plaited it into two plaits, she let it fall down her back and tied the kerchief well away from her forehead so that the curls around her temples could be seen. She looked at herself from all sides and could not help liking her own reflection. Satisfied and infinitely happy, she sat on the long seat to wait until other members of the family started getting up.

She looked around the room. Spacious and light, it extended along the whole facade of the house. Large windows on three sides looked out to the Charshija, the Barracks, and Mount Glavica. Furnished from among her dowry, it reminded her of Savka's large room, the same carpet, same runners over the long seats, same embroidered cushions, except that everything was new, fresh, bright. The white, newly painted walls were furnished with shelves, crowded with the presents she had received before the wedding. There were silver-plated bowls and ewers, copper dishes, coffee cups in colored porcelain, glasses, decanters and carafes, and a censer of chased silver.

It bothered her that the windows were still without curtains and that there was not one icon there. "Leave it as it is for now," she thought, "and later I shall ask Janko to buy me an icon of the Mother of God with Baby Jesus and an icon lamp, a silver *kandilo* to hang in front of it, then we won't need anything else. I can make the curtains myself out of white woven cotton, doubled and with frills."

When she heard a door open somewhere and someone descended the stairs, she took her new jug and basin, towel and scented soap, then left the room silently so as not to wake Janko, and went to the upper house where Ratko's and Simuna's room now was.

"Who is it?" asked Ratko, impatiently.

"It is I, Jelka," she answered, a little frightened.

"Come in, come in, bride, may God keep you happy," he welcomed her cheerfully.

Jelka went in, wished them "good morning," placed the basin and jug to one side, then approached the cushions on which they were seated, already dressed. She first kissed Ratko's hand, then Simuna's. "I have brought water for you, if you have not yet washed."

"We did, so to speak, splash our faces to rinse the sleep from our eyes. But if you are going to pour some water for us, it will be a pleasure to wash again," Ratko said, pulling up the sleeve of his jerkin and approaching the basin. "Why is it covered? I can't very well wash through the lid."

"But, Adzo, it is perforated so that the water can flow through."

"Look at that, I ask you, how artfully it is done, pierced and cut out like the finest lace. How did they tin it that it shines so much?"

"They are silver-plated, the basin and the jug. Uncle Jovo bought them for me as a present when he went to Saravejo."

"The Sarajevo craftsmen are better than any others. The main high street there, the Bashcharshija, is a real paradise! They say that there is none more beautiful in Istanbul itself."

When Ratko had washed his hands and face, Jelka handed him the towel and poured water for her mother-in-law, who had approached quietly. "This is from Saravejo too, there are no such fleecy towels here," Ratko continued. "Something is written on it. Do read it for me, I am not literate."

"Neither am I, but they told me it says 'Good Morning.' Janko and I have identical ones."

When Simuna had also finished washing, Ratko took the jug and examined its workmanship. "This is even better decorated than the basin. The ornaments are curly and interwoven, somehow in Turkish fashion. There, copper can be carved as if it were wood. Ah! truly, nothing can escape the hand of a man if God breathes talent into him."

"I am now going to wait upon Janko, if he is awake," Jelka said when he returned the jug to her. Then taking the basin, but leaving the towel and soap with them, she left the room.

As soon as she closed the door behind her, Ratko turned to Simuna. "You see how well-bred she is, yet does not look down on us, but shows us all due respect. She's very much taken by Janko." He smiled thoughtfully. "When they wanted to give her to another, she told Janko, 'You or the grave'." Afraid that he might have become too soft, he continued in a harsher voice, "But one mustn't spoil her, and we shall keep her on a tight rein, as we did our own children."

Jelka went to the pump under the stairs, poured more water into the jug, rinsed the basin and went up to Janko's room. He was still sleeping. She did not want to wake him, but went quietly to a shelf, took from it a copper set for serving coffee and headed for the kitchen quarters. There she found Petrija, her youngest sister-in-law, and kissed her cheek.

"I won't kiss your hand, you are younger than I am."

"No, certainly not my hand," said Petrija shyly.

"Do you want me to call you 'sister' or by the name of some flower, as a young sister-in-law may also be called?"

"As you wish, but if you like, call me 'sister'."

"You are preparing coffee for Adzo and Nana?" Jelka asked when she saw a large coffee pot placed against the embers in the hearth.

"Yes, I am, you can take it to them if you like."

Jelka made the coffee, poured it into her jug, placed it on the tray and carried it away. She walked slowly across the courtyard because the flagstones in the Kojics' paving were lumpy and uneven, and the soles of her slippers smooth, and she was afraid she might slip and spill the coffee. That would be a bad omen for her happiness in the new home.

The morning was warm, the sun had risen from behind the mountains and scattered its rays among the magenta shadows. The copper of the new tray shone with an iridescent glow.

When Jelka appeared, Ratko leaned against the cushions, lit his pipe, and began to watch her contentedly. She served them, then stepped aside, waiting to refill the cups.

"So, you say you are not literate," said Ratko to start the conversation.

"No, Mother did not allow me to go to school so Adzo Jovo engaged an old priest to come to our home and teach us, and he taught us letters from the church books, the old script, *az*, *buki*, *vjedi* and so on.[3] We also knew a lot by heart but could not read and write properly, so he was told to stop further work with us. I only learned to write my full name and my family name."

"More you won't need. Let Janko teach you to write our family name too, and that is enough for you. I, too, my child, know as little and have learned the numerals for my craft, but now I don't even need them. I sum up everything in my head quicker than my sons do on paper. In commerce one has to be shrewd, that is more important than any amount of schooling."

Jelka refilled their cups for the third time and, when they had finished, she went to wake Janko.

Once they were alone, Ratko said to Simuna, "Why are you so silent?"

"I feel rather ashamed of being so peasant-like."

"You must not be. She knew who we were, so why else did she come to our home?"

"She came because of Janko and perhaps she does not like us."

"I don't care whether she likes us or not, she has to respect us; we gave birth to her Janko."

"He may also be ashamed in front of her."

"My God, if that is how it is going to be, for our children to start being ashamed of us, we shall certainly part. We are nobody's burden. We'll hire servants to wait on us hand and foot. Ratko has money and can live like a Pasha." He patted her shoulder and added with a smile, "And you will be my Pashinica."

"Oh! May God our savior protect me! I would rather be buried than have servants around me instead of my children. You go too far. Pay no attention to my being silent, I am like that until I get used to things and am at ease. When we moved into these houses I did not know where to turn in buildings of this size, I could hardly make out which door led to what room, and now I can find my way even in the dark."

They sat a while longer, then put on their shoes and went to the small house for breakfast.

Janko got up, washed, dressed, and groomed himself, then sat by the window to wait for Jelka. When she entered, he lifted her in his arms and carried her across the room, kissing her. "Is it true that you are mine, my jewel, my golden bird of paradise?"

At first she playfully tried to wriggle away, but when Janko started unbuttoning her shirt, she arched out of his arms and sprang to the floor. "You have made me all disheveled by your foolishness. What a disgrace if anyone came into the room and saw what you are doing."

"Why a disgrace? In Vienna, I hear, they kiss in the parks in daylight."

"Harlots perhaps, but a decent woman would not kiss in front of anyone, not even in Vienna."

"But you are my lawful wife."

"Even so, now is not the time for kissing. Restrain yourself, what

61

do we have the night for?" As she saw Janko moving closer to her again, she ran out and added from the door, "If you are so idle that all sorts of ideas slip into your head, I'm not."

She ran down the stairs and went to Petrija to decide with her on how they should share the work.

Many things changed in the Kojics' home after Jelka was brought there. She introduced new ways in cooking and serving, and in the running of the entire household. No one interfered with her, nor obstructed her. Simuna gave everything into her hands and withdrew, partly because she was ailing, but mainly because she did not know how to run a house in town fashion.

The way of life became better and richer, but the outlay greater too, yet no one protested, not even Ratko who was thrifty. He knew how to accept changes when new conditions demanded them, and was generous when he wished to show off or when it was necessary in business. The former peasant style of life had cost him less, but it was no longer suitable for their house since they had begun to be included amongst the gentry. He therefore ordered all that was needed in the running of a proper household to be bought for Jelka, especially as she demanded nothing for herself but only for the family home.

They bought new pots and pans of best copper, a larger tray with a special set for serving preserves which they now offered to guests, a sewing machine, and the icon of St. Stevan for the visitor's room. At Jelka's request, the old plain runners and divans were discarded from that room and a new Bosnian carpet bought with matching covers for the long *secija* seats, on which firm homespun dark red cushions were arranged in rows. Jelka made curtains for all the windows in both large houses, while any other changes were left for later.

Most affectionate towards Jelka and most attached to her was Stevo's daughter, Olga. She could not remember her mother and, although Simuna and Petrija had brought her up well, Jelka was more tender toward her, more fun, and had a way of cuddling her and surprising her with presents, however small. She was always patient and knew how to play with and comfort her when she cried. Jelka, too, grew very attached to Olga, who was a lovable and beautiful child, because she too had lost her father early in life and knew what it was to be without a parent.

Six weeks after the wedding, Savka came with Jula on a visit. All the Kojics were pleased by the visit, and gathered to welcome them, from Ratko—although he had been annoyed with Savka at the wedding because it seemed to him that she was cold toward his family—to his daughters, who had come from the Mocevac to see Savka. They were all competing as to how best to entertain them, and Jelka looked happy and contented, yet, in spite of everything, many things in their home were not to Savka's liking. She tried to hide this, but left for home with a sad heart.

As soon as she and Jula appeared on the Golubinja, Joka caught sight of them and ran on to the street to meet them. "How is Jelka, how has she settled in?" she asked.

"She's well, thank God, happy and contented," Savka said loudly so that the neighboring women who were sitting by their gates could hear. "She sends her regards and has asked you to come with us next time. She misses you very much."

When they entered the house, Savka went to her room, locked the door and began lamenting quietly. "My Jelka, my great sorrow, you have broken your mother's heart. Although you hide it, I can see how you live. They are rich, but their peasant shoes protrude everywhere. You think you can endure this now, but you won't find it easy in such a family."

After a good cry which unburdened her heart, she changed her festive garments for the clothes she wore at home. When she came down, she told neither Jula nor Joka that she was not happy about Jelka's marriage.

Savka's brothers-in-law did not want to visit the Kojics themselves, but when their wives told them that Savka had been there, Jovo immediately went to her to hear what she would say as to how she had found Jelka.

"Well, how is your daughter?" he said as he sat down.

"She says she is happy, praises Janko and his people, but the family is large, her mother-in-law ailing and cannot help much in the house, and the sister-in-law young and unskilled. What's more, her brother-in-law's child is on her back too. Had she listened to us and married Pavle, she would be living in luxury now."

"What can one do now?" Jovo said. "She fell and she hurt herself. That's how it is when mothers allow their daughters to flirt with young men. In the past a girl did not dare exchange a word with a man, except her closest relative, but now she knows how to scheme with him and send him messages."

Savka said nothing, but felt the sting and became dejected.

"I'm not reproaching you," Jovo added. "My Staka is just like you. She has spoilt Persa and now cannot forbid her seeing fat Lazo whenever I am away from home. I am afraid I too will have to give her away against my will as we have given Jelka, although they are not made for one another."

"Perhaps she likes his looks. He is not so very small but, being podgy, he looks that way."

"Well, I would not care about even that, but they don't get along. They are already arguing so that the whole neighborhood can hear and laugh at them. A few days ago, he was angry, and in front of our house started shouting, 'Eels, who wants eels?' just to jeer at her because she is so long and thin, and she, instead of hiding away, ran to the window and shouted back, 'There is nothing for dogs, not even eels.'"

Jula came in to serve refreshments and, hearing this, she burst out laughing, put the tray on the table and ran out.

"See how they are?" Jovo said angrily. "Instead of being embarrassed, she laughs."

Savka, too, found it difficult to stop herself laughing. She pretended not to hear him, as if preoccupied with her own thoughts. "Not only mothers are guilty. You are a father, it is easier for you to keep her in line, you can beat her."

"How can I beat her when she defies me, the wench? 'One head but a thousand tongues.' She openly told me, 'If you as much as touch me I shall run to the other side of the Crossroads into the Medovic house, and shout from their balcony, "I'm Lazo's, I came to him of my own free will," and once I have taken your honor away, you will give me to him whether you like him or not.'"

"What does Staka say, would she give her to him?"

"She's on her side, like all mothers, allows her everything because she is delicate, fears she may be ill and indulges her."

"God be with her, she's not ill, but picks at her food and is fussy like my Jula. Perhaps she is hurt because Lazo is not to your liking and so pines, poor child. Youth is youth. To tell you the truth, I think Lazo is a good match. If she marries him, she would be near you and would live in clover; the Medovics always keep two servant girls at least."

"There you go, now, defending her like Staka, as if I wish her harm. However, I shall have to give her to Lazo, although I cannot stand the sight of him. Otherwise, I am afraid that he will steal her from me and there will be a scandal."

Jula was eavesdropping and, as soon as Jovo left, she sent a message to Persa that she had heard her father say he would give her to Lazo.

The second year after her marriage, Jelka became pregnant. Everyone was delighted, hoping that she would bear a son.

Ratko intended to name the boy after himself. As he sat on the divan with his legs crossed, he would light his long pipe and reflect: "How wonderful it is to see the continuation of one's own male line as if one were born again, because there will be one more shoot sprouting from my name, even when I am no longer in this world. And thus it will be repeated without end. Everything is forever continuing, nothing comes to an end, praise the Lord! Leaves fall and the following year new ones come out, grass dries up and in its place new grass grows, winter comes and shrouds the hills and valleys in snow. Then in spring the snow thaws and everything becomes green again, insects crawl out, and that's how the world eternally exists, since God is eternal . . ."

He wished to give his grandson the upper house on which was a plaque with the inscription "This house was built by Ratko Kojic and sons in the year of our Lord 1880, in the month of May." He mused proudly, "Ratko built it, let Ratko inherit it."

When Jelka gave birth to a daughter, they were all deflated. She too was so upset that for the first few days she could not feel the joy of becoming a mother. She even reproached the Mother of God, for she had on countless occasions prayed before her icon, looking at the Baby Jesus, hoping that she too might bear a son.

Ratko was hit hardest, and for three days he did not want to enter Jelka's room. It was with some difficulty that Simuna forced him to come with her and present the customary gifts to their granddaughter. After she had put a small golden coin on the child's pillow, he, too, placed a napoleon on it, then, looking sideways at Jelka, made himself mutter, "May she be happy and respected, God willing."

Only Janko was as happy as if a son and heir had been born to him. Often, after Jelka had bathed and breast-fed the child, he would stand for a long time by her cradle and revel in watching her rosy face with a fine dew of perspiration on the rounded forehead, and her sleepy eyes slowly closing.

But after a few weeks, when the baby began to smile and coo, they all grew to love her and even Ratko could not resist her. When Simuna asked for her to be brought into their room, he would stand over her, clicking his fingers to attract her attention, and would light up when she smiled at him. "There is nothing more beautiful than a tiny child's smile."

They did not christen her for a long time because she was born during the great frost around St. Sava's holiday and Jelka would not allow them to take her to the monastery for fear she would get a chill during the christening. (In the Orthodox Church the baby is immersed in water.) When it became warmer, Ratko personally went to Mrzovic to invite Godfather Colovic to christen his grandchild. By his wish, they named her Djana, as it was the name of a girl from Podpec with whom he had fallen in love and had often walked miles to see. Ratko intended to marry her, but his father had forbidden it because it was rumored that she suffered from consumption.

Not long afterwards, Stevo married again. He, too, took the daughter of a squire from an old and well-known family. Rosa was good looking, strongly built, diligent, and very religious. She paid little attention to her looks, and dressed modestly and in an old-fashioned manner. She did not like chatting or joking and when she had finished her work she retired to her room to read the Holy Bible. She was proud of her literacy, prayed frequently, and looked down on the Kojics as if they were heathens because they did not fast on Wednesdays nor during the holy festivals and because they did not attend church regularly but only on the major holidays.

Of all the members of the family Jelka was the one she could least endure, and she was glad that their rooms were not in the same building. She thought to herself, "It is obvious what sort of a woman she is, making herself beautiful all day long, laughing aloud and singing at the top of her voice whenever she sits at the sewing machine. She doesn't leave anyone in peace . . ."

Jelka also disliked Rosa from the very first day, but she was more skillful at concealing it.

Soon, small squabbles started between them which grew more frequent and more bitter, so that the other members of the family began noticing that the two of them did not get along. If something was bought that Jelka desired, or someone praised her, or a blind eye was turned to her breaking something of value, Rosa would be angry with the whole family and would not speak to Jelka for days. The other would then come up to her, wearing a provocative expression of disingenuous innocence on her face. "Sister Rosa, why are you so silent? Did I do something to upset you?"

"Leave me alone, go away and mind your own business. You keep everyone under your thumb and think you can do the same with me. Well, you can't! Let them all grovel to you, I shall not."

"How do you mean, grovel? You yourself see that I work like a slave."

"Yes, you like working, but you also like bossing people about. You've mesmerized them and they all humor you, so that you have become conceited and think you can make me crawl too. Not me, let that be quite clear to you! I carry more weight here than you. My man is Ratko's eldest son and it is only right that I should have precedence."

"No one is taking away your precedence. God knows, I don't understand what you want." She sighed deeply, making a sad face, whilst she thought to herself, "I am not taking your priority away because I have never given it to you."

They continued thus to needle one another, but they took care not to embark on an open quarrel.

One day, however, at lunch, when there was talk of which daughter-in-law should first be presented with the *libade*, the formal gold-embroidered jacket and jewelry, the two confronted one another. Jelka wished them to come to her, as she had been the first to be brought into the home, and Rosa to her, because her husband was the eldest of the brothers. This annoyed Ratko and he threw them both out of the room.

As she was leaving, Rosa said in a whisper, "You'll see, they will buy them for me first. Justice will prevail, it is stronger than your willfulness."

Jelka hid under the stairs to conceal a rude gesture. "That much for your justice being stronger! My injustice will blast your justice to hell."

That evening, in bed, Jelka began to cry and to reproach Janko. "Is that how much you love me! Not one word to show you are on my side. Silent as though you were dumb, letting Rosa push me aside."

"Listen, Jelka, you are not so green any more, stop your play-acting. We buy you everything you can think of, and if that's not possible now, you start crying like a spoilt child. I must give in to Stevo in some things. I can never forget his goodness at the time I was in trouble, when he agreed without a murmur that I should marry before him."

"So, you would allow me on the day of the Holy Trinity to go to the monastery dressed like the wife of an artisan, whilst Rosa is covered in gold from head to foot! I don't mind for my own sake, but what will people think? Everyone will assume I am some kind of poison, disliked by the family. Or, God forbid, that I am lazy, or have some other defect—and that's the reason you won't buy me the *libade* and jewelry after so many years, but adorn her as soon as she arrives. Now you listen to me. You can do as Rosa demands, but from now on I won't budge out of the house, nor shall I wear the necklace or the headdress or *libade* after her, even if you all beg me on bended knees. Let it be known that I count least in this home." She got up, and spread another mattress for herself. "And if you just try to sneak close to me like a tomcat, I'll scratch your eyes out."

Janko tried to convince her that she had no reason to be angry and finally began pleading with her to give in to Rosa this time and next year the same would be bought for her.

When she heard this, Jelka got up and started for the door. "I am going to run up to the attic and won't come down even if my child cries her eyes out, do you hear? Make a fool of yourself tomorrow in front of your own people for having to drag me out of the attic by force."

"Don't be so silly, now, come back to sleep. Tomorrow we'll think of something; if it's at all possible it will be bought for you too."

She threw him an accusing look, but came back, sat on the mattress, then turned to him even more furiously. "'If at all possible!' Very well, I won't let you touch me ever again. You'll get nothing from Jelka from now on, and that's that!"

The night resolved their quarrel. Janko weakened and promised her everything, and she fell asleep contented because she could show Rosa what her "justice" was worth.

In the morning she came down meekly and started talking to Rosa in a conciliatory tone, so that the other thought to herself, "Look at her, with her tail between her legs like a beaten dog. Janko must have given her a hiding last night." Assured of her victory, she forgave Jelka yesterday's argument and continued talking to her as if nothing had happened.

On the first occasion when all three of Ratko's sons were alone with their father, Janko announced that he would buy for Jelka with his own money all that Rosa would receive from the family funds, and so keep the peace in the house.

Ratko flared up, "I knew that trouble would come to my house with daughters from the upper classes. They have destroyed many a home and that's what will happen to mine. You had better understand that from now on nothing will be bought for either of them with the family funds, but you will have to pay for it with your own money, so, if you wish, you can dress them both up to look like birds of paradise." Having said that, he left the room in a furious temper.

Petko followed, afraid of being involved in the argument that he was certain would now arise with so much money in question.

Stevo too was seething with rage, which he controlled for a while to avoid exploding, and only after he had calmed down a little did he say to Janko, "Don't take offense now, but Jelka is a big trouble-maker and you are a weakling to keep giving in to her. Why must we waste so much money when it could all have been paid for by the family, this year for one of them and the next year for the other? If I don't buy the things for Rosa, and your hussy dares provoke her, it'll be worse. People will start avoiding us—already there's talk that we are at loggerheads and that our home is not a happy one. Enemies cannot wait to gloat over our discord. They hate us as it is and are envious of our success." He paused, then slapped his knee angrily. "All right, you buy for yours and I for mine, but from now on not another sound from either of them. Since those two met, there is no joy nor peace for us. Once Petko also marries, everything will go to hell."

Janko said nothing because he never contradicted his elder brother. Deep down he knew that Stevo was right, but nevertheless he felt hurt because they all wanted Jelka to be second to Rosa.

The feast of the Holy Trinity drew near. Everything in the house reflected the approach of the holiday: windows were cleaned, carpets beaten, curtains washed, starched, and ironed, floors scrubbed; everything was in its place, neat and cozy. Jelka and Rosa made plenty of meat and cheese pastries and stored them in wooden cases; baklavas and similar delicacies were left in the baking dishes to soak in sherbet, while other cakes were placed in wooden containers and covered with cloths to set. Roast lambs were taken to the lower store-room where it was as cold as an ice house.

On the very eve of the feast Simuna fell ill, so it was decided that only the men should go to the morning service in the monastery on the first day, Rosa and Jelka in the afternoon, and Petrija on the second and third days when the town's *kolo* dancing was most beautiful because the place was less crowded, as by then the peasants would have dispersed to their homes.

On the day of the feast Jelka and Rosa got up before dawn to finish all the housework, so that after lunch they could make ready and dress up at leisure. Their husbands had renewed their wardrobes from top to toe. Not only did they buy for them the *libade* and jewelry, but also silk robes, ready-made petticoats with frills, shoes of fine black leather with buttons at the side, bought in Goldberg's shop where Viennese fashions were sold, and lace scarves which were worn folded across the chest and gave special distinction to the town dress of Serbian women.

When they sat in the coach next to each other, all dressed in silk, velvet and gold, their husbands thought that they both now had contented hearts and so there would be no more discord in the house.

In front of the monastery forecourt, they stepped out of the coach and ascended the broad stone steps. Making their way through the crowd of people who watched them with admiration, they humbly entered the monastery to venerate the icons and to light candles for the health of the living and peaceful rest of the souls of the dead. They bowed before the altar and went out. Then, skirting the *kolo* dancing which had spread over the entire forecourt, they fought their way to the wooden stairs and climbed up to the long balcony of the monks' cells.

Having found a place from which everyone could see them, they sat down right next to the balustrade supported on its carved pillars. From their pockets they took small mirrors and, with hairpins, smoothed the hair under the velvet headband, held in place by a large golden ring in which a precious stone glittered, lifted the curls on their foreheads, and seeing how their necklaces and headdresses shone in the sun, leaned with satisfaction against the balustrade to observe the people around them. A conciliatory conversation started between them, guarded to avoid a quarrel, which they managed to keep up for a while until it turned into ambiguous bickering and whispered argument.

"See, you hussy, you are the reason why Janko and Stevo had to spend so much money. If you'd only had patience, all the things would have been bought, now for me, next year for you, and the family would have paid for everything."

"You'd have liked that, wouldn't you?" Jelka delicately concealed with one hand a rude sign which only Rosa could see. "Why didn't *you* wait? You'll not be the first! I shall be either the first or equal with you, but never second to you, understand that once and for all."

When the quarrel flared up and people around them began to take notice, they got up and left for home. Shaking with anger, they hurried to the coach which was waiting for them and continued to wrangle all the way home.

Rosa gave birth to a son in the first year and started showing off and looking down on Jelka. She considered herself blessed by God for her righteousness, for she had indeed conceived straight away and borne a male child.

This, for Jelka, was like a dagger in her heart. She now began to make herself even more beautiful so that in this way at least she could torment "that usurper," as she referred to Rosa in her thoughts. Of the entire family only Rosa noticed that Jelka was using make-up and began to remark on it to upset her the more. "You paint yourself like a harlot."

"You too would benefit from some paint, then Stevo might pay you more attention."

"I don't need attention, I am not a flirt like you."

"I suppose you held hands all night long and stared at the moonlight. So where did you get the child?"

"Quiet, you bitch, all you think of is lust. Have you forgotten God and the fear of God? You neither pray nor go to church, but seek new ways to seduce Janko; the whole house can hear your kissing and teasing."

"And you, poor soul, you don't even know what passion and desire are. True, not everyone has the gift of enjoying the pleasures of life, so you'll leave youth behind without knowing what it was spent on."

"I am not a harlot, thank God, but a good housewife and a decent woman. If I were like you, I would fear God himself."

"You ask *Him* about such things too?"

"You are talking like a Lutheran. Don't involve God in your shameless affairs."

"It is you who should leave Him in peace. Go and dress, and make yourself more presentable. Your man will soon be coming from the Charshija."

They continued to spite one another like this. Jelka discovered Rosa's weaknesses and retaliated in her mischievous way. If she saw Rosa secretly collecting fresh eggs from the henhouse for her own use, and hiding them in the pockets of her *dimije* trousers, she would in passing slap her playfully across the hips, breaking the eggs, then in astonishment apologize for everyone to hear. "Please forgive me, how was I to know that you hide raw eggs in your pockets?" Another time she found a freshly baked bun, still hot, wrapped in a cloth hidden beneath a beam in the kitchen quarters. She called Petko and the two of them ate it, put a large stone in its place, then, hiding nearby, they waited to see what would happen next. Soon Rosa appeared, went into the kitchen and reached for it. She turned furiously, but when she saw them, said nothing so as not to give herself away.

Rosa saw that, although she had borne a son, she could not take Jelka's place or undermine her standing because of that, so she decided to tell her father-in-law in front of everybody that Jelka was using make-up. She would not say anything behind her back when she could say it to her face, and on the first occasion, during dinner, she summoned her courage and began:

"In this house some people save and others squander."

Ratko felt that an argument was going to start again and stiffened. "Come on, say who is squandering. Could it be Jelka by any chance?"

"Yes, it is. She changes her clothes three times a day, wears her necklace not only on holidays but on working days as well, and also does other things . . ."

"What other things?"

"She spends money on cosmetics, a whole *medgedia* each month, and what I suffer from her God only knows."

"Come, say openly what you do suffer from her."

"She is turning Olga against me, giving her dates and sweets, spoiling her, so the child is turning away from me."

"Now listen," Ratko cut in, "this is the last time you accuse one another. If you begrudge her spending on cosmetics, I shall give her my own money for it." He opened his money pouch, took out two *medgedias* and put them in front of Jelka. "Here, you can make yourself up as much as you wish. You can also change dresses three times a day if it pleases you, as you already have them, and wear gold day and night if you choose—such use won't wear it out." He then turned to Rosa. "You, too, can paint yourself like a Turkish *bula* if your husband allows you. I shall give you the money as well."

Everyone was silent. Jelka took the *medgedias*, stood up and wanted to kiss Ratko's hand, but he withdrew it angrily and continued staring at Rosa:

"As for your remark about Olga, it is unjust. The child was a baby when Jelka came here and she nursed her as if she had borne her. If she is still attached to her, that's in her favor. It is charitable to look after an orphan. Olga will learn to love you and will become attached to you if you behave in the same way towards her as to your own child." He sighed, scrutinizing them both angrily. "Now listen. If you don't give up arguing, I shall send you both packing back to your families to have your way and throw your tantrums there, as you used to. In my home the daughters-in-law must be willing to obey even the smallest child, as is the custom with us in the country. If your men give you a loose rein," he threw a sidelong glance at Stevo and Janko, "and discord arises in our home, I shall divide the family and let everything collapse, as has already begun."

He did not touch his food again, but got up from the table and went to his room. Jelka sprang to her feet and left the room also, and Rosa ran out after her.

In the courtyard a whispered argument began. They both contained their fury with great effort, their faces burning red, eyes flashing.

"So, you got your reward for announcing in front of everybody that I use make-up!"

"You trollop! Admitting so readily that you paint yourself. Your skin must be thicker than leather, you haven't an ounce of shame in you. I would rather the earth swallowed me up than accept money so openly for what even *bulas* are ashamed and hide, just as the snake hides it legs."

"You are now beside yourself, dear, because Adzo allows me to make up. Go on, explode, I am loved by everyone in this house. Stevo, too, used to love me as a sister, unless you've turned him against me." Someone opened the door of a room nearby and they ran, terrified, each to her own quarters.

Petrija, Ratko's youngest daughter, reached marriageable age. She was more beautiful than her sisters, of medium height, slender, with big blue eyes and black hair. Her mouth was small, with full lips, always red and fresh. From her sisters-in-law she learned to dress well and arrange her hair, to hold herself gracefully, embroider in gold, crochet fine lace and do tapestry, to cook, bake, and receive guests. In other words, how to run even the grandest household.

Her brothers were proud of her and loved her the most because she was the youngest and had a gentle nature, unselfish and sensitive. They wished to marry her into a good family and decided amongst themselves to give her a large dowry and so find for her a better home than those of her elder sisters who had married beneath themselves. When the first opportunity presented itself to raise the question of Petrija's future with their father, they suggested this to him.

Ratko bristled angrily when he heard about the dowry and opposed them from the start. "I did not give one to the other two, nor did my daughters-in-law have any to speak of when they were brought here. Why, then, should it be given to this one?"

"Listen, Adzo," Stevo said, "when you were marrying off Mara and Stojana you were not what you are now, that's why you gave them to artisans of slender means, but God has now made us prosper, let us at least marry off this one well."

"But that would not be right, you see. We allowed the others to go barefoot, so to speak, whilst this one would, beside her rich trousseau, be bringing money with her as well; I would not do that if she were the very light of my eyes."

Janko now interrupted, hoping he could soften Ratko's heart. "All right, Adzo, I also hold that it would be a sin against the other two if we should even now overlook them and abandon them to their present poverty, so let us determine a share for them too; it is never too late to undo an injustice."

"What do you mean?" Ratko was astounded. "You now want three dowries at once, as if the family coffers were overflowing?" he said, and began to puff at his pipe more rapidly, a sure sign that his anger was rising. "Do you realize that we would soon be scraping the bottom if we were to take out recklessly and put little in?"

Stevo began to explain to his father that they would not be able to marry off even Petrija as well as they should because the family were not yet sufficiently well known and, without money, her beauty would be worth nothing. He tried to convince Ratko that amongst her suitors would be young men from the best families as soon as it became known that she had a big dowry.

"No!" Ratko flatly refused. "I don't want to break into the family wealth, so you, if you are that softhearted about your sisters, can pay for their shares from your own pockets. There are three of them, so let each of you give to one."

Having no other choice, they agreed that Stevo would give to Mara, Janko to Stojana, and Petko to Petrija.

The next day, at the same time, they all assembled in Ratko's room. Simuna came too—only the daughters-in-law were told not to enter. Mara and Stojana did not know exactly what was to be decided, but they had heard some rumor that it concerned Petrija's dowry, and they were both on edge.

Mara was tall, bony, dark, worn, and gray, with premature lines around her eyes, always frowning, as if she had never in her life laughed or been happy. Stojana was small and fat, with faded blue eyes and blonde hair. She was never satisfied with anything. She complained because she had married a man who was ill, and wished that her husband would either recover or die so that she could marry again. When she became a widow, she continued to complain about her husband for leaving her with nothing; about her father and brothers giving her too little support; about her son being a tie, as she could not remarry because of him since she did not wish to burden him with a stepfather. Yet she had a good heart, often visiting the sick, bringing them gifts and spending days nursing them. She took her little Diko everywhere and God alone must have looked after him, for he never contracted any illness but was healthy, with cheeks always as rosy as apples. On every All Souls' Day, she would go to the graveyard and light candles for the dead whether she had known them or not, and give money to the poor to pray for their souls.

The three sisters sat next to each other, their brothers facing them, and at the head sat Ratko and Simuna. When they had settled down, Ratko began to speak as if he were delivering a sermon.

"Hear, my daughters, that your brothers wish to make you happy and give each of you equally your share of their own money. For you two, Mara and Stojana, this will mean a great help in your need, and it will make you, Petrija, a well-endowed bride-to-be."

When Stojana heard that they were to receive equal shares, she started crying. "That's not fair. Mara has a house and rent from it, she's alone and profits from everything, a little from the embroidery which she sells through *bulas*, a little from your help, so she's been quite comfortable. Whilst I have nothing. I pay the rent and I've a child to support. What you give me I eke out as far as I can, but there is never enough, always only 'ninety *grosh* for a hundred days,' as they say, and I cannot make ends meet."

"There'll never be enough to satisfy your grudges," Mara snapped. "You have always found my morsel bigger than yours. You think I am happy because I am alone? If I had just one child the whole world would belong to me, even if I were destitute. I'd have turned every stone to earn a living in order to nurse and cherish it."

Ratko grew angry and wanted to throw them both out, but Stevo wouldn't let him.

"Leave it to us to speak to them, Adzo. We have made ourselves responsible for them and we can come to a just decision even without you."

Ratko said nothing. It was the very first time that someone had disregarded his orders. This surprised him, but he realized that he had no right to interfere as it was not a question of his money.

Stevo addressed Mara: "Tell me, sister, how would it be best for me to pay your share? Do you want it all at once, or to be given to you monthly?"

"The first," Mara said without hesitation, "and all to be recorded in writing stating exactly how much you are giving me and stressing that it is not given out of charity but instead of my dowry."

Stojana did not wait for Janko to ask her, but began hurriedly, "I am asking nothing from you, my brother, but to build me a small house so that I have a roof over my head."

Here Ratko could not restrain himself from interfering. "Ah, Stojana, you are asking too much. Do you know what it costs to build a house? It is not a birdcage, to be hung on a branch . . ." He paused, then suggested, "Let Janko build you a medium-sized house, four rooms with a corridor in the middle, and let him give it to you for you to enjoy without any payment for as long as you live. All this to be registered at the Town Hall so that the documents are in his name.

If your Diko can buy it when he grows up, that is all right. If he cannot, then after your death it would remain Janko's and his children's."

Both Janko and Stojana agreed to this.

When it was Petrija's turn, she was too shy to tell them what she wanted but said that she would be satisfied with whatever Petko provided for her.

"Petrija, I could buy you the *libade* and all the jewelry when you get married, the same as Rosa and Jelka had."

Joy set Petrija's face aglow. "I would wish that most of all," she whispered, delighted.

"Why wait until she marries? Why don't you buy it for her now and let her take it with her together with her trousseau when she is led away?" Ratko again intervened. "One must strike whilst the iron is hot, Petrija, or your brother could go back on his word later; he's a bit unreliable and tight-fisted!"

When Petko saw that his father was relaxed and in a better mood, he did not spare him either. "True, Adzo, I am of your blood. You are not unreliable, but your fist is indeed tight and you keep it tighter than any of us."

Simuna had remained silent all this time and was holding her hands pressed firmly over her stomach. Since she had begun ailing, she felt a constant dull pain there and was indifferent to everything around her. She seldom left her room and was mostly in bed.

Once it became known that the Kojic brothers had given dowries to their sisters, suitors from good class homes were soon asking for Petrija's hand, but she found fault with them all.

Janko became suspicious, and one day he asked Jelka whether Petrija had confided whether she was in love with someone. The two had become close friends and Petrija talked to her about the young men who came to their gates to court her. However, she had said nothing about Djoko Adzipetrovic until a few days previously, because he was rumored to be a keen womanizer and she was afraid of being forbidden to see him. Jelka had discovered by chance that he was frequently seen around their house and had guessed that it was he who appealed most to Petrija.

It happened on the day it was Petrija's turn to prepare dinner. She had baked a *burek* and had put it out to cool on the flagstones beside the kitchen doorstep. When she went to take it in, she was flabbergasted to find the dish empty. As she looked round, wondering what had happened to a whole *burek*, she heard Djoko's voice coming from Glavica Hill:

"Oh, what a pastry, succulent and tasty, a regular feast for us!"

She looked up and saw him sitting on the slope nearby with his friends, laughing.

"Don't stand there staring, better go and prepare another one for dinner."

Petrija could never be angry with Djoko, she had learned to love his jokes and mischief, so she laughed too, then ran to Jelka's room to tell her what had happened and ask her advice about dinner.

"You never told me you knew Djoko Adzipetrovic," said Jelka, looking quizzically at her.

Petrija blushed deeply and turned away to hide her embarrassment.

"You rather like him, it seems," Jelka said.

Petrija whispered, "Yes."

"Is he in love with you?"

"He says he is."

"Is he going to ask for your hand?"

"He never mentioned that."

"Oh now, Petrija, take care. He has swept many a girl off her feet, then slipped away and washed his hands of her. Should Adzo and your brothers hear about him, they would kill you."

"What shall I do about dinner? It's too late to start another *burek*." Petrija was trying to change the subject.

"Have you got anything else ready?"

"I have a meat and potato stew, that's ready, what else should I add?"

"I'll quickly mix the dough for a pudding, it will soon rise if I put several eggs in it, and you can prepare something good to start with, smoked meats, pate, and cheeses, to be eaten with raki as an aperitif, then bring out the stew. By then the pudding will be ready too."

After that evening, Jelka could find no peace of mind. She worried about Petrija because she knew how difficult it was for a girl to remain chaste. A male is a male. How clever she had had to be to protect herself from Janko. And Janko was honest, he would have married her even if the worst had happened. About Djoko all sorts of things were being said, and she therefore wondered whether to tell Janko about him. So, when he approached her first, she felt relieved.

Janko was not too displeased when he heard about Djoko, because he came from an old and noble family and was the only son. The Kojics knew him by sight, a small wiry young man with lively, intelligent eyes, dark hair, and a thin mustache. It was known that his grandfather had been the first man from Plevlje to visit the Holy Land and that in their home were many relics brought back from Jerusalem and Christ's tomb—precious crosses carved from yew, the staffs of the holy hermits, bones of the saints, a piece of wood from the cross on which Christ was crucified. And it was rumored that several pots of gold were buried in the foundations of their house.

Whilst Janko and Petko held that Djoko was a good match for Petrija, Stevo did not agree.

"I have heard," he said, shaking his head firmly, "that he is a flirt and has deceived many a girl who later had great trouble in finding a husband."

Janko smiled confidently. "Perhaps, if he found easy pickings somewhere or a girl who was unprotected, but with us he would not dare touch her. He knows who he would be dealing with: we would break every bone in his body."

"Even so," Stevo went on, "if he does not ask for her hand soon we shall have to forbid her to see him."

The Kojics waited for Djoko to approach them about Petrija, but when they saw that he continued coming to see her and did not ask for her hand, they became uneasy and forbade her to stand around talking to him at the gates, so for a while he did not appear.

One evening, when they returned from the Charshija, Stevo and Janko heard whispering in the forecourt, and when they opened the gates someone hid behind them. They stopped to look and were astonished to see Djoko and Petrija crouching in the corner. They grabbed him by the shoulders, but Petrija ran upstairs, flew into her father's room and burst into tears.

"Quickly, Adzo, Stevo and Janko want to give a thrashing to Djoko Adzipetrovic!"

Ratko came out on the landing and paused to see whether they were fighting or just arguing. Stevo's voice could be heard:

"Come on, why don't you speak up and give us an answer? What were you looking for at this time of the day in someone else's forecourt?"

"I was chatting with your sister," Djoko answered defiantly.

"And you, you rogue, chose to chat in here?"

"What else could I do when you hide her away like a Turkish *bula*?"

"You are lying, dog, we are not Turks to be hiding her, but we wouldn't allow her to talk to a rotten philanderer like you even outside the gates, let alone hiding in dark corners. You spend all your time fooling around with girls without any thought of marriage."

"I shall get married when I please. Are you by chance trying to force your sister on me?"

"Who is forcing you, you scoundrel? Get out of here before we thrash you."

"Just you touch me, if you dare!" Djoko began to provoke them. "I have done nothing to her to make me afraid of you."

Ratko was getting worried that they really might come to blows, and he called from above, "Wait until I come. Don't you touch him."

They released Djoko, then posted themselves at the gates to prevent him from running away. When Ratko arrived, Stevo said angrily:

"This scoundrel wants to bring shame on our house. He sneaks and steals into God knows where and because of him many a girl has got a bad reputation; but he won't succeed here. We'll break his nose so that he will remember as long as he lives, nor will that wench of ours get away lightly."

"Calm down, children," Ratko soothed. "He is neither a scoundrel nor a sneak, but a young man from a good family, of the line of Adzipetrovic. Come inside, let us talk things over quietly. Why are you making such a fuss? Anyone would think that something had really happened."

They all went into the visitors' room, where the family guests were received, and when they were seated, Ratko turned to Djoko:

"Listen, young man, if you are interested in our Petrija and she is in you, and if your intentions are serious and honorable, you ought to ask for her hand and I would give her to you; but, if not, leave our house alone. I have saved you this time but if you once again hang about anywhere near our courtyard we shall give you such a beating that even God himself won't save you."

Djoko sat mute, staring rigidly in front of him as if someone had drenched him in cold water.

Ratko now addressed his sons sharply: "I forbid you to say another word to this young man and I want no more noise this evening. Calm down and escort him decently and quietly to his house. It is getting late, someone else might attack him and everybody would think it your doing since he was seen earlier in front of our gates."

Djoko approached Ratko and shook hands in silence, then went out with Petrija's brothers.

They did not utter a word all the way, but when they arrived at the Adzipetrovics' house, Stevo said:

"Go now, but if we see you once more with our sister, we'll wring your neck like a chicken's, even if it lands us in jail. "

Entering his gate, Djoko shouted, "If I want to, I shall come again!"

They ran back to seize him, but he shut the gates in their faces and locked the heavy iron-bound doors.

"You'll pay for this too, one day, you bastard!" Stevo shouted after him, overcome with fury.

"I wouldn't give Petrija to him now, even if he begged us on bended knees," Janko added bitterly.

Djoko stood still until the sound of their footsteps grew faint, then took off his shoes, crept upstairs in stockinged feet so that his father would not hear him, and went into his room. He sat on the *secija*, took off his fez, and scratched his head. "Well, well, I was in a tight spot this evening! Ratko saved me, otherwise I was in for a tough time!" As he began to unbutton his gaiters, his thoughts still lingered over there on the Hill, with Petrija. "I do care for her, devilishly. The thought that those tyrants might be beating her now makes my whole being ache for her. I didn't realize till now how truly fond I had grown of her." He stretched, tired, listless, and flat, as after some illness, then undressed and lay down. Worries absorbed him again.

"I don't dare go anywhere near there or they'll wallop me. And get married . . .? No! What do I need with all that aggravation? Children being born and, with them, all the worries and other troubles. No! I'm happy as a lark as I am. I shall get married as my father did, when I tire of bachelorhood. There's plenty of time."

He was tossing and turning in his bed, trying to fall asleep, but sleep evaded him. As dawn was breaking, he was still awake, rummaging among his thoughts. Determined to get some sleep, he got up and closed the window so as not to be disturbed by the sound of voices around the fountain where people were already gathering to fetch water, the din of the ewers and jugs, and the arguing of the women. Angry and exhausted, he lay down again, pulled the cover over his head and fell asleep.

His mother, Sara, came twice with coffee to wake him, but having peered from the door of his room and seen how deeply he slept, she went back. When she heard that her husband Gavro was awake, she went to ask whether he would like her to bring his food first, as always, and later coffee, or would it be better if he drank some hot raki with sherbet for his cold.

"Bring whatever you wish," Gavro said morosely. "He came in late again last night, I heard noises outside the gates."

"Yes, as usual. You know his habits, it's not the first time he's done it."

Gavro said nothing. He got up and began to dress. When Sara brought him the raki and asked what he wanted for breakfast, he waved her away.

"I want no breakfast, nor anything, when I know what is waiting for me. I shall have to marry off that vagabond so that he settles down once and for all!"

"Steady, Gavro! You were no better. There was plenty of talk about your goings-on with dancers in Salonika. I have heard lots of things, even since we got married, and when you were being so jealous about me. For two years you did not allow me to look out of the window in case any man should see me."

Gavro stamped off, not wanting to listen to the same reproaches for the thousandth time. "As soon as he gets up, tell him to come to the store to help. It's market day and there will be a big rush."

Sara accompanied him to the gates, brushing the back of his coat with her hand. Whenever she reminded herself that he had kept straying even after he married her, she consoled herself that at least now, in old age, he belonged to her alone, forever, and she enjoyed feeling her own possessions under her hand.

Djoko woke before lunch. He got up, went to the window, and looked towards the Kojics' houses. Now everything seemed clearer and simpler. Even the thought of marriage did not seem impossible. On the contrary, it appealed to him more than giving up Petrija. Without her, nothing was worth while any more. "I'll marry, there's no other way."

Sara came in, bringing coffee. "My God, son, you're late, and your father said you were to go to the store at once!"

"All right, all right, I'll get ready quickly. Will you bring some hot water for me to shave?"

When she left, Djoko washed and dressed and as soon as his mother returned, he began to shave and drink his coffee. Sara noticed that he was very preoccupied and silently withdrew from the room.

In his thoughts, Djoko continued talking to himself: "I have some regard for Ratko. A peasant, yet a wise man. His sons are fine too, presentable and hard-working. They have gained respectability, especially the two older ones; the youngest is quiet and only a few people know him. They did call me all sorts of names yesterday evening, especially Stevo—a dog could not swallow what he said to me even if it were buttered. But, to be honest, they had some reason for it. They were defending their sister's honor. I would do the same if I had one. They would make good brothers-in-law, someone to be seen with in the Charshija and show off in front of people."

It was clear to him now that marriage was imminent. He only wanted to find out how big a dowry Petrija would bring. He had heard something but only vaguely. It would have been better if he could have sounded them out before he asked for her hand, and learned how much it was, but there was no time left for waiting now. He was afraid that her brothers might forcibly give her to another, to spite him. "Why beat about the bush? I shall go there this very day and ask them openly."

As soon as he got to the Charshija, he sent a message to the Kojics that he would come after *icindija*, the call for afternoon prayers, and talk to them about an engagement.

Ratko was glad to hear this, and even Stevo and Janko were not displeased, although they were angry with Djoko. They refused to be present during the talks and decided to go to the Charshija and stay there until after *aksham*, evening prayers. Petko went with them to avoid being involved should any dispute arise about the dowry.

At the appointed time Djoko arrived. He met Stojana in the forecourt and bade her ask her father whether he would receive him. When she went upstairs, he glanced into the kitchen quarters and saw Petrija there. Stealing up behind her, he tried to kiss her, but she pushed him away.

"Go away, for God's sake, you clown, there will be trouble if anyone sees you near me. I had enough last evening, never in my life have I been so terrified."

"Did they beat you?"

"No, but they said I wouldn't get away lightly if they saw me once more with you."

"I came to ask for your hand—so you will become the clown's wife."

Petrija was bewildered and tears of happiness filled her eyes, but she still did not let him near. "Go now, please," she said gently. "Perhaps Adzo is angry and could beat me if he finds you here."

Stojana now arrived and told Djoko that Ratko was waiting for him in the visitors' room.

Ascending the stairs, Djoko straightened the collar of his jacket and pulled his waistcoat closer to his chest, whilst Stojana and Petrija peered from the kitchen, laughing.

"Cold feet, by heavens, toeing the line now we've got you," Stojana said in a whisper.

"Hush, now! Adzo may not give me away."

"Of course he will, you fool, indeed he'll give you away. Who could ask for a better match? Why did your brothers clear off, if not to let Father maneuver Djoko into marrying you? Why aren't they here now to send him packing? When you become engaged, they'll pretend nothing ever happened and will be proud to have got such a brother-in-law. Had Mara and I gone to better homes, they would be looking after us better even now. It is not for nothing that the saying goes 'A wealthy sister has loving brothers.' Everyone looks after his own interests, that's how it is."

Jelka and Rosa came in. They were dressed up and had prepared refreshments, waiting only for their father-in-law to call them. He had ordered that Petrija should not come until he sent for her.

Djoko went to the door of the visiting room, opened it slowly and entered timidly.

Ratko got up from the *secija* and came to meet him. "Greetings, and welcome," he said cordially.

They shook hands and sat down next to one another. Djoko was glad to find that none of Petrija's brothers were in the room. He took out a cigarette case and offered it to Ratko. The other refused with a wave and pointed to the pipe lying beside him.

"Thank you, I smoke this, but please go ahead."

Djoko rolled a cigarette, waited for Ratko to fill his pipe, then lit up, first for Ratko, then for himself.

"I can see that you're a decent young man and that you know how to show respect for your elders. Nowadays not all young people do."

Encouraged by such a reception, Djoko decided to tackle the matter straight away. "I have come to discuss the engagement. I have not told my father anything until I have enquired how big a dowry Petrija would be bringing. If we two settle this, my father would also agree."

Ratko frowned. This approach displeased him, but he tried not to show it because it was a question of Petrija's happiness. He adopted a stern tone of voice, but without shouting or being offensive. "To tell you the truth, young man, you have surprised me somewhat by the manner in which you begin discussing an engagement. I am not selling my daughter nor buying a son-in-law, to be now 'settling' this with you, as you put it."

"I only wanted to know this before I advised my father that I wish to marry her. He will certainly ask me about it. That, I think, is not an insult at all. In the merchants' world it is customary."

"Yet, you see, it is not so everywhere. My sons are merchants, but when they got married they did not even mention a dowry. That would, in their opinion, have been embarrassing."

Now Djoko felt offended and went on stubbornly, "If the dowry is an embarrassment, why did you give it to her and let the news be rumored about?"

"But, my dear man, that's another matter. It was our desire to endow our girl well, as a gift to her, not to give to whoever should wish to marry her. And as for haggling about it, it is out of the question here." He paused, then continued angrily, "Now, I am asking you, do you love Petrija and do you intend to marry her whether she has a dowry or not?"

"I do love her, I would not be here now if I did not, even if she had the treasure of Tsar Radovan![4] If she brings money with her, that's fine, and if not, I'll take her with nothing at all!"

"Ah well, young man, that's how you should have started and not from the wrong end. I shall now give you a plain answer." He cleared his throat, drew a few times on his pipe, and said, "Had it been up to me, I would not have given her a farthing. What does a good girl need a dowry for? But my sons decided to buy her a headdress and necklace such as my daughters-in-law have, to take with her trousseau."

This seemed too little to Djoko, but he did not venture another word on the matter, and changed the subject. "I would wish us now to decide the dates for the engagement and the wedding. The Christmas feast is approaching, so let's seize the time before then, as winter will set in afterwards."

"I will talk it over with my sons and will send word for you to come to decide on the exact day of the wedding."

Djoko wanted to leave immediately, on the pretext that his father was waiting for him in the Charshija, though in truth to avoid meeting Ratko's sons, but Ratko would not allow him to.

"Sit down to drink at least one glass of raki with me, for your and Petrija's happiness. That much time you have."

Having said that, he left the room and called from the landing, "Petrija, congratulations my child, the engagement is arranged. Bring some raki for your Adzo, my dear, to drink health to you both. Hurry up, Djoko must leave as his father is awaiting him."

In the kitchen quarters, the kissing and congratulations began. Stojana burst into tears of happiness. "How fortunate you are, my sister, getting married to a healthy man, entering a wealthy home and, what's more, you love him. Thank God you at least are happy, and you won't forget us two, either."

Petrija was stunned, and unable to move, but her sisters-in-law put a tray in her hands and helped her to cross the courtyard. She entered the room quite confused, served raki to her father and to Djoko, then started for the door, but Ratko stopped her.

"Hey, wait, bride-to-be, where are you going? Come, let Adzo congratulate you." When she approached, he kissed her forehead. "May this be happy and forever!" He turned to Djoko, clinked glasses with him, then raised his own. "May it bring happiness to you too, God willing! Come on, shake hands you two, why are you so wooden?"

Djoko went up to Petrija and they shook hands. "May we be happy," he said, then pinched her arm so that Ratko could not see.

She covered her face to hide her laughter, while Ratko thought, looking at her, "That's women for you, pretending to be embarrassed, yet she knew how to sneak behind the gates with him. One cannot trust them, even if they are holy. They are all Eve's daughters, even the holy Mary herself, may God forgive me."

When Djoko set off, Ratko accompanied him to the stairs to show him every courtesy. Rubbing his hands contentedly, he returned to his room and said to Petrija:

"This has turned out well. 'The wolf is satisfied and all the sheep are accounted for,' as the saying goes. He wanted to ask for money beside the dowry, the fox, but I anticipated it."

Petrija looked at her father absentmindedly, without hearing what he was saying. "God, is it true . . ." she thought, "that I will be Djoko's?"

She collected the glasses, left them on the table, and ran to her mother's room.

"Nana, I'm engaged. I shall marry into the Adzipetrovics' house."

"May it bring you happiness, child," Simuna whispered, then began to cry.

Petrija sat beside her mother, lowered her face into her lap and she also began to cry. "I'm so sorry to leave you, Nana."

"That is as God ordained, child. I too left my mother when I married, and I had to go into another village, whilst you will be near me."

Jelka came in just then, bringing coffee for Simuna. She congratulated her, then turned to Petrija. "Don't cry now, but wash your face and comb your hair, then go to receive guests. Some neighbors have already come, and Mara came too, furious because we promised Petrija without asking her."

"God, how odd she is," Simuna said. "I am the mother and I am not annoyed that they did not ask me."

"She is difficult," Jelka smiled, then joyfully reminded Petrija, "Go on, bride-to-be, lots of people will soon be arriving."

Petrija went out of the room and Jelka helped Simuna to dress in festive clothes, then tidied her room a little in case someone came in with congratulations, as Simuna did not leave it any more because of the dull pain in her stomach.

4

After Petrija's marriage, Simuna's illness worsened and confined her to bed. She was racked by stabbing stomach pains, felt sick and could not eat. Stojana nursed her and brewed healing herbs for her to drink, rubbed her with raki and vinegar, applied poultices to her navel, and even steamed her over hot bricks, but she felt no better.

They called the priest to say prayers for Simuna and took her to the monastery of the Holy Trinity, where they helped her to slide beneath the casket in which Saint Sava's staff and the bones of some unknown saint were kept, but even that did not help.

Finally, Mara secretly brought a famous soothsayer, Majra, to see her. Majra pressed her hands all over Simuna's body then, with a forefinger on the roof of her mouth, looked at her throat and tongue, and questioned her as to where and when the pains attacked.

"I will now cast the embers and melt the lead so that I can predict, to a hair's breadth, where your illness has settled and how you contracted it," she said.

She cut off a strand of Simuna's hair, pulled a few threads from her shirt and went with Mara to the kitchen quarters to begin her divining. With tongs she spread the embers in the hearth, and gripped a few live coals to singe the strands of Simuna's hair together with the threads, then melted the lead in a small pan and poured everything into a bowl of water. The embers hissed in the water and the molten lead hardened again into a few small nuggets of various shapes. Majra sat on the floor with the bowl on her lap and, bending over it, began her soothsaying:

"I see here some brushwood in the grass, also a lizard and a large snake. Evil spells lie in wait in the grass on which the ailing woman stepped, and because of it she became ill. The illness is gnawing at her secretly, as the snake gnaws the roots, and is poisoning her as the lizard with his slime poisons everything around him. It has struck at her guts now, and later it'll spread its threads to her legs, arms, under her ribs, until it reaches her heart." Glancing at Mara and seeing how pale and frightened she had become, she changed her tone to console her. "But do not fear, I can cure her. With those coals I have removed the spells, you heard how they hissed; they cannot harm anybody from now on because I have destroyed their threads. And now I'll give you a potion which will heal the gnawed guts." So saying, she took from the pocket of her *dimije* trousers a small bottle corked with a piece of corncob and handed it to Mara. "Pour this into a bottle of beer and add strong raki to it, preferably from the first brew. Your mother should every day drink a small glass of it first thing in the morning. Take this water with the embers and lead nuggets outside the gates tomorrow before dawn, and pour it out on four sides, left, right, before, and behind you, and that's how the illness will pour away from your home. If you do all this, by my Turkish Allah, your mother will be cured."

Mara paid her, then led her down the back yard and out through the narrow garden gates, fearing that someone might see. She was most afraid of Rosa, who would be angry because she had brought a heathen into the house and so would tell Ratko, who would raise hell if he found out that divining and soothsaying had taken place in his home.

Simuna drank Majra's medicine, and many others which women

neighbors kept bringing her, but she felt scarcely any benefit from it all. She could eat a little and move around, but the dull pain in her stomach persisted.

One day, when they were all assembled in Simuna's room, Rosa said, "How would it be if now, around Lady Day, we took Nana to the church of Our Lady of Miracles in Cajnice? Whoever goes there has been healed, especially if they spend the night in front of the altar where the icon of the Mother of God is placed. The blind have found their sight, the lame have walked again, the paralyzed risen . . ."

Ratko interrupted her, "Leave those stories be, daughter Rosa. Were this so, nobody in Cajnice would ever be ill."

"Don't talk like that," Simuna pleaded. "Perhaps the Mother of God would help if I went to her and appealed to her gentle heart."

"If that's what you wish, I'll take you, not only to Cajnice, but also to Saint Vasilija of Ostrog, and if you wish, to the foot of Ostrog Mountain. Though I don't believe much in such help. God alone can save you, and he will do so without your asking."

"Why couldn't we all go with Nana, Adzo?" Stevo suggested. "There is a big feast there on Lady Day. It lasts three days, and there's a large fair too. People gather from all parts, so we might do some trading there as well."

"But how can we leave our home and business here?" Ratko asked, anxiously.

"We could close the shop and the store for a few days," Janko suggested, "and leave Jelka's cousin, Vaso, at the Inn. He knows a bit of German and will manage to make himself understood with the soldiers. Mara and Stojana can move into our houses here to look after them."

Ratko paused a little to reflect. "All right, so be it," he said, looking at Simuna with concern. "God knows whether we'll all ever again travel somewhere together."

Jelka was delighted about the trip, not only because of the festivities, but also because she would see her aunt, who was married to a prominent merchant in Cajnice, Petar Adzilukic. Without delay, she sent word to her mother to come and help her decide what presents she should take.

The following day Savka arrived all excited, and even as she entered the door she began, "I am delighted you are going to see Nasta, she's my favorite cousin. We are the same age and grew up together. I myself shall send her a gift also, but for you it would be best if you took the family a large bundle of special gifts for everyone. Get something gold for her, a brooch or earrings, she always loved jewelry."

"Oh, Mother, I can't tell you how glad I am to get away from all this hard work for a while, and go somewhere where people are rejoicing and having a good time. When one is in a large family, one can't move, like it or not."

"Couldn't you take Jula with you, my dear, as a favor?" Savka suggested diffidently. "She doesn't see any life or even go outside the gates, nor has she any girlfriends dropping in, or that she could visit. She has a strange nature, like her father, my Tane. But he had a business to occupy him and used to mix with people, however casually, while she buries herself in the house as if she had already gone gray, and she'll be only eighteen this coming Shrove Tuesday." She sighed, then went on, afraid that Jelka would interrupt her, "Neither does she court like other girls. Young men began to stroll in front of our house but gave up. Perhaps they heard that she had found fault with each one. Nor does she have any worthwhile suitors, and I fear if it stays that way I'll find it difficult to marry her off."

"All right, I'll take her with me as you suggest. Who knows where happiness is to be found, and which path one's destiny has ordained?"

Savka sent Jula ahead to help Jelka prepare for the trip, and in her wake a bundle containing her clothes and shoes.

Jula differed from her sister in every way, in looks and in temperament. Shorter and slimmer, she was long-legged and had small feet like Savka, a darker complexion, but blue eyes and light hair which deepened into a wild chestnut glow. She was proud of her good looks, and so obstinate that her mother had to indulge her in every way. Joka, too, was afraid of her and tried to please her even harder than Savka, whilst Jelka could never feel really close to her, nor help with advice, as Jula thought she knew best about everything.

The preparations for the journey were in full swing. Afraid that everywhere would be booked because of the Fair, Janko wrote to Jelka's relative in Cajnice, Petar Adzilukic, and asked him to find them somewhere to stay. The women baked pies, savory biscuits, and plain cakes which they decorated with sugar cubes; new dresses were made for Simuna, who had to be persuaded that she could not go to Cajnice in peasant clothes.

Soon, a reply to Janko's letter arrived in which Adzilukic wrote that he was looking forward to their visit, and had not tried to find lodgings for them because he and his family were offering the hospitality of their home. There was room for everyone, they were eagerly expected, and he sent his best wishes.

On the day before Lady Day, early in the morning, in front of the Kojics' houses two coaches arrived, ordered by Stevo and Janko from Osmo Hodzic, who hired out the most expensive coaches in Plevlje.

When Ratko set eyes on them, his mood turned sour and he went to Simuna's room grumbling: "Our sons are real spendthrifts! They've taken the dearest coaches, as if they couldn't find something cheaper! We would have been no worse off if we'd taken an ox cart, as I wished. We could all get on it, and there'd still be room for the bundles of clothes and food. How shall we two sit all the way to Cajnice with our legs hanging down? In an ox cart we would have put cushions on the straw and relaxed crosslegged; you could lie down too, if you felt unwell."

"Don't be angry, for God's sake," Simuna whispered, trying to calm him. "Let them do as they like, it is their turn now."

When the others heard that the coaches had arrived, they rushed to finish dressing, then began to carry out and load up their bundles and take leave of Mara and Stojana, who were staying behind to look after the houses. They would also supervise the employees assigned to help in the gardens and stables, and with the livestock, while the Kojic shops and store were closed. Finally, they all took their places in the two coaches and set off: Ratko, Simuna, Stevo and Rosa with their little son Pavle on her lap in the first, and in the other Janko, Petko, Jula, and Jelka with Djana.

The autumn was early that year and nature's changes could already be felt. The leaves had begun to turn all shades of green, yellow, brown, and crimson. Cool, fresh air whipped their faces, the horses raced as if they had wings and their manes flowed in the wind. Everybody was in a good mood except Ratko. As they were crossing the barracks grounds, Simuna looked around her spellbound by the splendor that spread before her. Broad, even paths led through the avenue of wild chestnuts behind which stretched the dense forest of beech, oak, and acacias. There was no hint of a military background and the barracks could not be seen for the greenery. The artificial lake with its small central island glittered, water gurgled in the bronze fountain, the brooks murmured as they branched out and channeled the water across the grounds, and narrow lanes twisted like pale serpents amongst the flower beds and shrubs.

"Do you see, Simuna, how the Shvabas have settled their asses in our valleys? They brought in their army, planted their camps, and built their nest as if they would stay here for centuries. But, God willing, we may soon see the back of them."

"And do you think the valleys are ours?" Stevo said sadly. "Nothing belongs to us, we are slaves."

"They were once ours and will be again, with God's help. It is said that Saint Sava's father and his descendants ruled here until the Turks overran them, after the battle of Kosovo, and now this evil has also moved in. But all power fades and misfortunes come in series. Their empires will dissolve too, and they'll turn tail and settle down wherever their native soil is. Our dawn will break: we can't be slaves for ever."

"Do you really have hope, Adzo, that we'll ever be free?"

"Of course I have, now more than ever; we are not alone any more, there are others who think about us too," said Ratko, and glanced meaningfully at the coachman's back.

Only now did Stevo remember that the coachman was a Turk. He was afraid they might unwittingly say more than could freely be said except in front of Serbs, so he changed the subject, and asked his mother how she felt.

"Far better than when lying or sitting all day long in my room," Simuna said, radiant.

The morning was free of mist, which was rare at this time of year. When they emerged from the valleys, before them lay a wide highway which led through the slopes of the bare hills covered only by thin yellowing grass, stunted bushes, and clumps of juniper. The higher they went, the denser and greener these bushes became, until they entered woodland.

95

"We'll soon arrive at Boljanice," Stevo said, "where we can rest and have a drink. Somebody has opened a small inn there now, and I hear it is doing well."

"No," Ratko broke in. "We'll continue to Metaljka and rest at our own inn." He turned to glance at Jelka, but could not see her face. It was rumored that her father had been killed by Turks near Boljanice and he wanted to pass quietly through that area.

When they heard that they were driving through Boljanice, Jelka and Jula grew sad. They had been very young when they learned from a neighboring woman that somewhere near this highway the Turks had cut their father's throat. Although Mother had told them this was not true, and that he had died by falling off his horse and hitting his head against a boulder, they had always harbored a hidden pain and doubt.

After the woodland, they drove through pine trees which grew ever denser and became a real pine forest. Metaljka was situated there, a small settlement with a few soldiers' huts and several houses, some log cabins and a few tiny shops, neither a town nor a village. They stopped in front of a low-lying inn from which Ratko's relative, Risto, and members of his family ran out to welcome them.

"We won't stay long," Ratko said, stepping from the coach, "only a little while for Simuna to rest."

"We'll see about that," Risto protested as he came up to help Simuna. His wife took Rosa's child in her arms, and his son and daughter-in-law went to the second coach to give a hand to the others. They greeted Janko and Petko, but did not venture to approach Jula and Jelka, somewhat stunned by their good looks and distinguished bearing.

When they all entered the inn, Risto invited the coachmen too to take some refreshment as soon as they had covered the horses with blankets and fed and watered them.

Settling their visitors on benches around two tables, they put a cushion stuffed with straw behind Simuna's back and wrapped woolen shawls around her and the children, as the air at this altitude was much cooler than in Plevlje.

"Don't you start preparing anything, Risto," Ratko said, seeing that the other was whispering something to his wife and daughter-in-law. "I meant it when I said we wouldn't stay long."

"Upon my word, I won't let you leave without lunch! Everything will soon be ready, the chickens we've just plucked are already roasting on the spit and the women will prepare the rest. Leave as soon as you've had lunch. You'll arrive before dark, so don't you fret."

Seeing that everyone wished to relax a little, Ratko gave in. "All right, if you insist, but I fear we'll overtax your hospitality, we are so many."

"And so you should be. Ratko's kin should branch out and, God willing, there'll be more of you still. Don't feel sorry for me. I have everything I need and I'm not the pauper I was when I came here. Thanks to you I prospered. Now I have livestock too, twelve sheep, a dozen goats, three cows, let alone poultry and the rest."

Whilst they were talking, the women brought raki and white cheeses as appetizers, also giblets fried with onions, and a wheaten loaf. "See how quickly it is all done! Soon the roast meat from the spit will follow, and the pies, hot, straight from the hearth. You'll have plenty of time for traveling," Risto said, and began to lay out tin plates on the bare pine tables, clean and yellow like buttercups, scrubbed down with caustic soda.

Ratko was not in a good mood and conversation languished, so lunch was soon over.

The highway was much better now, broader and firmly packed with stone chips leveled by steamroller. The forest was becoming denser still as they drew closer to Cajnice. The horses, fed and rested, raced like lightning. The whips swished and cracked round their girths, and the coachmen, wined and fed and merry, burst into song:

"Will you regret your rich auburn hair . . ."

Rosa crossed herself and began to protest in a whisper, "God save us, what song is this? As if we were not going on a pilgrimage but out on a picnic to enjoy ourselves."

"Quiet!" Simuna said softly. "Don't you see they are drunk? What would they know about a pilgrimage to the church when they are not of our faith? Let them sing what they wish, as long as they don't spill us into a ditch somewhere."

They drove so fast it seemed to Simuna that it was they who were motionless whilst toward them flew pines, firs, oaks, junipers, beeches, and aspens. Sometimes they would emerge into more open scrubland, then plunge back again into the rich Bosnian forests. All around them was the scent of fir and juniper. "How well this air makes me feel," she said, refreshed by the heady atmosphere.

"It's not only the air but the miraculous power bestowed on you by the Mother of God, glory and mercy be to her," said Rosa, and crossed herself.

Simuna too crossed herself, attempted to rise a little and, losing balance, she would have fallen had not Ratko caught her.

"You'd have fallen flat in the middle of the highway if I hadn't grabbed you. Sit quietly and cross yourself when you get to the church," said he, half jokingly but with a touch of temper.

Stevo observed his father with concern because he noticed that Ratko had grown sullen since Metaljka. "Is something ailing you, Adzo? Perhaps the driving is too fast for you?"

"Nothing's wrong with me," Ratko growled.

"Are you annoyed about something?"

"I am cross with Risto. My inn, my equipment, my provisions, yet the profit we share is slim. He must be swindling me. You seldom call on them. I can't read the accounts, and you just glance at them, so he does them to suit himself. His sons are literate, he is sly and they've grabbed the opportunity; they can steal to their hearts' content."

"Don't feel like that, Ratko," Simuna tried to calm him. "Thank God we have enough, as long as we keep our health. One mustn't become greedy. Wealth is in God, and people should be content with whatever His mercy bestows on them."

"You keep quiet and don't meddle in things you don't understand. You've become too forward since your illness and you go too far."

"I think, Adzo . . ." Stevo tried to justify himself, but Ratko cut him off:

"You think. If you thought at all, things wouldn't be going so sluggishly with that inn, nor with the other one in Zlatno Borje. I'll sell them, understand that, I won't let anyone make a fool of me."

"There, Ratko, don't be angry and don't be unjust," Simuna began again. "Risto does not sell only the drinks that you supply, but also milk, mature cheeses, ham and the rest, which all sell in a flash when the soldiers arrive hungry. You know yourself that we also earned quite a lot with those very things when we were here."

"And where did he get so much livestock? One can't make a profit on such products without having cows, sheep, and goats to milk. How did he obtain all these?"

"He bred them, began with little and it multiplied. Livestock is quickly raised. Many years have passed since we moved down to Plevlje, he has prospered during that time. They are diligent and active, and can turn their hands to anything. I've never tasted such good cream cheese or curd as theirs, and Shvabas like such things. They don't gulp raki on an empty stomach like our peasants."

Rosa did not join in the conversation but thought to herself, "True, they are diligent, but thrifty too; had they been squandering as we do in our home, they would have soon closed the inns and surrendered the keys."

A similar conversation went on in the other coach between Janko and Petko.

"Ah, how crafty Risto is," said Janko, "pretending to work for half the profits and sending us barely a quarter."

Petko laughed, amused that Janko found this surprising; as if it was self-evident. "We should have foreseen it long ago. We've no time to visit and control them, and who wouldn't take advantage if he had the chance? 'A stranger's hand does not scratch the itch.' While we worked only in the inn, one of us could always go to Metaljka and Zlatno Borje, but how can we do it now that our business has expanded? If we install someone else there, it would be the same, and if it comes to stealing, better our relatives than strangers. Such are our times. Nowadays everyone tries to grab something whilst the Shvabas are still here, for once they go, there'll be bugger all to be earned under the Turks."

"You really think the Shvabas will leave Plevlje? That's what Stevo's put into your head."

"I don't need Stevo or anyone else. I was told by a train driver from a Czech regiment that the Shvabas are here only for the time being, only temporarily. He says that it would be better for us to

The kitchen was roomy, with a big built-in stove on which dishes simmered in enamel pans. Along the wall was a row of cupboards containing china plates, tureens, and cups for black and for white coffee, all decorated with gold rims, and on the other wall were sinks of white enamel.

Nothing impressed Jula so much as the brick stove with its large oven which could accommodate even the biggest baking tray. "How wonderful this is, Auntie Nasta. It doesn't smoke, the dishes don't get sooty, and no coals or flames can be seen, yet there is room for still more dishes to be cooked. There is nothing like this at home."

"Yes, it's much better than the hearth, but it is too big for us now. There were eight of us before: father and mother-in-law, two sisters-in-law, and our two sons; then the sisters-in-law married, our sons went to Sarajevo to study, and the two elders died, may God bless their souls, so only Petar and I are left in the house. We keep one manservant, but he doesn't eat with us; he is a Turk and we cook with pork fat. I don't usually light the stove, as it's easier for me to cook something quickly on the hearth in the kitchen quarters and not dirty anything in the main house."

They arranged the appetizers on the plates, which Jula took in on a large silver tray while Nasta followed with the raki.

Rosa and Jelka were exploring the bedrooms. All the furniture was modern: manufactured beds, cupboards, bedside tables, washstands, coffee tables, chairs, and divans. At the windows were factory-woven curtains, and on the walls, beside the icons and family photographs, a few landscape paintings. Big lamps with rounded bases and tall narrow cylinders had silky white shades that spread a soft light, making everything look silken.

When they had put the children to sleep and arranged their things on the cupboards, they paused by a large mirror to smooth their hair before going down to the dining room for dinner, which soon began.

With food and drink, conversation flowed pleasantly and even Ratko cheered up. After dinner, Petar Adzilukic went to reserve a place in church for Simuna because she wished to go there that same evening.

"You may give a good donation, if necessary, and I'll repay you tomorrow," Ratko said.

"Of course it's necessary to give to the church, and to tip the priests as well," Petar laughed. "'Their heads may be holy but not their behinds,' as the saying goes. They too must live."

Ratko arranged with his sons that throughout the night someone would always be with Simuna to look after her. "I can stay with her until *jacija*, as I can't anyhow fall asleep before hearing the *hodja*'s midnight prayers from the minaret," he suggested. "Stevo and Janko can come afterwards and stay until dawn, when Petko could replace them." This was agreed.

As soon as Petar returned, he and Ratko accompanied Simuna, whilst his servant, Use, carried the mattress, pillows, and covers.

The church was full of ailing people who lay on stretchers, rush mats, and carpets, and they had to fight their way to the altar, where they laid out Simuna's bedding right under the miraculous icon.

The whole night through, Simuna did not close her eyes. The entire church hummed with murmured prayers, the wail of the sick, and suppressed moans and sighs. She too prayed in whispers to the Mother of God, but more for her children and Ratko than for her own health.

Before the morning service, the priests announced that the sick must now leave the church to make room for people waiting for the service.

Petko and Petar Adzilukic, who had relieved Stevo and Janko, helped Simuna to her feet and folded her bedding, which they gave to the verger to carry, then slowly walked out. They were almost the last because the exit was crammed.

Supporting his mother's arm, Petko almost collided with a fair girl of medium height and gentle countenance. She was accompanied by a tall, middle-aged, distinguished-looking woman, dressed all in black.

Once out of earshot, Petko asked, "Who are the two women we just passed?"

"The wife and daughter of the merchant Dejanovic. He suffers from consumption. All his children have died except for this daughter, yet there he is, still living."

"And is the daughter healthy"

"Yes, both she and her mother are. They haven't contracted consumption."

"She's very beautiful, this daughter of Dejanovic," said Petko fervently, half to himself.

103

"Beautiful and virtuous, there is none like her in the whole of Cajnice." Adzilukic smiled, then added, "Her name is Pava. She's now the only child, and they say she'll inherit all the Dejanovic wealth."

When they arrived home, Petko washed and combed his hair, then set off for the church again. He could not get inside, for it was filled to overflowing. Even in the doorways the faithful stood pressed against one another as they prayed. He decided to wait in the churchyard until the liturgy was over and the people started coming out.

When he saw the Dejanovic girl again, she seemed even more beautiful in the brilliant sunlight, as if she alone was illuminated by it. He smiled. She looked at him as if in recognition and, blushing slightly, went past him. He let her and her mother walk on a little further, then started after them and followed them all the way home. The girl turned back on entering the forecourt, and when she saw him, smiled. Overcome by a joy he had never before experienced, Petko felt all the blood surge to his face. He stood there for a while, then left, still dazed.

Without noticing where he was going, he wandered until noon, and all the time his thoughts were on the fair girl with the tender smile, shining in the sunlight. He returned home just before lunch. At the table, he knew neither what he was eating nor what went on around him, and as soon as the meal was over, he went out for a walk again for fear of betraying his confusion and absence of mind. He walked around, viewing Cajnice, until he found himself in front of the Dejanovics' house. Stopping on the other side of the street, he stared at the lace curtains in the open upper floor windows.

A small hand appeared at one of the windows after a short while and dropped a red carnation down. He ran across and, reaching for the flower, looked up, but the hand had disappeared, only the curtains swayed in the window. He stood motionless, staring at the sleepy facade of the house, and, as nothing stirred again, he tucked the carnation in his buttonhole and left.

He continued strolling through the town, which now appeared to him enchanted, and prolonged his walk along the road through the pine forest, thinking all the time of the Dejanovic girl, Pava. Having made up his mind that only she could be his wife, now he was afraid that her family might not consent if he asked for her hand before returning to Plevlje. Petar had told him they were wealthy and he doubted whether her parents would let their only child and all the inheritance go into a home about which they could learn little in so short a time.

At twilight, he once more arrived in front of the Dejanovic house and waited. Although impatient, he decided to remain there until he saw Pava, at a window at least. He waited in vain, for no one appeared, nor could any sound be heard from the house, as if it had been deserted.

Finally, he began singing softly, hoping to attract Pava's attention:

"The wind carries the scent of carnations . . ."

Before he could finish the song, Pava came to one of the windows. Overjoyed, Petko took off his fez in greeting and, gathering all his courage, asked, "Will you come tomorrow to the churchyard and the fair?"

"I cannot; I still don't attend festive gatherings. We are in mourning because only a few days ago it was the first anniversary of my remaining brother's death. Today is the first time I have left off mourning clothes."

"Please come. I have something important to tell you. We shan't dance, just watch the crowds and talk."

"I'll ask, and if they allow me, I shall come. Wait for me in front of the church. But go now, or Mama will scold me and, please, don't sing again in front of our house."

As she closed the window, she smiled at him and he went away brimming over with happiness.

That same evening, he told Jelka everything and begged her to come with Jula tomorrow to meet Pava. Seeing that he was quite bewitched by the girl, Jelka agreed, a little out of curiosity, but also to take Jula out amongst young people.

On the following day, she and Jula tidied up and swept the rooms, fed Djana and gave her to Nasta to keep an eye on her, then left with Petko for the church.

Cajnice was swarming with people. Most had flocked in from the surrounding villages, but many had also arrived from Sarajevo, Gorazde, Rogatica, Vishegrad, Priboj, Nova Varos, Prijepolje, and Plevlje. The fair was held near the church. Everything was booming with loud voices, music, and songs which could be heard on every side. The three of them forced their way to the churchyard, and waited there watching the *kolo*. Petko was restless and anxious, whilst Jelka and Jula were amused by everything, especially the young men who made eyes at them and hung about nearby, though they pretended not to notice. Several youths who were standing in a group and looking at them finally asked Petko to come over and, when he joined them, began to question him in whispers. He stayed a little time to exchange a few words, and, when he returned, said:

"They asked whether you are my sisters and are you both married."

"And what did you tell them?" Jelka asked teasingly.

"I told them everything as it is."

"What a beast you are! Why, for heaven's sake, didn't you say that I, too, am not married?"

"I didn't dare because of Janko." He laughed and, turning to Jula, pointed discreetly at a tall young man wearing a town suit. "He is from Sarajevo and can't take his eyes off you."

Just then Pava arrived. She greeted them with some reserve and timidly exchanged a few words with Jelka but, although the others tried to make her feel at ease, it was difficult to keep the conversation going. Jula kept in the background, more interested in the young man to whom Petko had drawn her attention. Finally, Jelka excused herself from Pava saying that they must return because of Djana and Simuna, and led Jula away.

Petko felt easier once they were alone, although they remained silent, watching the *kolo*. Gradually, struggling for words, he began to tell her how much he liked Cajnice and its wooded surroundings, then fell silent again, too shaken by her nearness. At long last he gathered enough courage to whisper, "I like you very much."

"I like you too," Pava whispered back.

"Would you accept me if we came to ask for your hand?"

Pava blushed and bowed her head, staring in front of her and twisting her handkerchief, then she said softly, "I think I would, if my parents agree."

Silence descended again, but it now drew them closer to one another and was more soothing, as if words would only disturb them. They stayed there for some time, immobile and mute from excitement, then Pava said she must go home. She did not allow him to accompany her, and afraid of forcing himself upon her, he let her go alone. On his return, Petko walked aimlessly, in a dream, not knowing what had happened to him. When he found himself in front of the Adzilukic house, he was astonished. Noticing on the other side of the street the men from Sarajevo whom he had met near the church, he smiled. They came over to ask whether Jula was going tomorrow to watch the *kolo*, how long she would be in Cajnice, where she came from, from which family, and who was her next of kin. Engrossed in his own thoughts, he answered impatiently and could not wait to be rid of them, but took care not to be rude for Jula's sake.

When at long last he entered the house, Jula ran to meet him and asked excitedly, "What were you talking about with the Sarajevo men?"

Seeing her so flustered, Petko laughed and started to tease her. "What Sarajevo men? I didn't even see them."

"Don't tease me now. I was watching from behind the curtains and I saw you talking to them."

"If you tell me which one of them you liked best, I will tell you everything."

"They are all nice, but the tall, distinguished one with the small black mustache appeals to me most."

"Well, it was he who asked most about you." He told her what they were interested in and that they had begged him to tell her that they would wait for her tomorrow in the churchyard.

Jula's eyes sparkled with joy when she heard this. "Please, call on Pava and let's go together tomorrow."

"I don't dare to hang around their house now, nor do I know whether I will see her even if I did."

"Write her a letter and send it by someone."

"Perhaps she's not literate."

"Of course she is. All Bosnian girls of our age have been to school, Aunt Nasta told me," Jula said impatiently, then ran to Jelka to tell her about the men from Sarajevo.

Jelka was pleased that someone had finally appealed to Jula, and agreed that she could go the next day with Petko and Pava to watch the *kolo*, but advised her not to stand talking at the gates until they were better acquainted.

"God forbid. What do you think of me?" Jula was offended. "I would not stand at the gates for any man, not if he were the son of the Tsar. I hold my head high, not like you."

Jelka said nothing. Their mother had told her that Jula was difficult and the smallest thing could make her angry, and she was afraid that whatever she said would make her fly off the handle. It would be a disgrace if anyone heard them arguing, especially Rosa; she would revel in it, now more then ever, because she had found it hard to put up with the hospitality of Jelka's relatives and acknowledge her obligation to Jelka.

That evening Petko announced to his brothers his intention to betroth the daughter of the merchant Dejanovic, and told them how they met and that he had given her his word.

"We won't object if Adzo allows it," Stevo said.

"It would be best if Petar praised her. He knows the family well. Let him say that she is the only child and the heiress to a large fortune. Adzo is quite greedy and I bet he'll agree."

Janko burst out laughing. "You mock him, while you are the one who takes after him!"

This annoyed Petko and he turned on Janko. "I am proud to be like him, and not spendthrift like you two."

"You are like him in this respect but in no other," Janko continued to chaff him.

Petko got up angrily and started for the door. "I won't utter another word about it to you, I'll talk to Petar and Father instead."

When, the next day, Petko and Jula arrived at the churchyard, the men from Sarajevo were already waiting for them. They came over immediately and introduced themselves to Jula. The name of the tall man who so appealed to Jula was Spasoje Lusic. With him were his two brothers and some other relatives. Pava arrived soon after. Petko saw her from afar as she squeezed through the host of people assembled in the churchyard around the townspeople's *kolo*. This time she was accompanied by an elderly servant from whom she parted as soon as she saw Petko heading toward them, and came on alone.

After a short while, Spasoje's brothers and relatives left. He moved to Jula's side and started talking to her in a low voice. They did not notice that the jostling crowd had separated them from Petko and Pava until they found themselves next to a group of Austrian officers who openly gawped at Jula. Annoyed by this, Spasoje suggested that they join the *kolo*, but did not say why, afraid of offending or upsetting Jula.

"I don't care much for dancing," Jula said, "and I'm really not interested in watching the *kolo*. I would rather we went for a walk."

They walked toward the fairground where the crush was greater still and could hardly make their way through the multitude of people. Time and again Spasoje tried to protect Jula from being roughly pushed by someone, and his attentiveness was so pleasant to her that she did not object when he, as if by accident, would put his arm gently around her shoulders to guide her.

All about them was commotion and jostling, everything vibrated with songs and music, and with the cries of vendors who pushed purposefully through the crowds:

"Buns, buns! Fresh and hot, straight from the oven!" shouted the baker, balancing on his head a long plank on which lay rows of plump, golden-yellow buns.

"Sherbet! Lemonade!" cried the seller of soft drinks. In one hand he carried a glass tankard and in the other two pitchers.

"Sweet, sweet! Halva, fudge, nougat! This way, folks, to sweeten your lips!"

"Ice cre-e-eam, ice cold and honey sweet. Ice cre-e-eam!"

After some struggling, they reached the place where the stalls had been set up, covered by makeshift canopies and festooned with hanging merchandise: scarves and shawls of all colors, halters made of fine rope decorated with baubles and tassels of multicolored wool, strings of beads and imitation ducats, mirrors, slippers, woven wool sashes, chains of threaded hazelnuts and bunches of walnuts. On the counters were the smaller wares: combs, hatpins with glass heads, knitting and sewing needles, bead necklaces, clasps, buckles, threads, purses, round enameled pictures of Franz Josef and Empress Elizabeth, flutes, nutcrackers, rings, earrings, whistles, trumpets . . .

They stopped in front of the stall selling posies of flowers to which small mirrors were attached by thin spirals of wire, making them vibrate with every move.

"They also sell these flowers back home, too, in front of the church on St. Elias's day," Jula said. "Young peasants buy them to adorn the girl of their choice. If she allows it, it's a sign that she also likes him, so it is a token. No one else is allowed to pin flowers on that girl. Later, their parents get together and sometimes a betrothal takes place that same day, or even a wedding. They settle everything in one go for the same cost."

"And if the girl does not let him adorn her?" Spasoje asked, looking with admiration at her smiling face.

"Then the young man looks for another. There is always someone who wants the one the other has rejected."

"Would you allow me to pin a flower on you?"

"I don't know. I think it isn't enough for a man just to attract the girl. First she must know who he is, what he does, what kind of home he comes from, and what he possesses."

Spasoje became serious, poised as if to collect his thoughts, then took Jula's hand and said, "I will tell you everything and there are people here who know us and can confirm it all. Your relatives and the Adzilukics can verify it for themselves." He began to talk about himself and his family and she thus learned that they were merchants, and owned several houses and an estate at Kozja Cuprija where they holidayed in the summer or went for short outings in their own carriage.

Jula was pleased that he was well off because she was determined to make a better marriage than Jelka and her girlfriends, but she feigned indifference. She also said, casually, that her sister and she would inherit the large house where she now lived with her mother and an old servant woman, her father's shop, her mother's valuable jewelry, land on Zlatibor, and cash in ducats which was at her uncles' for safekeeping.

Spasoje listened, although he knew all about it through his friends from Cajnice and had heard it from the people from Plevlje who had come to the fair.

Pava and Petko left the churchyard when they noticed the others had gone, and wandered through the noisy crowd until they found themselves by the outer walls of the church, where several women wearing black head scarves were sitting on the grass. They had spread

their laps with black cloths on which were placed combs, razors, tobacco pouches, tinder boxes, items of jewelry, and other small objects, mementoes of their dead over which they each lamented in
turn. The refrain of the laments merged and mingled, voices floated
in the oppressive heat, vanishing in the echoes of music and songs . . .

"Dear brother . . .," ". . . your poor mother," ". . . daughter, my
little lamb," ". . . with three children, your three orphans . . ."

Pava became sad and tears filled her eyes.

"Let's get away from here," Petko said. "Don't be sad now, when
we were so happy."

He led her toward the jolly peasants' *kolo*, hoping it would cheer
her up. To the sound of shepherds' pipes, young men and women
hopped on one spot and, swinging on their heels, moved impercepti-
bly left and right whilst their numerous multicolored bead necklaces
tinkled rhythmically on the bosoms of the girls. The dress of the
Bosnian villagers was simple and home-made: a shirt of thickly woven linen, waistcoats, skirts, and breeches of broadcloth, and on their
feet, embroidered woolen socks and strapped, soft-soled leather shoes.

The *kolo* was split in two, on one side the girls and on the other
the men. When the music stopped, the dancing continued to the sound
of alternating songs:

Oi, you maiden, oi, oi, oi,
Oi, you maiden flower.
Have you got a sweetheart?

How could I, oi, oi, oi,
How could I spend my youth
Without a sweetheart?

As they moved on, different songs mingled from another direction, sung in high-pitched women's voices:

Don't take for a wife
A dainty little waif,
Take someone like me
And your heart won't waver.

Pava paused and looked up at him pleadingly, "I can't go where there is merriment, either," she said. "Let's look for Jula and Spasoje."

They headed toward the fairground. At this end of it was the live-stock market, on one side the horses, cattle, and smaller animals, and on the opposite side wool, earthenware, skins, copper and wooden household utensils: saucepans, basins, cauldrons, frying pans, baking trays, coffee pots, ewers, tubs, barrels, casks, kegs, and drums. They did not stop there but continued toward the stalls, where they caught a distant glimpse of Jula and Spasoje. When they drew nearer and saw that the couple were talking to one another softly, as in a trance, they exchanged looks and withdrew quietly for fear of intruding.

Suddenly the sky darkened and a wind blew up and started to lift the canvas covers from the stalls, catching small objects and sweeping them ahead like a monster broom. The cattle began to bellow, horses to whinny and lunge against their tethers, while the sheep huddled together bleating. Angry shouts were heard, arguments and curses from vendors who were collecting their merchandise from the stalls or trying to rescue it from the wind and from the looting va-grants, delinquent children, gypsies, and vagabonds of all kinds who materialized out of nowhere, it seemed, and stole whatever they could lay their hands on.

Everything was in a turmoil as people ran for shelter from the rain, which first started to fall in large sporadic drops, until the storm gathered force and it poured down in sheets.

In the pandemonium it took some time to find one another at the entrance of the church, which was already crammed with people. When the first onslaught of rain subsided and the crowd began to disperse, they decided to part. Jula ran home alone, to avoid being caught again in the rain, and Spasoje went to the nearby inn together with his companions. Petko saw Pava to her home and, although they hurried, both got drenched to the skin.

When Jula arrived home, she stopped by the kitchen to ask Jelka to come to her room. As soon as they entered, and as she was shedding her wet clothes, she began to talk about her meeting with Spasoje.

"He told me he'll be coming to ask for my hand before we leave here and said that he finds me very attractive, that the whole of Cajnice seemed to light up after the he had met me, that my beauty could adorn a sultan's harem of three hundred wives." She said it all in one breath, as if afraid of being interrupted by Jelka.

"But would you wish to marry him?"

"I would indeed. I like him more than any man I have ever met, and besides, it's time I got married. Why wait and lose such an opportunity? He's well off, distinguished, and from a good background."

"You didn't give him your word?"

"I said I couldn't promise anything until I had consulted you. Let him come here so that you and Janko can meet him and his relatives and they can see you."

Jelka relaxed when she heard this. She was delighted that Jula was interested in someone, as she was so arrogant that no one in Plevlje could approach her, but was afraid to decide anything without her mother's approval and until they knew more about Spasoje. "I don't dare give my consent before asking Mother and our uncles," she said firmly. "I'll speak to Nasta and, if she and Petar allow it, Spasoje can call on us, but the betrothal cannot take place here."

Jula looked at her with hatred in her eyes. "You are peeved, my dear, because I stand to make a better marriage than you, and you want to spoil my chances. Well, I'm telling you, I belong to Spasoje, come what may, and I'll declare it now in front of everybody."

She ran toward the door, still in her chemise, but Jelka got to it first, turned the key, and hid it inside the bodice of her dress, then, keeping her voice down, began to scold her:

"Shame on you, to give us a bad name. Control yourself and think of our reputation."

Enraged, Jula tried to get the key away from her, then, realizing that the other was stronger, began to scream and tear at her hair.

"Oh no, you shrew, I won't let you rampage here as you are used to doing. I'm not Savka. Stop it or I'll give you a good hiding." Grabbing her hand, Jelka warned her in a whisper, although she was trembling with fury. As Jula continued to yell and kick, she struck her and went on slapping her sister at random until she stopped struggling and sprawled across the bed, sobbing.

Jelka went to the window to cool down before going down to the kitchen to help Nasta with the dinner. She knew that everyone must have heard Jula's scream but decided not to mention it unless asked, in which case she would tell the truth. The rain continued to fall softly outside and wash down the window-panes. In the garden the wet, dark leaves glistened, bending under the occasional gusts of wind, then sinking back into the steady rhythm of the rain. She sighed deeply, smoothed her disheveled hair and turned to Jula who was sobbing softly.

"Wash your face now, comb your hair and change your clothes, then come down quietly. If anyone makes some remark to you, say that I won't allow you to get engaged without Mother's permission and that's why you were crying, but that you have now agreed that a betrothal should take place in Plevlje. Tell the same to Spasoje, too, or I'll ask Janko to take you back home now. Spasoje will only respect you more, you fool, than if we gave you away as though you were a burden to us, just to get rid of you."

When Jelka came down, everyone was already at table in the dining room, except for Simuna, whose dinner was taken to her. This made her feel better, because during meals the conversation was only held between the men and the oldest woman in the family. Younger womenfolk could answer a question if asked, otherwise it was not in order for youngsters, especially female, to intervene. Such was the custom, whether in the homes of merchants or others, even in the villages. She had to sit down next to Rosa, who glanced at her meaningfully but did not dare to speak to her. The others pretended not to have noticed anything, even when Jula appeared, still flushed from crying and angry with everybody.

Jula did not touch her food and could hardly wait for the dinner to end and the men to move to another room, there to smoke and drink coffee. As soon as they rose from the table she also left, slamming the door behind her.

Rosa stayed with the others to help clear the table and to hear why Jelka and Jula had quarreled, but when she saw that this would not be discussed in front of her, she went to see Simuna, who was being neglected by everyone except herself and Ratko.

Jelka waited until she was upstairs, then, bursting into tears, told Nasta what had happened. "Mother complained that she was difficult but I could not believe that she would be so beside herself because I can't let her rush into accepting someone she knows nothing about. How would I face my mother and the uncles?"

"Don't upset yourself, you are not staying with strangers," Nasta comforted her, although she was rather ashamed of the behavior of her cousin's daughters in front of her husband. Now she was relieved to hear the reason for their argument. "It's true when they say that there is no greater woe than being in love, yet without love youth would wither. It's God's will, I suppose. Don't worry, Petar can enquire about Spasoje, and he could also write to Sarajevo and find out everything about his family. Let them come here to see Janko and you, but one mustn't hurry with the engagement."

There was great excitement in the Adzilukics' house the following morning. The Kojics arranged for a visit in two days to discuss Petko's betrothal and they went to the best goldsmiths to buy a gift for Pava good enough for the Dejanovic home.

Before they were back, the Sarajevo suitors sent word that they would be coming in the evening to ask for Jula's hand. Petar answered that there could be no talk of an engagement yet, as Jula's mother and uncles had not been consulted. He had already enquired in the Charshija about the Lukics and discovered that they were well-known and respected merchants, among the richer in Sarajevo; that they owned a large house near the Bashcharshija, the main high street, and several smaller houses on Bembasha which they let; that their shop was one of the most beautiful, with windows in Franz Josef Street, and that they had an estate in Kozja Cuprija.

When the others heard about this, Jula's prestige suddenly grew. Rosa, out of envy, did not budge from her room, whilst Ratko was thrilled that his house would have some sort of link to the big Sarajevo merchants on this side of the family too. Only Jelka was even more worried now because Spasoje looked to her too gaunt and pale and, seeing how eagerly his relatives were pressing the betrothal, she feared he might be ill and they therefore wanted him to get married quickly, father a family and so leave behind his own flesh and blood, should he die soon. She did not dare confide her suspicion to anyone, especially Jula, knowing how she would interpret it, and waited to hear what the others would say.

Everybody in the house joined in receiving the guests with the utmost courtesy, but the gift token was not accepted; instead, they were asked to write to Jula's uncles in Plevlje and arrange with them the date of the betrothal. Spasoje took to everyone, though they too shared Jelka's opinion that he was not in good health, but did not say this to Jula.

Ratko had asked Adzilukic several times how big a fortune Pava was to inherit, but the other said he didn't know exactly and that this was not important if the girl was of good repute. In fact, he had heard that Rade Dejanovic had incurred some debts, but he thought it was only a small amount, as none of his possessions had been sold so far, neither his house, nor his shop, nor the brickworks, nor the village land whose produce he received. He toyed with the idea of mentioning these debts to Ratko but, seeing how greedy he was, he deliberately said nothing.

On the day of the visit to the Dejanovic house everybody was wearing rich Hercegovina attire, embroidered with gold thread and decorated with braids of thin gold wire. Only Petko was in a modern town suit.

When Ratko saw him, he burst out laughing. "Go and change into your usual clothes, you fool. In them you look passable, but this fashion suits you like a cassock on a piglet."

The others kept quiet because Ratko was right. The suit was not made to measure but bought off the peg and in it Petko looked even shorter and fatter than he was.

He was not offended though. "Nothing for you to get upset about, Adzo. Pava loves me as I am. She said she wished me to wear a modern suit as her late brothers did, and I obeyed."

Ratko had to give in and set off with Petar, followed by his three sons.

At the Dejanovics' they were met in the courtyard by the maids who led them to the visiting room, old-fashioned but opulently furnished.

The floor was covered by a Smyrna rug of oriental design in soft colors, woven out of fine wool which shone like silk. The narrow divans and the cushions were of red velvet, and the shelves shone with silver ewers, platters, and bowls. On the three-paneled screen glowed the golden frames and engravings of the icons, in front of which small wavy blue flames flickered in red glass lamps with silver holders, suspended by silver chains from the carved ceiling of rare wood.

Next to the built-in stove with shiny green ceramic inlays stood a high-backed sofa. Flowers of various colors were woven into its silken plush covering, as though spilled over the scarlet base. Rade was seated on it, dressed in *shalvare* trousers, leggings, and polished kid leather footwear, with a sable-lined jacket thrown round his shoulders and a fez on his head. He was gaunt, with sunken chest, his cheekbones flushed and his deep-set eyes black and glittering as if aflame. A long thin mustache framed his pale lips. Next to him stood Zorka, his wife, wearing a long dress of heavy silk and *kalkan* headdress.

When the guests approached, Zorka bowed low, her right hand on her bosom, Istanbul fashion, and Rade rose, lightly touching his forehead and chest.

Once the guests were seated along the narrow divan, Adzilukic started the conversation. As was the custom he first enquired about Rade's health and assured him that he looked better than when they had last seen each other.

"Thank you," Rade smiled obligingly, and gave Zorka a sign to offer the guests tobacco from the amber box that stood on the copper tray beside him.

They all filled their pipes but nobody lit up.

He noticed this and showed them his own lit pipe. "Don't refrain because of my illness. As you can see, I also smoke, although I cough a bit. I can't stop, nor do I wish to, because without tobacco and the rosary . . ." He glanced at the string of jet beads that lay on the table in front of the sofa. "I don't know what I'd do." So saying, he stretched out a large thin hand, dried as if it were made of wax, took the rosary and began moving the beads between long fingers with swollen joints and polished mother-of-pearl nails. Everything about him spoke of the grave as if he were already dead, only in the glowing embers of his eyes smoldered the remains of life.

The conversation progressed slowly, led mainly by Adzilukic and Dejanovic. Only when Pava's betrothal was mentioned did Ratko speak up. Although somewhat tongue-tied when he arrived, he now regained courage and began to talk so calmly and sensibly that Rade responded.

"Pava told her mother that she met your son and wished to marry him, and I understand from Petar Adzilukic that your house is reputable, for if it were not, he wouldn't have brought you here. I would not oppose Pava getting married soon after the betrothal. My days are numbered, why avoid the truth, and I would wish to see this festive occasion with my own eyes. I have not yet had the good fortune to marry off any of my family. They died and I buried all four in the flower of their youth."

Zorka was silently wiping away the tears that ran down her drawn but still beautiful face.

On Petko's suggestion, they decided that the betrothal should take place at once and the wedding in a week's time. Although he didn't say so, everyone knew he was worried that Rade would die before the wedding if they did not hurry and that Pava's wedding would then have to be postponed for at least a year until the customary term of mourning was over.

Pava was summoned to declare in front of everybody that she liked Petko and wished to marry him. Her parents gave their consent and bestowed their blessing on her, and Ratko with his two elder sons presented the bride-to-be with the ring, the pendant and chain, and earrings, all in gold set with precious stones.

Rade was greatly moved and her mother led Pava out of the room, afraid that he might start to weep. Lately he could not look at his daughter without shedding tears, which caused his temperature to rise and further upset his frail health.

The servants brought in refreshments and raki for the guests and coffee for Rade, which calmed him. Zorka served the guests with the refreshments passed to her by her servants.

The following day the Kojics sent a message to Mara and Stojana to say that they were prolonging their stay in Cajnice and would be bringing Petko's bride home with them. Stevo instructed his sister-in-law in Rogatica to bring over Olga—who had been staying with her for almost a year—so that she too could attend the wedding. Simuna and her illness were forgotten by everyone except Ratko, who now spent all his time at her side. Afraid that her health might deteriorate, and upset by the delay in their departure that Petko's wedding caused, he worried about the business and the property at home. It also annoyed him that in his confusion during the betrothal he had not asked how big Pava's dowry was.

"It is still not clear to me why they agreed to all this haste. We had no time to enquire what belongs to her or if she has anything definite in writing, or brings with her any capital."

"Ah, Ratko, I don't know why it is that you have become so greedy, trying to squeeze profit out of everything," Simuna reproached him. "If they love each other and are happy, let them enjoy life for as long as God allows them. Should she bring a dowry, fine, but if not, that will still be all right. We have everything, thank God, and she will have a home to come to. When you married off our other two sons, we had less, yet you were not so upset, although their wives brought nothing but their trousseau with them. We are old and death awaits us. Then we leave everything behind and depart empty-handed, arms crossed, and nailed inside four planks, to go where there is no return. Stop worrying, my dear, and give yourself another few years' peace and good health."

"Don't talk nonsense, for heaven's sake, and don't start lecturing me now," Ratko cut in angrily, although he secretly felt she was right. He too now suffered from rheumatic pains contracted during the night spent with Simuna on the stone steps in the church of Our Lady of Miracles.

When Spasoje found out that the Kojics were staying longer in Cajnice, he also stayed on, although his brothers and relatives returned to Sarajevo. Every evening Jula came out and they stood at the garden gate talking for a long time. She wanted to walk with him through the pine woods but Janko threatened to take her straight back to her mother if she moved a step further from the gate.

As the Dejanovics had requested, the wedding ceremony was conducted quietly, without great rejoicing. The Kojics hired three coaches and immediately after church set out on their journey home. Spasoje, with two accordion players, took a fourth coach to accompany them as far as Metaljka, but did not allow any music to be played until they were out of Cajnice. With Petko and his bride sat Stevo, still wearing the best man's kerchief, and once they had left Cajnice, they were joined by one of the accordion players sent by Spasoje to cheer

119

up Pava. From time to time she smiled at Petko, but whenever she thought of her father and remembered the expression of hopeless sadness on his face which he could not hide from her as they parted, she was close to tears and controlled herself with difficulty.

Petko was blissfully happy. It seemed to him that all the riches of this world were his, but he tried not to show it, for fear it should upset Pava that he could be joyful when she was sad. Stevo was lost in thought, having gathered from conversations with Petar and his friends that the changes Austria planned would not be good for the Serbs either in Bosnia or Herecgovina, especially those in Plevlje. He had decided to say nothing about this to the others to spare them worry, as there was little they could do but remain silent and wait.

In the other carriage everybody was dispirited because Jula had not stopped crying quietly at the thought of being parted from Spasoje. Janko could hardly control his impatience to reach Plevlje, knowing they had suffered considerable losses by keeping their shop and store closed for so long and had not managed to do any business in Cajnice.

This time they did not stop long in Metaljka, so that they could get home before darkness fell. Risto and his family brought out drinks and food which they consumed standing up. When the time came to say goodbye to Spasoje, the accordion players began to sing "Are you so sad that we have to part?" Jula burst into sobs and Jelka led her to their coach. As they drove off, Spasoje followed them for a while, waving his kerchief until they were lost in the dense greenery.

Simuna shrank into the corner of her seat, pressed her arms over her stomach to relieve the pain and continued looking at the scenery around her. She did not regret being taken on such a long journey to Our Lady of Miracles, although she felt worse now than she had when they left Plevlje.

A few days after the Kojics returned to Plevlje, Pava's trousseau arrived. It was not bigger than Jelka's or Rosa's, but everything in it suggested quality. The trunks were crammed with expensive silk clothes, shirts and underwear for Petko, Pava's frilled petticoats, long corsets trimmed with lace, chiffon scarves, handkerchiefs edged with gathered tulle—delicate as cobwebs—dresses bought in Sarajevo, court shoes with button trimming, and lace-ups with high heels, stockings of silk thread which rustled in the hand, boxes full of hairpins and tortoise shell combs for chignons with fanlike ornamental tops, and bottles of oils and scents with cut glass stoppers. In the small rattan baskets lined with silk there were aromatic bon-bons wrapped in gold paper, biscuits and other delicacies which could only be bought at the Sarajevo confectioners. Because of those rare sweets, Stevo's Olga and Janko's Djana hung around Pava's room and ran in at any opportunity, and so were the first to make friends with her. She was never disturbed by their visits but always received them kindly and allowed them to examine her things. She was especially patient with Olga because she had been left motherless. Pava answered her endless questions, telling her about the carousels in Ilidza Spa, about the Bascharshija and the Bezistan quarter, and about the source of the River Bosna with its seven springs. Olga liked Pava's scented dresses, her sad smile, and the tender touch of her hands when she combed her hair. Pava would take out her boxes of silk ribbons and plait them into Olga's thick long tresses "to prevent the evil eye from harming healthy, rich hair."

Because of her gentle nature, Pava soon captured the affection of all the other members of the family, even Rosa, whose moods were not easily soothed. Brought up in a home dominated by chronic illness and devastated by frequent deaths at an early age, she had come face to face with all the worst of human suffering and had gained the wisdom to realize that life is but once given to man, and that it must be lived with that knowledge. She visited Simuna every day, bringing her gifts and knowing how to comfort her with the right words. To Ratko she showed the customary respect due to the head of the family, which flattered him, for not only was his son married to an heiress but she also respected him. She addressed her brothers-in-law as "brothers" and her sisters-in-law as "ladies," which Rosa correctly mocked. "What a way to address yesterday's peasant!"

Pava's sisters-in-law regarded her with great esteem, partly because of Ratko's attitude towards her and partly because she dressed in Viennese fashion. Petrija was so overwhelmed by her dresses, bought in Sarajevo from the foremost Viennese merchants, that with Pava's help she immediately sent for their catalogues and ordered two frocks of pure silk, two parasols with frills in matching colors, and a pair of lace gloves as well as a pair of mittens which were lately being worn by daughters of the richest men in Plevlje. Even her Djoko ordered tails and top hat, the kind that fat Lazo had. Rosa, despite her dislike of Austrians and their fashions, felt gratified now because Jelka was being overshadowed not only by Pava but also by Petrija, whom they used to regard with condescension. Pava was equally courteous towards Rosa and Jelka, although she liked Jelka better, a fact she tried to hide, having realized from the outset that the two did not get along. She wanted to reconcile them, but as soon as Rosa felt this she flared up:

"Your intentions are useless! I won't make peace with that hussy for as long as I live. You'll have to choose which of us you wish to be your friend. Both you cannot have. If you favor me, I accept, for you are a decent woman; if her, I don't care, but don't count on my friendship any more."

"Sister Rosa, I don't wish to interfere in your affairs but I don't think there are any big disagreements between you and if you both give in a little and live in harmony, it would be better for everyone."

"Pay attention to what I say, sister Pava. You'll soon find out what she is and what I am. With me everything is open and just, I fear God and speak only the truth, while she's a schemer and sly as a fox. She flatters you now to spite me, and wants you to fall under her spell like all the others in this house. She could lead a thirsty man past water, and I advise you to watch out because she will soon disarm you and make you follow her like a dog. Her magic keeps everybody spellbound except me, even my Stevo. How many times has he given me a beating because of her. No one but God knows my troubles. I curse her in all my prayers and hope my curses will catch up with her one day."

Pava was aghast when she heard this, but said nothing to Jelka, who was prepared for a reconciliation, and remained on good terms with both.

Barely a month later, Pava received a letter from her mother telling her of her father's death and the big funeral in which the whole of Cajnice had taken part. She begged her not to grieve too much because it was God's will and, for the departed, death was a release which he had eagerly awaited. She also asked Pava to forgive her for keeping it from her until after the funeral—it was Rade's wish. At the bottom of the letter she added that their creditors had sold everything they had, as their debts were much bigger than Rade was aware of, but Pava should not worry on her account because she was allowed to keep the house in which they lived, during her lifetime, and so she could lease out the upper floors. Pava's health and happiness were a great consolation to her and she thanked God for it.

Having read the letter, Pava collapsed on the floor, curled up in despair, and burst into tears. Although she had long anticipated her father's death while his strength had gradually waned, she had not realized how heavy the blow would be. It seemed to her that her heart was torn in two and she could not breathe with the pain. Only later, when she was a little calmer and read the letter once more, did she realize that they were now destitute. She knew they owed money, but no one, not even Rade, had suspected that their debts had accumulated to that extent. Her main concern was for Petko, because Adzilukic had told him she had a large inheritance. Before her wedding Rade had written to his creditors asking exactly how much money he owed but, to spare him sorrow, they had assured him it was not large. It concerned him that he did not know how much Pava would inherit, but he was confident that at least the brickworks and the house would pass to her mother and later to her. Pava was afraid of what Petko would say when he found out, and decided that if he or his father were to utter one word of reproach, she would pack and return to Cajnice, where she and her mother would stand up to their poverty together.

When Petko came in she did not stir but waited, silent and rigid, to see what would happen. Beside her lay the letter. He immediately realized that her father had died, lifted her gently from the floor, and picked up the letter. As he read it, he began to frown, turning angrily to Pava, but when he saw her pale face and the pain in her eyes, he paused, stock-still. She squared her shoulders and stared back proudly, ready to confront his fury. He flinched, felt ashamed for having reacted as he did and, afraid of losing her love, put his arms around her and drew her to him.

"Don't be sad. You poor father is free from his suffering now.

Have no regrets about your inheritance either, because I have none. Don't say anything to anyone, because of Rosa. She hates me and would thrive on it. Don't worry about your mother. I shall send her money secretly and when we separate from the rest of the family, we'll bring her over to care for our children, God willing."

Now Pava gave in to her sorrow, leaned her head on Petko's chest, and sobbed.

No one in the family learned about the loss of Pava's inheritance. It was kept secret even in Cajnice at first, but the poorer section of the population soon heard about it from the servants, and the whispered rumors spread faster than if it had been announced by the town crier. The rich feigned ignorance, but deep down they gloated over it, because Rade's distinction and wealth had been for many of them hard to swallow. When the poor hate, it is because they are hungry and because God has shared out the riches unequally, leaving some destitute and giving opulence to others. But when the rich hate it is because they are no longer unique and so they wish to ruin whoever possesses more. Thus there is no end to their envy and greed until death overtakes them.

Zorka Dejanovic accepted the loss of her entire fortune calmly and tried not to show how much this had affected her home. As soon as the funeral was over, the creditors informed her that all her accounts were closed, but she decided to keep her servants so that the customary running of Rade's house could be maintained for as long as possible, because it was important to her to keep her status and dignity during the period of mourning. She took two diamond rings and one of the gold coins set in a necklace, and sent them by her servant to the *begum* in her neighborhood with a note asking her to send as much money as she thought the jewelry was worth, or to keep it as a guarantee for a loan she would repay later. In reply the *begum* returned the rings and coin and sent her twelve florins. This was enough for the memorial services on the seventh and fortieth days. Zorka did not wish to save on these rites and held them as befitted Rade Dejanovic. She invited a great number of people from the most prominent houses, as well as the poor, who were always more numerous than the wealthy. Three hired cooks prepared the dishes, not counting the relatives who were helping. Cases of provisions were delivered from the Charshija, veal, beef, and selected cuts of pork, as well as countless lambs and chickens from the butchers. Wine poured generously from casks, and cases of beer, *mastika*, brandy, and rum were served. Tables were set in all the rooms for all the relatives and friends, and in the courtyard and the gardens for the poor. Beggars and vagrants flocked in from everywhere, as this was a rare occasion when they could eat and drink to their hearts' content, for which privilege they prayed wholeheartedly to God for the peace of Dejanovic's soul. He had remembered them during his lifetime too, and on all the main holidays he had distributed baskets of food equally amongst Serbs and Turks, as well as others, even the gypsies.

Zorka did not mind spending on anything given in Rade's memory. She knew that besides jewelry she could also sell other valuable objects, gold incense-burners, candlesticks, and similar things which were hers. She inscribed Rade as a benefactor of the church of Our Lady of Miracles and had a headstone of black granite erected, more beautiful than any in Cajnice. She also financed memorial services for the half-yearly and yearly commemoration of his death and, having thus expressed her devotion to her life's companion, she found peace in her sorrow. "He lived nobly and was nobly mourned."

Zorka regretted having written, in the first moments of despair, to Pava, and soon afterwards sent her a message that she had found Rade's account books and had managed to recover money owed to him. As a matter of fact, she had asked for the money to be repaid, but no one returned a penny and instead avoided being seen near her house. None of her debtors attended the funeral or the memorial services. Not wanting Pava to know that she was selling her jewelry, and in order to convince her that she lacked nothing, she immediately returned Petko's money and started sending them expensive presents.

Pava knew that the cash could not last long, even if all the debts had been repaid to them, because there was no income from their estates, nor from the once profitable brickworks. She lost both weight and color, and often withdrew to her room to brood about everything that had, like a nightmare, befallen her family. In less than five years her father's health had collapsed, her four brothers fallen ill and died, their assets had been lost, and her poor mother left in poverty to mourn her great misfortune. She remembered the life before her father's relapse. Mother was cheerful, she looked beautiful and as stately as a sultan's wife. Her long, thick plaits were wound like a crown around the *tepeluk* headdress, she wore bright *libades* and long silken skirts with trains. She often gave parties during holidays. On such occasions the whole house would be illuminated, all the rooms, corridors, kitchen quarters, courtyards, even the streets, where large lanterns were suspended from the gateposts, spreading shafts of light over the whole neighborhood. *Kolo* dancing, songs, and feasting sometimes lasted until dawn. Savory pies, baklava, and other delicacies were lavishly served, washed down with sherbet or lemonade, and various alcoholic drinks for the men. Everybody was joyful and happy as if neither sadness nor want had ever existed. And how low had her mother fallen now. What fate lay in store for her in old age? Pava realized how much pride mattered to her when she returned Petko's money with a message that she would not need any in future. She also knew that her mother would never agree to move into their home, even if she had to live on bread alone.

Although Pava tried hard to hide her worries, Jelka noticed that beside her sorrow something was haunting her. One day, when they were alone, she came up to Pava, gently took both hands and said:

"Sister Pava, are you unwell? Perhaps life in a large family does not suit you—it's hard and you are not used to work. Perhaps you are not so fond of Petko as you were in the first days of your marriage? I can see that something is tormenting you other than the grief for your father. Don't be afraid to tell me, I can keep a secret to my grave, and it would make you feel better."

Pava embraced her and through tears told her what had happened after her father's death, that she worried about her mother as much as she mourned her father. Jelka led her to a *secija*, sat beside her and tried to comfort her:

"Listen, dearest, your mother is not destitute, she'll manage, everybody says she is a wise and capable woman. Even if at first she has to sell some objects of value, it is nothing to be ashamed of, and it can be done without anyone knowing. And later you can help her."

"Petko sent her some money one day, but she returned it," Pava murmured.

126

"She won't refuse it from you. A son-in-law is not the same as one's own child. Petko doesn't have to know. My mother and sister also live frugally but no one knows it, not even Janko. I put aside a little from the money he gives me to pay the women who do weaving or spinning for me, or buying jute and thread for embroidery, and for my own clothes, and so I collect as much as a gold florin or more, which I hand to my mother. That's not a sin, even God would forgive it. If He dealt in human affairs, He himself would take at least a little from those who have and give it to one who has not. Your Petko is a skinflint, but good-hearted and devoted to you. He would not refuse if you asked him for the money to buy clothes, or for needlework, beads, make-up, or anything you need to make yourself pretty."

Pava hesitated. The relations in her old home had been quite different. No one had had to resort to such measures in order to obtain something. "I'm afraid he may become suspicious if I start spending more and would love me less."

"What a real child you are not to realize that a man likes nothing more than when his wife makes an effort to look attractive for him! The first year of my marriage, I changed three times a day and Janko was delighted because I wanted to look different every time he saw me, and it was never easier for him to part with money! When we separate from the rest of the family, we'll both be able to save more."

Pava felt relieved, although she was not sure whether she could follow Jelka's advice. "But how could I send the money to my mother in Cajnice?"

"When you collect a gold florin's worth, I'll change it into paper money with a woman who does weaving for me. That's how she is paid by the Shvaba women. You can put it in an envelope with a letter and drop it into the Austrian post box by Pekara. That's where Janko puts his letters for Bosnia. We could always go for a walk there together in the evenings. No one would know the reason why."

"God bless you, Jelka, you really are kind. Please don't let anybody know what I have told you."

"I swear by my father, may he rest in peace. My faith is strong although I don't cross myself and genuflect all day long."

"Thank you from the bottom of my heart," Pava said, and kissed her.

At that moment Rosa entered the room then, seeing them kiss, rushed out as if she had been scalded, and from then on counted Pava among her enemies.

"Poor Rosa," Jelka said with a compassionate look. "She'll never be happy. I didn't know it at first and thought she was plain spiteful until a relative of hers told me that Stevo has never kissed her, nor does she know what real conjugal pleasures are. He is not passionate like our husbands, and without love there is no joy in the life of a young woman even if all the riches of this world are hers."

"Perhaps it is her own fault. See what she looks like. Even if she doesn't wish to preen herself as we do, she could at least be well-groomed and dress decently, and not go around like a menial. If we were closer, I'd tell her not to present herself like that, in front of Stevo at least."

"I told her that the first year she married into the family, and if you knew how she responded! She called me a slut and a spendthrift. She thinks she's protecting the family fortune which will be ruined because of me."

A few months after the death of her father, Pava became pregnant. Whether because of her sorrow or because of her unconscious fear of bearing children, having come from a family devastated by tuberculosis, she did not rejoice in it, felt constantly sick, and could not even enter the kitchen quarters without feeling ill. Having no appetite, she lost weight and became so pale and weak that Petko began to fear for her life. He asked Jelka to take over her share of work and her shift in cooking the family meals, had to force her to take small quantities of food more often—which he himself served her—and frequently dropped in from work to see how she felt.

Soon afterwards, Jelka too became pregnant. She was very happy, hoping that it would be a son this time, and ran to tell Pava. "Good news! You have company now."

Pava grew worried that she might have burdened Jelka with too much work. "Are you feeling sick? Is your pregnancy as difficult as mine?"

"I feel fine in the beginning but later I grow too heavy and my legs swell. When you stop vomiting and start feeling better, I'll be swaying from side to side like a barrel."

"By then, I'll be able to replace you. We'll find a way of sharing the work as soon as I get better, and Rosa will help too."

"I doubt it. She touches nothing outside her duty."

"Let me talk to her. If I ask her nicely she won't ignore it."

At the first opportunity, Pava told Rosa that Jelka was also pregnant and begged her to help them. Rosa did not even bother to answer her but sent word through Stojana, who had come to visit them.

"Tell those two spoilt wenches that I don't intend to lift a finger on their behalf. If they whisper behind my back, they can find a way of managing without me. They are afraid of pregnancy as if they were made of glass, yet all people on the face of the earth are born of mothers. I am with child too, it is two months since it began to move, but I don't talk about it, nor do I ask for help. If they were different women, no one would know about this shame which God has inflicted on us as punishment for Eve's sin. So we conceive in sin and bear children in pain. Had that bitch not sinned and led Adam astray, we would conceive and bear children differently. The Mother of God conceived from the Holy Ghost and bore Christ from her chest, and so would we, still living in Eden, innocent as angels. But what decent women hide, others make public, as if it were something to be proud of."

Stojana repeated it all to Pava and Jelka, then quickly slipped out and ran, afraid of being asked to help and of becoming involved in their dispute.

Just as Pava stopped vomiting and recovered, resuming her shifts in the housekeeping, Rosa gave birth to a child and fell ill. She did not want anyone to know about her confinement but delivered the baby, a second son, herself, and tied and cut the umbilical cord. As she could not expel the placenta quickly, she tried to scrape it out with a spindle, and lost so much blood that Stevo found her barely alive. He immediately called Jelka to look after her and rushed to the Austrian hospital to fetch the doctor, who arrived in time to save her from septicemia. When Rosa regained consciousness and saw that Jelka had bathed and wrapped her child in diapers, it was worse for her than the pain she had suffered. She straight away called Stevo and told him to send someone to old Marta from Mocevac and ask her to come and look after her and the child until she recovered.

Old Marta was a renowned midwife, a good cook, soothsayer and fortune teller. She knew how to read cards, how to discover the latest news and spread it with lightning speed, and to create intrigues which no one could unravel, and she stirred up such quarrels that "two eyes in the same head would fall foul of one another." For this reason she was seldom engaged, despite her diligence and capabilities. When Mara heard that Marta had been summoned, she rushed over to tell Jelka and Pava that they should avoid her like poison. By the second day after her arrival Marta had already managed to inflame Rosa to the point of sending a message to her sisters-in-law not to enter her room. For no visible reason, she became angry with other members of the family too, and did not spare even Simuna, although she had genuinely loved her until then.

Rosa's illness was long and her recovery slow. The doctor visited her regularly and instructed Stevo not to allow her to leave her sickbed until all her strength had returned. Stevo had already had a bitter experience over the death of his first wife and was afraid he might become a widower again with three children to care for.

To stop old Marta from intruding into the kitchen quarters, Jelka and Pava shared all the work of preparing the family meals, with occasional help from Mara and Stojana, who dropped in to lend a hand. The order that had previously reigned in the household was lost and an unhealthy atmosphere took over; everything began to crumble, foretelling the dispersal of the extended family. Just then, Jelka had to drop everything and go to her mother because a message came from Sarajevo that in a few days Spasoje would be coming with his party to ask for Jula's hand. When she told Janko about it, he was worried.

"How can you leave home now? Rosa is still ill and cannot take over her duties, Pava weak and inexperienced, and Mother bedridden. The whole house will be in chaos and Adzo will raise hell . . ."

"Don't bother to tell me all this! I have to go and I won't ask you or Adzo for permission. Jula is my only sister and I must help her, even if everything in the Kojic household would turn upside-down. Isn't it enough that I have slaved here for four years, haven't seen the light of day, and suffered Rosa's moods and Adzo's tyranny without a word? Let them manage as best they can. They are not poor and Petko can hire a servant to help Pava."

"He wanted to find help for her before, but Adzo would not allow it and won't agree to it now either."

"Why did you ask him? Stevo didn't ask whether he could bring in old Marta. I hope you won't burden poor Pava with everything. She's exhausted as it is from hard work she is not accustomed to."

"Well, you know yourself what a despot he is."

"I do know. If he wasn't, his wife would not have wasted away as she has. She's been ill ever since I came, confined to bed like a cripple. She's aged before her time; she's not much older than my Savka but looks as if she were her mother. Will you allow him to destroy your wife too? He now pretends to be good to Simuna, but when she was young he drained all her strength, gave her six children, and saddled her with farm labor as well as housework until he reduced her to this state."

Janko was silent. He realized that Savka needed Jelka now more than ever and that he must give in. "All right," he finally said, "slip out somehow so that Adzo does not see you. As for the others, I don't care."

"I'll pack all my and Djana's clothes into a bundle and you can send it over tomorrow by one of your men, and I'll only say goodbye to Pava and Nana. I know they'll understand and won't be angry."

And so she left, escaped through the gardens and down their meadows, then over the Muratbeg's field to Mocevac and straight across Citluk to Golubinja. Janko visited her every day at Savka's to bring the latest news. He told them that Petko had found help for Pava, that Ratko was furious and thundered around, that Pava's maid quarreled with old Marta and that such confusion had been created in the house that nobody knew who was doing what. One day he took Jelka aside to tell her something in confidence.

"Do you know that old Marta has found out in Mocevac that all Pava's inheritance is lost? Some woman from Cajnice said that the whole of Dejanovic's possessions were sold to cover his debts, even Zorka's house is mortgaged to the hilt, but she is allowed out of charity to live in it during her lifetime. And Petko was hoping his wife was a big heiress."

"Don't tell anyone and pretend you know nothing."

"Everybody knows. Old Marta told Rosa, she passed it on to Stevo and he to Adzo." He went on to tell her how Ratko had immediately summoned his three sons and given them the usual dressing down.

"You imbeciles, why did you let those liars and cheats deceive you?" Scandalized, as if everything had belonged to him and somebody snatched it away from him, he looked daggers at Petko, as though it were all his fault.

"What do you want from me?" Petko had lashed back. "Dejanovic was counting his last days and wasn't concerned with anything, and Adzilukic did not know."

This enraged Ratko even more. "Don't talk nonsense. You yourself told me that Adzilukic said Pava had a large inheritance. That's why you married her."

Petko did not give in. "Firstly, I did not marry her for it but because she attracted me, and secondly, if anything had been left she would have inherited it. Now everything is lost—and that's that. The loss is not yours but hers."

Ratko paused and, not knowing how to answer, began to complain, "I really have no luck, not only have my daughters-in-law come penniless, but my own daughters squeezed dowries from me, I had to pay for expensive jewelry for two daughters-in-law and now this one will also demand it . . . Everybody robs me and nobody contributes a penny to my home."

At that point Stevo intervened. "You have grown old, Adzo, and you have things mixed up. Be calm, and sort things out now. First of all, not one of your daughters-in-law has come empty-handed, but brought with her a fine trousseau as is the custom. As for their jewelry, you didn't buy either for Rosa or for Jelka. We did, Janko and I, with our own money, and Petko will buy for Pava. As for our sisters, it is we who gave them a dowry, of our own free will. They neither asked for it nor had to 'squeeze' us for it. I don't know why you are grumbling or what you want. Let the matter of Pava's dowry drop and let's not talk about it any more. Such a wonderful young woman came to our home, yet sorrow and worries fell upon her, so let us not add to her misfortune. You must allows us to manage our own lives. The time for it came long ago. You are not young any more, nor hale and hearty. You should take a rest. We respect you, but we cannot allow you to rule our lives forever."

Janko sighed when he recounted it all to Jelka, as if something pained him.

"And you said nothing?" Jelka asked. "Why didn't you too tell him what you think?"

"He didn't address me, and when they both turned on him, I felt too sorry for him to attack. Although he has lately become hard, one cannot say that he was not always wise and hard-working, and he has created our wealth. We have helped, but had he not known how to lead us, things would not have developed so fast. I agree that it is time for us to control the business, but we can't exclude him from everything. One must let him manage something if he so wishes."

"And what did he say when they gave him a piece of their minds?"

"He was quiet at first . . ." Janko smiled, remembering how Ratko answered them:

"Wait until we finish the houses by Dubure. It is already decided which will go to whom, then you can separate, as matters have come this far. Each of you has his money with which to start, and as for the family capital and the land below Dubure, I won't give it away for as long as I live, but when I die you can share it between you. Go now and make up your minds what you want."

Jelka was overjoyed. "Oh, well, it is good that he has so easily agreed to the separation. Did you decide when?"

"No, we didn't. No one mentioned the separation again. We'll see what will happen when the houses this side of Dubure are built."

As Jula wanted, her wedding was conducted in the European fashion which was being introduced in the houses of Plevlje merchants, many of whom were now traveling to Vienna on business. She did not want anyone but the closest family and a select number of guests to be invited. There were to be no *kolo* dancers or gypsy musicians, everything restrained and rather formal.

When at last Jelka returned to the Kojics, Janko could not allow her alone to be without help. Petko had decided to keep Pava's maid throughout her pregnancy and until the baby grew strong, so he too hired a servant.

Ratko's authority declined as soon as he let the management and control of his home slip out of his hands. The traditional order, which was the very foundation of the extended family, disintegrated and everything began to deteriorate. Whilst Rosa and Jelka tried to hide their intolerance of each other, their maids began to quarrel openly, and old Marta added to the trouble by mixing and passing on bits of gossip all round, thus involving all the family in their intrigue. Chaos reigned in the house until finally the three brothers went to Ratko to ask that the separation be hastened.

Frowning, Ratko heard them out, then said, "I won't allow you to separate until I have built everything I intended, even if blood flows between you. Whoever is not satisfied can collect his possessions and go his own way. I won't give him anything that belongs to the family. Shame on you! Can't you bear up a little longer and, when everything is completed, divide it properly and in peace? Tighten the reins on your wives, get rid of the servants and let the three of them do as much as they can. They don't always have to cook different dishes and pies. One day we can eat seasoned maize porridge, another day baked potatoes and cheese, if they have not time for something else. We won't suffer because of it. Our immediate aim is the construction. Can't you see what dangerous times are upon us? One must invest in something safe. Who can tell, one day those houses may become our only means of support. Why can't you obey me? I can't take everything to my grave; everything will be left to you."

Stevo and Petko said nothing: only Janko ventured to suggest, "Why don't we divide the houses we have, move out and settle down without feeling so confined, then continue further building?"

"No, that wouldn't work. Once the family disperses, there's no common undertaking or working harmony. You don't get along even now when you have interests in common, but without those everybody would only be working for his own advantage."

Silence descended as they sat deep in thought. Finally, Janko asked, "How far do you intend to build, Adzo?"

"It is up to us. If we apply ourselves, everything could be ready in a year's time. We've got our own workforce and gained experience whilst building these houses. We can also bring in our relatives from Mrzovic to help out. I have bought the old Turkish inn which we'll pull down, and the whole of this side of the street will then be ours, not a foot anybody else's. All the land on the other side belongs to the Barracks, and the Shvabas won't allow anything to be built there. No one will disturb us, or interfere with our rents. This quarter here is dry, high on the hill, and healthy, so we will easily find good tenants."

"And on the site of the Turkish inn we could build a hotel?" Stevo asked, with a gleam in his eye.

"We could, too," Ratko confirmed, "in the same position but on the corner between our street and the Dzada, to give it two facades. Besides, the place attracts trade."

The prospect of building the hotel appealed to the brothers, and each secretly desired that it should fall to him when they divided the property, whether by getting less of the residue or buying it out. For that reason they began its construction as soon as they completed the work that had been in progress. But when they measured the grounds and started to dig the foundations of the hotel, Ratko discovered that the Austrian brothel was being moved from Jalija to the two-story house right next to their land facing the Turkish graveyard. The news devastated him and he immediately gave orders for all work on the hotel to be stopped and called his sons.

"It is all over with our construction plans for the hotel or any other building, nor do I want anything that belongs to us to be next to that filthy house. Until the Shvabas leave and take with them that monstrosity which has brought shame upon our town and citizens, we won't build anything there. Let the land stay idle, it disturbs nobody and demands nothing. Everyone knows it is our land and when better times come we'll realize all we've planned. If I die before then, you will continue, I'll pledge it to you."

His sons were silent, as if in two minds.

"Don't you know what misfortune that filth has caused up to now? The Shvabas hushed up the matter of the massacre that took place between the Serbs and the Turks because of those Viennese whores. They ordered the investigation to be stopped, but two lives were lost, that of the Turkish beg who died from the knife of a Serb and the priest's son who committed suicide when the police surrounded his house. His poor wife fell ill with sorrow and disgrace, and died, leaving two orphaned children." Sensing that they were still hesitating, Ratko went on, "And it is said that such a house spreads a dirty

French disease. The Serbs run to Sarajevo and secretly seek a cure, whilst the Turks are covered in scabs on the face, their noses drop off, and they perish silently like beasts. But no one dares open their mouth because of the Shvabas and we have to suffer that infamy which has diseased our Plevlje. Are our Kojic houses to be next to that horror? We'll divide what we have and, God willing, when better times come, we'll build the rest."

When all the work was completed on the new houses, and Ratko had turned the land on the other side of Dubure into fields and meadows, the family separated. Stevo got the houses under Glavica, two large and one small. He also kept the inn and the store that they contained. Ratko and Simuna continued to live with him. Petko inherited one large and three smaller houses, and Janko two three-story houses opposite the Krstata Barracks and the small one in the back garden. Petko immediately opened a new inn in the big house and Janko took over Stevo's shop in the Charshija.

5

All the Kojic houses were built after Austrian plans; Ratko himself supervised the work and he chose and obtained the building materials. As soon as they had separated, Janko hired the Shvaba gardeners who had laid out and maintained the park around the barracks to arrange the flower garden in front of the house which stood back from the street. In the middle they made and planted five circular flower beds edged with turf, and the paths between them were strewn with white pebbles. At the street end of the garden, they erected a spacious hardwood pagoda with a latticed screen and domed roof. Around it were planted vines, and along the fences grew quince and plum trees for their pretty blossom, as well as lilacs and jasmine. Janko also planted an ash tree there to remind him of the ash tree in Savka's garden under which he and Jelka had pledged themselves to one another. The first and second floors of both houses Janko kept for his own use, and the rest he rented to families of Austrian officers. He chose high-ranking tenants, amongst others a military doctor and, in the house where he and Jelka lived, a Major von Ries. In the first house facing the Krstata Barracks he opened a bar on the first floor, and employed Jelka's relative, Vaso, to run it. The small house in the garden contained the kitchen and dining room, and the servants' quarters.

The furniture was bought in Sarajevo and all the rooms were furnished in European style; only the main reception room had *secijas*, embroidered cushions, and curtains from Istanbul made out of purple woolen cloth, interwoven with gold thread and trimmed with silk braid of the same color. Even this room contained some pieces of European furniture: a cabinet and a grandfather clock made in Vienna, a round table with a set of chairs and, under the icon of St. Stevan, a small one displaying a tall candlestick and the incense burner, both of gold-plated silver. The carpets were woven to fit the rooms, two for each room, for everyday use and for holidays. The corridor was long and wide, with doors on each side leading to all the rooms and a tall window at the end which had the same curtains as the reception room. Under the window was a long seat with cushions on it. Hidden underneath and covered by a lid was an opening leading to the "blind store" which stretched the entire length of the corridor and had no windows. This was a secret hiding place. A set of carpets was also woven for the corridor.

Jelka was much happier since they had moved, free of Rosa's presence and the laborious work of an extended family life, as there were now fewer family members to care for and the house was new and easy to maintain. Her friendship with Pava had become even closer since Jula had married and moved to Sarajevo. She often visited her mother to make her feel less lonely, because Jula had taken Joka with her to help her settle in the new environment. The only aspects she disliked were the Austrian tenants and their wives, especially because Janko enjoyed talking with them and exchanging pleasantries in a language she did not understand. Sometimes she reproached him. "What made you bring them here and fill our house with foreign hussies?"

"Don't say that, Jelka, they are not living here for nothing, but are paying high rents," Janko tried to calm her. "Besides, the women are not hussies but decent housewives. They all come from very good Viennese homes and are married to high-ranking officers. We haven't anyone of low rank, not to mention the doctor and von Ries, who is an aristocrat, the son of a count."

"I don't care if he is a count himself, he is a Shvaba. There must be something wrong with him that he sticks a lens in a healthy eye for the sake of fashion."

"If only you knew what an educated and clever man he is, you wouldn't talk like that. He gave me, as a gift, those thick books about the history of Austria. Their culture is a thousand years old. Take a look at those pictures of monuments, their own and those they have excavated from all over the world."

"I still don't like it that he has persuaded you to put the money into Viennese banks. Petko is cleverer than you and Stevo, he is already building the second house since we separated."

"My money doesn't lie idle in the bank either, it multiplies each year and its interest is growing. Don't you worry, Janko knows what he is doing."

They were in the garden. Since Jelka had become heavier she often sat there, although she complained at first that it made her feel as if she were in a window display. Now she had grown accustomed to the severe outlines and the harmonious arrangement of the flower beds, which reminded her of the designs on the carpets, and she sometimes spent the entire afternoon in the pagoda, where she could knit or embroider in peace, whilst Djana was playing in the garden.

"How can I not worry when you are so anxious to keep up with Shvaba ways? I don't mind the furniture—it's better to sleep in a bed than put mattresses on the floor and keep the linen in chests—but why do you want to have a piano like they have? Who will play it?"

"I want our children to learn. We don't want to remain like peasants. All the Sarajevo merchants' children are being brought up in European fashion."

She softened a little and said with a smile, "Wait till they are big enough and there are many of them, God willing, a house full, then you can teach them whatever you like."

"All right, my Jelka, your man will do anything you wish." Janko laughed and took out a gold pocket watch he had bought in Vienna. It was attached to a thick chain with a seal at one end and his initials at the other. "But I mustn't tarry. People are waiting for me in the shop."

They got up and Jelka saw him to the gate. As they stepped into the street, he saw a young peasant girl, barefoot and in rags, and spoke to her sharply, "Why are you begging so young, why don't you work?"

"I am not begging, I am looking for work, if only for food. I haven't eaten all day except for a piece of corn bread which I took with me when I left home. I put a stone under my belt to stop my stomach rumbling."

Janko felt sorry and, turning to Jelka, asked, "Why don't we take her in to help you now around your confinement?"

Jelka also took pity on her at the thought that no one would take so shabby and emaciated a person into their home, and so dirty that one would not take a walnut out of her hand. "All right," she decided. "We'll try her out and if she is diligent and decent, she can stay."

When Janko had left, Jelka led her into the front garden. "What is your name?"

"Zlata."

"All right, Zlata, you have heard that we'll try you out, but first you must wash and change. I will give you some of my clothes to put on and later I will show you what there is to do."

Zlata quickly caught up with the housework. Jelka dressed and shod her and kept her clean, and she no longer looked so ugly. She went to church every Sunday and sometimes visited her relative who, with her husband, had moved from their village to Trlica where they worked in a pub. Zlata was quiet and obedient, learned many skills, and was a great help to Jelka. She had come at a time when the big preparations for winter were taking place: jams were being made, soaps prepared, various vegetables pickled, fruit bottled, farm stocks slaughtered for smoked and cured meat, and other chores were in full swing.

When the time for Jelka's confinement approached, she decided to take Djana with her and stay at Savka's for a week because later, with a new baby, she would not be able to visit her for a while. There was no need to worry about the house. She had told Zlata to wash the windows and scrub all the floors during her absence so that on her return everything would be in perfect order. Janko hired a coach to take them there, and as they drove together along the Charshija, Jelka thought that no other woman could be happier than she. Janko stopped for a while at Savka's, then left for work, and Jelka settled down with Djana. They spent a pleasant evening with Savka at dinner, but when it was time for Djana to be put to bed, she began to cry.

"I don't want to sleep here, I want to go home, I want my daddy!" They cajoled her, offered her toys, and tried all they could think of to soothe her, but nothing helped. Her cheeks flushed and wet with tears, she sobbed and screamed until, finally, Jelka said:

"I have no choice but to go back home. She's spoilt everything, the little rascal. She's too attached to her father and he to her. She's the very light of his eyes, he spoils her, lets her do whatever she likes and won't touch her, no matter what she does, nor does he let me smack her. I am afraid she'll become worse than a wild pup. A child cannot reason and if it is not afraid for its behind it becomes impossible. I will leave things here and send Janko's man to fetch them."

She said goodbye to her mother, took Djana's hand and left. When she arrived at the gates of her home, she took Djana in her arms and carried her through the garden because the lantern at the front of the house was not lit. Seeing that the lamp was burning in Janko's room, Jelka thought, "He's already back from the Charshija and must be reading. How surprised he'll be when he sees us." She quietly crossed the corridor and opened the door.

When she entered the room, Jelka screamed. Putting Djana down, she ran down the corridor as if possessed. Not knowing where she was going or how, she finally arrived at her mother's house, oblivious of everything, and banged with all her might on the door-knocker.

Savka came down to open the gate, and was frightened by the sight of her daughter so distraught. Jelka pushed past her, ran into the house, and threw herself sobbing on to the floor in the hall. Savka knelt beside her and lifted Jelka's head to stop her banging it against the floor. She also began to cry.

"Tell me, in God's name, what's happened?"

Jelka continued to sob, shaking and writhing as if in agony. When

141

Savka managed to raise her and make her lean against the wall, she opened her eyes and began to stare vacantly as if she were somehow looking into herself, rigid, frightened, desolate. From time to time shudders seized her.

"Calm down, my Jelka, calm down, please, or you'll miscarry, you'll bear a dead child."

Alarmed, Jelka stopped crying, sighed deeply and said, "I caught him . . . caught Janko with Zlata."

"Where is Djana?"

She burst into sobs again and began to bang her head against the wall, and grip her throat, choking. Savka tried to grab hold of her hand but she pulled away in a frenzy, and began to claw at her own face.

"Don't, you'll disfigure your face and leave permanent scars as if from smallpox."

"I don't care, what pretty face, what good are my looks, my eyes even? Had I the fortune to be born blind instead of beautiful, I wouldn't have seen such horror."

"Please stop, not for my sake, your poor mother, but for the sake of the child you are carrying."

Jelka paused for a moment to reflect, pressing her fists to her chest. "That I should live to see this! Had he found someone prettier, it would have hurt less, but that common peasant! When she came to ask for work, she was so filthy I couldn't let her into the house until she had washed. I took her out of pity because she was hungry. I fed her, deloused her, dressed her, made her look decent—to be so rewarded. I wouldn't be so shocked if she now looked any better, if she weren't so black and thin that dresses hang on her like rags from a scarecrow . . . that he should have been tempted by her. Where is my happiness now, my bliss? They have all gone. There is nothing left. It would have been better if I were not alive, Mother, if I were in my grave. Death is sweet compared with this insult, this shame."

"Cry all you wish, my child, but don't let the neighbors hear you."

Overcome by her sobs, Jelka suddenly felt a violent movement within her. The baby was almost visibly tossing from side to side. Terrified, Savka began to plead with her through tears. "Calm yourself, or you'll strangle the child and pay with your own life."

"So be it. There is nothing left for me but to die!"

The mother smoothed Jelka's hair from her forehead and pressed her head to her chest. "Don't talk like that, my love, think of Djana. What would she do if anything happened to you?"

"I can't. I can't think of anything now, Mother. All I can see is the sight I found when I opened that door. The horror of it. I could never have imagined that anything like it could happen, that I could hear about it, let alone see it."

As she spoke, someone knocked at the gate.

"Get upstairs, some neighbor may have come for a chat. Go into your room and don't come out, in case anyone sees you in this state."

After Jelka had climbed the stairs, Savka went to the gate and asked who was there.

"It is I, Janko, open please."

Opening the gate, Savka saw him carrying Djana in his arms.

"She fell asleep on the way."

"Wait here until I see what Jelka is doing. I daren't let her see you now." She went to Jelka and told her placidly, "Joka Tozovic is here. You lie down and calm the baby. I will tell her you are unwell and are already in bed so she'll leave sooner, I hope. Keep quiet as if you are asleep." She then went back, gave Janko a sign to come in, and let him into the sitting room. Taking Djana from him, she put her on one of the seats, took off her shoes, and, without undressing her, covered her with a shawl. Janko sat on the *secija* staring at the floor in front of him and Savka remained standing by the door, unable to utter a word. Janko began first.

"Savka, Mother, help me. You'll mean more than my own mother to me if you do that. Calm Jelka down and see that somehow she forgives me. I won't forget it for as long as I live. I'll get Zlata out of the way, marry her off, give money to arrange it, and no one would know about this."

Savka was silent, not knowing what to say to him.

He fell silent, too.

Finally she spoke. "Go, Janko, do as you think best, but don't show yourself to her until I send word."

He rose, said goodbye and left quietly. Savka locked the gate and the front door, tucked Djana up and went upstairs. Jelka was quiet, resting, her hand on her stomach with a vague look in her eyes, as if trying to listen.

"Did she leave?" she asked abstractedly.

"I told her I was tired and must retire early because of you."

"It doesn't move, Mother, could it be suffocated?"

"God forbid, the child has calmed down because you are calmer."

"Mother, I'm afraid."

"Don't be frightened, wait a little, it's sure to move."

Both became quiet, holding their breaths. Suddenly Jelka's hand moved and her face lit up. "Here it is, moving again, thank God."

Savka placed her hand on the other side of Jelka's stomach and waited to feel the movement. "There, it is moving here, too, pushing hard as if with its little legs."

They both smiled and cheered up for a moment, then Jelka became grave again, thoughtful.

"I worry about Djana. As for those animals, I don't want to think about them any more. From now on he is dead as far as I'm concerned, the brute. If only I could get Djana here. Please, Mother, go and get her."

"How can I? It's pitch black outside."

"I'm afraid I won't be able to sleep all night. All I can think of now is my child."

"How about going downstairs so I can make us some coffee? It would help us collect our thoughts."

"Let's," said Jelka, getting up.

They went down and Savka led the way into the visitors' room.

When Jelka saw Djana, she asked, flabbergasted:

"How did she get here?"

"Janko carried her over."

"He didn't come in, by any chance?"

"No, he just gave me the child."

"You didn't speak to him, I hope."

"No, I didn't dare because of you."

"That dog, I won't allow him anywhere near me. I wouldn't even look at that good-for-nothing now." She lifted Djana into her arms, carried her to the room and took off her clothes. Then she too undressed and lay down next to her.

Savka brought up the coffee and sat beside her. They exchanged a few words, then fell silent again.

After a while, Savka began tactfully, "My child, a man is a man. That bitch led him into temptation."

"Leave it, please, don't mention him to me. I don't want to know. Thank God he brought me the child, I need nothing else from him."

Savka spread a mattress next to hers and lay down. Neither could sleep. Before dawn, Jelka was eventually overcome by sleep but Savka remained awake.

Quietly, so as not to wake her daughter, she sat up and began to contemplate the situation. "What is going to happen now? Jelka is stubborn, she won't give in, and then what? Shame and disgrace, to be called a divorced woman. Her children to be branded by such disgrace, to have people say, 'Father a lecher and mother an abandoned woman.' If only she would forgive, God willing! Swallow the bitter pill, as many a woman has done, and covered things up so that no one is the wiser. The children would suffer most if they divorce. She'll have to be reconciled with him and get over this. One has to accept all kinds of misfortune. This is the first to befall her, and who knows what else is awaiting her? A man has to be harder than stone to endure everything that is in store, or he would crack like a nut. Everybody deceives himself, hopes for the best, and this deception carries us along to make living easier. Yet, if many knew what is bearing down from over the hill, they'd sooner put an end to their lives than face it. But no one knows, and when a sudden blow strikes, they think, 'It will be better once this is over.' Nor are all destinies the same. Some have quite a pleasant life and others, God protect us, have calamities that hem them in and squeeze like pliers . . . My Jelka, whichever way she turns, the best is to forgive and go back to him. That is how it will be, she has no choice."

Having thus concluded that she had found the solution, Savka felt a little easier, more at peace.

Dawn was breaking. She quietly stole out of the room so as not to wake her daughter and Djana, washed, combed her hair and dressed, then knelt in front of the icon and began to pray in whispers: "Almighty God, gentle Lord, have mercy on all the people and help them. Enlighten them and save them from sin. Forget not the traveler on the road, the sick confined to his bed, the prisoner in jail. Help my Janko to free himself from the Satan who has led him into evil. Help my Jelka, give her strength to endure her suffering. Don't forget my Jula either, alone in the distant world. Give us in this new day a new fortune." She crossed herself with a broad gesture of her right hand. As always the prayer brought her peace and serenity. She rose slowly and went to start her daily chores. Having fetched water from the well, she lit the stove, then mixed the dough for bread and for the breakfast pastry. Just then Fata arrived with the milk. Savka asked for more than she usually took.

"My elder daughter has come to visit with her child, so I need more milk."

"Has she now? Allah be praised that you have them." As she spoke, Fata poured more milk into the jug. "This is for good health."

"Don't, dear, it's too much."

"It's for good luck. May your granddaughter flourish."

Savka thanked her and asked her into the kitchen quarters for a cup of coffee. "Come, Fata, here is some tobacco, sit down and have a smoke, I have already put the coffee pot on."

Fata pretended to hesitate. "Why must you give me coffee every morning? You've got a lot to do today, I'll be in the way."

"Why in the way, woman? My daughter is still asleep and I don't feel like drinking alone."

When they had drunk the coffee, and Fata left, a woman neighbor dropped in.

Savka assumed a happy expression, saying, "Come in, come in, you're welcome. I have guests. Jelka is here with her child and will be staying with me for a few days. Her confinement is near and she needs a rest."

"I heard her arrive. You are lucky with your children. I hear that Jelka is happy and that Janko treats her as if she were the very light of his eyes."

It suddenly occurred to Savka that she perhaps knew something or had heard the comings and goings the previous evening. If she had seen Jelka when she came running as if possessed, she would have known there was something wrong and had come to spy out what had happened. Savka offered the coffee to her as well. "Yes, Jelka is happier than most. Jula too, she writes that she is well, so there is no mother more fortunate than I am. May God let it last."

They chatted for a while then Savka saw her out. She thought, "That snoop, why did she come so early? She must have noticed something. There are those who eat their own bread and worry over other people's troubles. They prefer the misfortunes of others to their own fortunes. I should think God created envy to punish the envious because they eat their hearts out and are never happy, as there is always someone to be envious of."

She was still lost in thought when Janko's servant arrived. He brought from the Charshija two bags full of goods and delicacies—meat, coffee, sugar, rice, raki and brandy, Turkish delight, sweets, nuts.

"Master Janko sent them."

Savka emptied the bags and handed them back to him, then took her purse from the shelf and gave him a large tip. Taken aback, he protested that it was too much, but eventually accepted it, and touched his fez lightly. "To your health, then."

As the man left, Savka thought, "Really, Janko is good, poor thing. What came over him? The Devil himself must have led him into evil." When she heard Jelka talking to Djana, she quickly tipped batter into the pan, poured coffee with milk into a jug, put cups on the tray, and took everything upstairs. As they breakfasted, Savka tried to amuse Djana, and dandled her on her lap, but she was afraid to even look at Jelka. When she darted a casual glance at her and saw how poorly she looked, her heart sank. Dark rings under her eyes, face rigid, her whole being radiating dullness and apathy. One wouldn't believe that pain and trouble could so change a person in one day, as if she was not the same person as yesterday.

"Come, put on a nice dress and make yourself pretty. Someone may call in, and it wouldn't be good if they saw you looking like that. No one can give your consolation unless you yourself find it in your heart."

"Let them see me, I don't care. Why hide it? They'll find out."

Savka hesitated a little, then decided to tell her what Janko had sent.

"You didn't accept?"

"Indeed I did, of course I accepted. Did you expect me to return it and lose face publicly, or snub Janko in front of his servant? Every servant is a paid enemy and rejoices when his master is in some trouble or disrepute. The moment it was out that we'd returned what he sent us, it would spread in no time." She got up and collected the jug and the cups. "I'm going to bake the bread and start preparing lunch and you can dress and tidy the rooms. You'll feel better if you find something to do."

Having delivered Djana, Janko had returned home and gone to bed, but could not fall asleep until dawn. "What now?" he thought. "What will happen with Jelka? I feel as if her horrified eyes are still staring at me and I can still hear her scream. What have I done? Cursed soul! What came over me? It's as if darkness had descended upon me and I didn't know what I was doing. Why did I drink so much rum? And that bitch, why did she come to take my shoes off? Why did she come near me when she saw I was drunk and staggering up the stairs? Still, it's no one's fault but mine. Why did I have to drink, curse upon me? Left without my wife for the first time and I get drunk as a lord. What will happen to Jelka? She could die in childbirth. After such a blow, something could happen to her even tonight. What should I do? If I could get rid of Zlata and Jelka forgives me, life will never be the same again, nor will our happiness. I have thrown it all away, I, myself. No one else is to blame. Destroyed her life and mine, curse upon me." Unable to rid himself of such thoughts, he got up and, not knowing what to do, took the bottle of rum, finished it, dropped on the bed and fell asleep like a log.

He woke in a sweat. His head was heavy, his chest so compressed he could hardly breathe. Having washed and dressed, he went out without breakfast to avoid seeing Zlata and decided to go to Adzo and Nana, as only they would be up so early. They were awake, sitting as usual on the cushions and drinking coffee.

"What a miracle, son!" Ratko welcomed him mockingly. "What can it be that you have remembered us? You seem to have forgotten us completely."

"No, Adzo, I haven't forgotten you, but there is so much work, there hasn't been time. I must see to everything, you can't rely on employees. Now that Jelka's relative is looking after the bar, I am almost all the time in the Charshija, rushing back and forth between the shop and the store-room."

"Didn't you hear that your mother was very ill these past few weeks?"

"No, Adzo."

"You should come and see how we are. We are old and can go any time. It is your duty to call on us and exchange a few words. Are you just waiting to receive the news that one of us is dead and then come? And that wife of yours too, putting on airs as if she were a pasha's wife, asking to be served on a silver tray. They say you've found a maid for her."

Janko was stung by this remark, and his heart began to beat faster, but he said nothing and lowered his eyes.

"If things were as they should be, she would keep visiting us. She's not up to her neck in work, even if you are. Rosa is looking after us, not a day passes by without her coming to bring something to her mother-in-law. There, she's abrupt but just and good-hearted. And we do care that our children do not forget us in our old age."

"You see, Adzo, Rosa is in the same house, it's nearer for her."

"And where are you, in some other town or what? The third house from ours, one could piss across."

"Jelka is ill, she's gone to Savka to recover."

Ratko became worried. "What is it? What is she complaining of? Is she in pain?"

"No, nothing, just . . . she's very heavy, close to her confinement."

This annoyed Ratko. "Confinement! Confinement! That word was never even mentioned before. It was shameful to say a woman gave birth to a child. One referred to it as a new arrival. But now our women are imitating the Shvabas' wives, short of asking us to take them to hospital to give birth in front of doctors and nurses. My mother bore me in a field, wrapped me in her apron, and carried me home. Those women were healthier and strong."

"Don't, Ratko, for heaven's sake!" Simuna interrupted. "You are telling us what used to be. Even I didn't bear children in the fields, never mind Jelka."

"And look what a lady you've become. If you were still of childbearing age, you would want me to send you to hospital. As if one can run away from those pains. Every female suffers, my dear, even a beast—'from a queen to a filly' as they say. If there was another way, the Shvabas would have invented it and their wives would bear children in a medicinal way." Looking at Simuna he added jokingly, "You've inherited it from Eve. She tempted Adam and was the cause of his sin, therefore God assigned to her the childbirth pains, not to Adam."

"Ah, but God is male and was on the side of man; if the Mother of God had been there at the time, she wouldn't have allowed it."

"Joking apart," Ratko continued thoughtfully, "I have found that those pains helped the birth. Without them neither a woman nor an animal could free themselves of the young. Once, in the village, our cow was calving; the calf was large and her pains ceased, she stretched out, didn't moo or strain, just looked at us. We pulled the calf out alive, but she died. At first I regretted the loss, good cow, big loss, but later I was more sorry for her, as if she were a person. I could never forget those big eyes looking sadly at me."

Janko could hardly stop himself from getting up and running away. He was afraid for Jelka because she was very big this time and because he had made her suffer so much. Having stayed for a while longer with his parents he got up and left. It seemed to him he was the worst man in the world. He had sinned against his parents too, because he had stopped seeing them. If they died he wouldn't forgive himself. Jelka could be excused, she was not of their blood and, besides, she didn't like to encounter Rosa, but for him, their son, there was no forgiveness. If everything was well with Jelka, he'd do all he could to make up for it, or he wouldn't be able to go on living. Having so decided, another thought occurred to him. "Good that Adzo mentioned the hospital. Should there be any difficulties, I will call the doctor who lives in my house, and beg him to save her at any cost. Let them sacrifice the child if there is no other way, just as long as Jelka doesn't die."

When he arrived at the Jalija, he regained his grip on himself and decided to go to the store to think things over. His immediate worry was to consider what do do about Zlata. He would have liked best to give her some money and send her away, but he was afraid of what people might say. To find her another place before Jelka returned was impossible: everybody would guess that something suspicious had been going on. "The best thing would be to get her married. I will spend money, I won't begrudge it, as long as I can get rid of her." Just as he was reflecting on this, he caught sight of his former employee, Relja. "My word, he would be better than anybody. He is a money-grubber, but lazy; he has it in his head to open a small pub but doesn't have the means. I will buy it for him, and all the stock, if he agrees to take Zlata." Janko headed straight towards him and, coming closer, slapped him on the shoulder as if they were friends, saying:

"Where have you been, Relja? I haven't seen you for a long time. Why don't you drop in some time?"

Relja looked at him suspiciously. "If you are thinking of asking me to work for you, I won't. You Kojics want one to slave for you but you don't pay more than others do. And even if there is some small gain, a penny or two, you wear a man out." Noticing that Janko frowned, he changed his tune: "On the other hand, Master Janko, you were always generous and gave us good tips, that's the truth. Still, I don't intend to work anywhere as before, I'm looking for something better, but can't find anything. I seem to have been born under an evil star."

"Listen, Relja, I'm on my own now and you wouldn't be working either for me or my brothers. If we come to an agreement on something, I will help you to get a better position and we'll both benefit."

"Oh, well, when shall I come?"

"Come today, between *icindija* and *aksham*. I live in that new yellow house on the lower floors."

"Right, I'll be there." Relja shook his hand as if they were partners.

"Look at that son of a bitch, talking liberties as soon as he heard that I need him," Janko thought. "They can spot it in the blink of an eye, that kind. He'll start haggling now. We didn't pay him well, he said, and he wore himself out working! As if we took him on to lie around on the cushions. If one could collect wages for doing nothing, everybody would become a laborer. They all envy their bosses, as though it was easy to be a boss."

When he arrived at the store, he called one of his men, filled two baskets with provisions and delicacies and sent them to Savka. Feeling better, he passed a row of sacks and went to the small room where he kept his account books. Glancing through them, he reflected, "Look at all the debtors whose payments are long overdue and they don't call in. What's more, they pretend not to see me, or sneak off to avoid meeting me. And the peasants are taking more and more all the time without settling old accounts. I must be mad to give it to them. I'll have to tell them I will charge interest if they don't repay on time. They are making a fool of me."

He pushed the books away, lit a cigarette and his thoughts drifted back to Jelka. "Perhaps she'll have a boy and will soften enough to forgive me. If she gives birth at Savka's, I will go there whatever happens. Anything will be better than it is now. The child will reconcile us." He sighed deeply, looking at the bluish rings of smoke dissolving under the low ceiling. "But there'll be no reconciliation if I don't arrange a marriage for Zlata."

Noon rang from the clocktower, Janko got up, called one of his men, and sent him to fetch a dish of meatballs. "As you go past the coffee house, tell Uso to send me one coffee and a glass of cold water." His throat felt tight and his thoughts wandered from one subject to another, always returning to Jelka. Trying to concentrate on something else, he once more picked up the account books. "What made me give them so much? How can one ever get it back from those paupers? They won't easily get out of trouble. And to stop giving them more until they have repaid, I cannot. Cap in hand they beg, implore . . ." He pushed the books aside again. "To hell with everything, why bother?" His lunch and the coffee were brought in. He quenched his thirst first, then began to eat but, unable to enjoy the food, poured himself some coffee. The coffee tasted good and he leisurely drank the entire contents of the pot, then went into the store-room to inspect the stock.

"Why did you put these skins in here in the damp to molder? Get upstairs and stow them on top of the sacks where it is dry. Do you have to be told everything? All you do is hang around by the door, looking up and down the Charshija to pass the time, not working."

He made another round of the store-room to examine other goods, took out his watch and decided to take a walk down the road to the Cotina, as it was still too early for the *icindija* and he did not wish to return home before then. When the muezzins announced the *icindija* from the minarets, he cheered up and headed toward the house to wait for Relja. He was impatient. As he entered the courtyard he called Zlata and, without looking at her, said abruptly:

"A man will come to ask for your hand. You know you cannot stay here any longer. If he marries you, I will buy him a *kafana*."

She bowed her head, saying softly, "Yes, master."

"He'll have to take you away before the mistress returns. Go now and get things ready. When I call you, come into the room."

"Yes, master," Zlata repeated, and withdrew.

When Relja arrived, Janko received him in the visiting room. He sat on the *secija*, leaned against the cushions, crossed one leg over the other, and looked at Janko questioningly, waiting for him to start.

Janko was annoyed by his insolent manner but had to hold back, having degraded himself to the point of discussing such matters with a former employee. Although pretending to be composed, he delayed the issue. He offered his tobacco case to Relja and asked, "Do you smoke, Relja?"

"Yes, I do."

"Here, help yourself."

Relja took and examined the case, turning it in his hand, then opened it carefully and began to roll a cigarette. "Even your tobacco box is made of gold! You landlords are doing well."

This angered Janko and he came straight to the point. "Listen Relja, here is why I asked you to come. We have a maidservant whom I want to marry off and send away as soon as possible. Would you take her?"

"Ah, I knew it would be something shady, otherwise you'd never have received me like this as a guest. But never mind. Is she pregnant?"

"No."

"How much are you giving with her?"

"I'll open a *kafana* for you, find a good position, and stock it up with drinks and all that is necessary. It may bring you good luck, you always wanted one."

"All right, I agree."

"Do you want to see her?"

153

"I don't have to, it doesn't worry me."

"But Relja, can you take her with you straight away? Do you have a room of your own? Where do you live?"

"I have a little house my father left me. He was an artisan, but I did not care to learn any craft. And whilst my parents were alive, life wasn't too bad. First my mother died, then my father, and I went into service. I didn't want to sell the house; if nothing else, it proves that I was somebody in the past. And I always had a premonition that the day would come when I would be my own boss, however small, and work in my own *kafana*."

"Well, then, in a few days I will have everything arranged and you will be your own boss in your own *kafana*. Will you take Zlata with you now?"

"Why not, brother? Straight away if you wish. Who could refuse you? No one ever had reason to complain about you. You are an honest man and your word is your bond."

Relieved that the matter was so easily solved, Janko rubbed his hands and said, "How about the two of us having a drink?"

"I'd like that, brother, good idea."

Janko went out and told Zlata to bring raki and coffee. When she came to serve them, he said, "Here, Zlata, this friend of mine wants to marry you. Get your things ready. He'll take you with him this evening. You will be wed as soon as I buy him a *kafana*. Go now and wait, and when he is about to leave, I'll call you."

Relja stayed a while longer, then got up and left with Zlata. Janko felt as if a stone had been lifted from his heart once this worry was over, and thought he had found the right solution for all of them.

Janko waited for Savka to ask him to come, but no message arrived. He frequently sent them goods from the Charshija which they accepted but remained silent. The worrying robbed him of any peace. He went to his shop or to the store-room and kept an eye on the bar, but could not stop anywhere for long. He tried to mix with people, had a drink with them, exchanged a few words, yet could not wait to get up and go. He now often called on his parents, took gifts to his mother and stayed with them longer because he felt best in their company, although he did not dare to confide his troubles to them.

When back at home, he tried to read but could not concentrate on anything as his thoughts wandered to other matters. One evening, he was overwhelmed by such despair and hopelessness that the thought of suicide occurred to him. He went to the cupboard where he kept his revolver, but as he was reaching for it, he started back and ran out of the house. Not knowing how to escape his wretchedness, he went to his mother. Simuna was alone in her room. In the pale light of the lamp her face looked exhausted and full of pain, but as she opened her eyes and saw him, she smiled.

"Where is Adzo?" Janko asked, concerned.

"He went out for a chat, had enough listening to my moans."

"Why did they leave you alone? Are they looking after you?"

"They all are, and Ratko is always beside me. He only sleeps in his room. He was never kinder towards me than he is now."

Janko sat next to her bed. "What is hurting you, Mother?"

"Everything, aches and pains everywhere, it's old age, that's all. I have no strength whatsoever. I pray to God to let me find peace soon, not to become a burden or wear anybody out. I don't fear death a bit." She showed him the tip of her bony index finger. "If I could only last until Jelka's confinement. I can't help feeling that it will be a son this time. I wouldn't mind dying the moment I lay eyes on your son, I so long for a rest."

"Why not call the Shvaba doctor who lives in my house? I'll ask him to see you and give you some medicine."

"God forbid, I don't want any doctors. If it is my time to go, then I'll go, I don't want anyone to hold me back. We all have to, one day. I have lived long enough and can't wait for the end to come. Since I can't do any work, life has become burdensome to me. It is drudgery to be always sitting for so long like a cripple."

"Don't talk like that. We won't give you up. We want you to stay with us if only to look at you. What would Adzo do without you? He'd die."

"Yes, I can see that he is very upset. We have had a good life together and lived to see a pleasant old age. When he was younger he was a little bit severe and bad tempered, but even then he never. hit me or degrade me, as some men do. It took a lot to persuade him to sleep in another room. He had no peace looking after me all night long. I made him go out this evening, too. He should be with people for as long as his legs support him. Later, he will also come to this."

Janko stayed with her for a while longer, then rose and said goodbye.

Following him with her eyes as he left, Simuna thought, "Who would believe that I, so tiny, gave birth to him? How tall he and Stevo have shot up, like giants . . . They take after my father. There was no more strapping a man in the village. Thank God, I have had a good life, married off my sons, found decent homes for my daughters, and now they have to go each with their own destiny. If only there weren't so many aches and stabbing pains. But one has to endure whatever comes, there is no death without illness, except from strokes."

Going out, Janko decided to take a walk up to Glavica. The night was clear and moonlit, and one could see the entire town and the hills around it encircling it like a wreath. As he climbed higher, the Charshija stretched beneath him, illuminated by lanterns. On the mosques *kandilos* burned. The minaret of the Great Mosque stood out, slimmer and more harmonious than the others. Lamp-lit windows in the houses twinkled like tiny burning points scattered all over the whole town. The deep blue sky was strewn with large stars which seemed detached from it, floating nearer the earth. Looking at Mount Ljubisnja he remembered Major von Ries telling him that enormous mineral wealth was hidden in the caverns of Hollow Rock—iron, copper, and perhaps gold and silver. "The Austrians don't want to dig it out because they don't know whether they'll stay in Plevlje for good and are keeping the location of it as a State secret. It would be better if they stayed than if Plevlje fell into Turkish hands, and if they started quarrying the ore, commerce would flourish, more people would be employed and there would be less poverty. Why should all these riches lie dead? And if the Austrians don't dig them up, the people of Plevlje certainly won't because we neither know where the ores are to be found nor how to quarry them. Whether the Serbs or the Turks would ever do it, who knows?"

Behind Ljubisnja the mountains of Montenegro were just visible. "There they live in freedom," Janko sighed. "God, will we ever free ourselves from slavery? Stevo's hope for liberation is firm, but I have doubts. Even if Serbia and Montenegro rose, they could never gain victory over the Turks and Shvabas. Serbia is small, Montenegro even smaller. If Russia helped, something could be done, but she won't. What does the Tsar care about us, although we are Slavs and Orthodox, as he is? And to start an uprising on our own, we would perish. What are we, a mere handful. One Serb to every dozen Turks. They would be helped by Austria as well, however much she pretends to be protecting us Christians from the Turkish tyranny. I can see how they hate Serbia. Stevo says Serbia upsets their politics. If we did rise, we would find ourselves between the hammer and the anvil, they'd crush us like worms. There is no hope for us, we'll remain slaves forever. God, how heavy my heart is, as if a stone were lying on my chest and I can't breathe." He turned toward Golubinja and tears flooded his eyes. "I can't wait any longer. I'm going to Jelka, come what may."

He came down from Glavica, taking a short cut leading to Mocevac, and started towards Golubinja. When he reached Citluk, he looked in the direction of the monastery and whispered, "Blessed Mary, you protect all mothers and children, save my Jelka too."

At Savka's, relatives and neighbors called to see Jelka. She received them, chatted with them, sometimes laughed and joked as if nothing had happened. Her pallor was ascribed to her pregnancy, and if anyone did notice a definite change, Savka explained that this time she was carrying with more difficulty.

"A little frightened too, like every woman. With the first child one doesn't know what childbirth is and is not afraid, but with the second, one knows what is in store."

Whenever she was alone with Jelka, Savka tried to lead the conversation round to Janko to soften her wrath. "My child, people are noticing that you are still not returning home. How would it be if I sent a message to Janko to come? You'll have to go back to him eventually."

"Not as long as I live. I would not go back, nor could I bear to look at him or her."

"But he said when he brought Djana that he'd send her away."

"It's too late. Nothing can be changed now."

"Don't be like that, my darling, he is the father of your children, the head of the family and a good man. He made a mistake, being a male. What man doesn't stray, but not every woman finds out. No one is sinless except God alone. We are all sinful, some in one way, some in another, and must forgive so that we also will be forgiven."

"No, this cannot be forgiven."

"What else can you do? Call yourself a divorced woman? Take the children away from their father, their own flesh and blood? Make them fatherless while their father is living? Not a day passes that Djana doesn't mention him, and what will happen when she grows wiser? And when that child is born? If Janko were dead you would tell it about its father and it would love his memory. There are children born after their father's death who are brought up to love him more than their mother, although they never saw him. What will you do or say when it learns that its father is alive and you have deprived it of him?" Seeing how much this conversation hurt Jelka, she changed her tone. "Do you want your enemies to revel in it? Those who envied and hated you, to feel as if revenged? I have thought a lot about all this, and whichever way you look at it, it is best to return to your home. Janko begged me to reconcile you with him."

"When did he beg you?"

"That first night when he brought the child."

"And you said you didn't speak with him."

"I didn't dare mention it. I told him to wait until I sent him a message."

"So, you are making arrangements behind my back."

"What else? Who would have dared to talk to you about it then?"

"I can't, Mother, I can't."

"You have no choice. Think what would happen if you divorced. He could marry better than any bachelor. Some woman couldn't wait to take your place. I hope you don't want to lose such a man. Young, good-looking, and rich, there's no woman who would refuse him. And your heart would break. You still don't know how difficult it is for a woman without a husband, someone to care for her and protect her. You yourself know how you and Jula fared after your father's death. And you have been sheltered by your uncles. But who would your children turn to? You mustn't bring misfortune upon them. They did not ask to be born, and having borne them you have become their debtor. Many a woman suffers worse things for the sake of the children, for the reputation and well-being of her family. Without a head of the family, a home is sad and empty. Do you want to start working for others, God forbid, become a servant or a cook? You think you could stand it, but do you really believe it is easy to stop being the first and become the last? And to remarry? Even if someone would take you with two children, how could you do it when you are still in love with Janko? You do love him. If you didn't, you wouldn't suffer so much. And he loves you. You should have seen how he begged and pleaded with me to reconcile you. My child, if we didn't forgive one another, no one could live with anyone."

"I can't forgive him, Mother, please don't talk to me about him. Whenever I remember, my heart still bleeds from the wound he has inflicted."

Savka wanted to say more, but Jelka interrupted her.

"Please, for God's sake, Mother, don't keep on about him to me any more."

But as time went on Savka skillfully and patiently prepared for a reunion. Whenever she spoke to Djana, she mentioned Janko, showed her the presents he was sending them, reminded her of her home, the garden, asked her whether she missed her father. And so, as one day succeeded another, she noticed that Jelka did not mind when the two of them spoke of Janko, although she was not yet ready to see him. Savka thought it best to wait, and was more and more confident that the time would come.

When Janko knocked at the gates, Savka anticipated that it was he, and without asking who it was, went down and let him in. She was pleased to see him. He greeted her, then anxiously, lowering his voice, he asked, "Where is Jelka?"

"She's upstairs with Djana, they are still up."

She led him into the same room as on that fateful evening. He sat down and she remained by the door, as she did then, but was more composed now.

"It's good that you came," she told him.

"Savka, Mother, free me of this torture, I can't endure it, I'll go mad from worry and despair."

"Let me go up to tell her you are here. I have done all I can, but she still cannot forget. She has suffered a lot, poor soul."

"I know, and I did too, this ordeal has distressed me more than anything in my whole life. I love Jelka above all and can't live without her. Even Djana seems little compared to her. Or my father and mother. My whole world is empty and barren." Saying that, he burst into tears as if a barrier had collapsed and a whole mass of suffocating torment poured out.

Savka had never before seen a man cry, and no one's tears shook and upset her as his did. She too began to cry. "Wait here, I'll call her," she whispered.

Entering Jelka's room, she just said, "Go downstairs, I'll stay with Djana."

Jelka turned pale when she saw Savka's tearful face and, without asking anything, descended. She stopped by the door for a moment to compose herself, then went in. Janko rose, approached her and knelt down. "Forgive me, please. Here, I'll kiss the ground you stand on, as is done before the Holy Mary." He bent down and kissed the floor in front of her feet. "Forgive me and come back to me. I'll kill myself if you don't. Without you there is no life for me."

She lightly placed a hand on his head and whispered, "Get up, I forgive you. We are sinners, like all God's creatures."

"Jelka, my happiness, I was drunk, believe me, I didn't know who I was or what I was doing. From now on, I won't drink, nor will I ever betray you for as long as I live. Better to burn down a church than to wound you. Because of what happened, because of that calamity, I feel cursed, as if I were a traitor, as if I'd desecrated the cross, changed my creed."

Holding back her tears, she went out and from below the stairs she called her mother. "Bring Djana down, her father is waiting," she managed to say, then went into the pantry and locked the door behind her. She sat on the floor and began to sob spasmodically. When she had stopped crying, she got up, wiped her face and smoothed her hair, then returned to the visiting room.

Djana was on her father's knee, her small arms wound around his neck, while he was kissing her hair. When Jelka entered, he lifted his cheek from the top of Djana's head and embraced her with his look. "I believe you will soon give birth."

"I think so too."

"Shall I send a carriage for you tomorrow, and perhaps Mother could also come?"

Jelka relaxed. She still could not accept the thought of being alone with him in that house.

Savka brought in refreshments. Silence fell upon the room. Even little Djana was quiet; her head pressed against her father's chest, she was falling asleep. Janko stayed a while longer, then seeing how pale and distressed Jelka was, he looked at his watch and said, "It's time for Djana to sleep. You two also need a rest." He tenderly picked up Djana and handed her to Savka, said goodbye and left.

The third night after her return, Jelka's confinement began. She woke her mother quietly and told her that the pains were upon her. Savka was glad. "Good luck, I'll go quickly to the kitchen to light the fire and put water on to boil. You keep quiet so as not to wake Djana and Janko. There's still time, these are the first pains, heralds of good news. We'll have everything ready before the real ones start." When she returned, she took out clean sheets for the bed and everything needed for a new-born child, all prepared beforehand. Jelka was pacing the room, stooping and bending when the pains gripped her, but did not utter a sound. When Savka saw they had become more frequent, she prepared the bed. "Lie down, my love, stretch a little and rest your back. It is not good to stoop so much."

Jelka lay down. The first spasm did not occur until dawn, after which Jelka was overcome by complete exhaustion and began to faint. Petrified, Savka brought raki and sugar. "Here, drink a glass of this. It will give you strength. Have some sugar as well, it's good for the heart," she said, trembling like a leaf.

Soon after came the second spasm, followed by a third. Jelka strained with all her might and the child slipped out as if soaped, and began to yell. Savka wrapped it in a diaper and placed it beside Jelka's feet, too frightened for Jelka's life to look at it.

"Tell me, Mother, is it another girl?"

"Why, no, *mashallah*, it's a boy, and big, a whole armful."

Jelka felt as if darkness was disappearing before her eyes. Her whole chest expanded with a deep breath which relaxed her and filled her with a sense of bliss. "Thank God it's a boy, he won't have to suffer like this."

Savka cut the umbilical cord, tied the child's navel with silk thread, then wrapped a shawl around him and gave him to Jelka to hold until she brought a jug of warm water and a small wooden bath.

"*Mashallah*, he's beautiful," she said as she took the child to bathe him. "I have never seen a lovelier child, God protect him."

By then, Jelka was free of the placenta, which Savka placed in a bowl of water, to wash it and make sure it was whole and healthy. "It's not good if a part of it stays inside the woman and rots. Many have developed childbirth fever because of it, and there's no cure for that." When she had satisfied herself that everything was all right, she took out the placenta and buried it under a rose bush. Having tidied the room, she poured water for Jelka to wash, helped her changed into a fresh petticoat with frills and a white blouse embroidered in white, then went to wake Janko. He threw on some clothes, came into the room, approached Jelka's bed and, taking both her hands, said, "Thank you, a thousand thanks for giving me a son."

"You haven't even looked at the child," she reproached him mildly.

He went to the crib, kissed the child, then returned to Jelka and, studying her pale face with concern, asked, "Was the birth difficult?"

"Not at all, couldn't have been easier," Savka interrupted.

The child thrived as days went by, but Jelka was not recovering. She lost weight, and was very pale and listless. She avoided entering the room in which Janko's infidelity had happened and had it cleaned and tidied by the woman who worked for them during the day. They never spoke about the event, or mentioned Zlata, but some hidden trace of sin was felt throughout the house and, like a crime, was itself a constant reminder.

Because of Jelka's ill health, they waited for the christening, but when forty days had passed, they could no longer delay it. Janko decided to choose a godfather amongst his friends from the town, who would be more suited to his present social standing than their old godparents, but did not do anything about it until he had advised his father. When he went to tell him about it, Ratko was shocked.

"What did you say?" staring at his son as though he couldn't believe his ears, and his face began to change as anger rose in him. "You would dare do it? Do you realize that the Colovics have been our family's godparents since the olden days? If you, my son, broke the tradition, I would put a curse on you. To a Serb a godparent is what Saint John the Baptist was to Christ. Would you, shame on you, change this for the sake of the nobility that you have now assumed—nobility that goes like chalk with cheese? Hold your horses, don't raise your head so high. 'The higher the flight, the deeper the drop,' as the saying goes."

"No, Adzo, that's not the reason, but they themselves have withdrawn. They only come for christenings or for *slavas*, and a godparent should be like a relative, a close friend. If we saw each other more often, our friendship would be firmer. And even if they do come, they seem embarrassed. They themselves feel out of place amongst other guests."

"They wouldn't feel so if Jelka and you were not such frosty hosts. Now don't you lie to me and pretend. I know everything and see everything. You are both giving yourself airs lately, none of us is good enough for you any more, you only mix with the gentry. What's more, I hear that you are seeing the Shvabas, some major?"

"But we all work with the Shvabas."

"It is not the same working with them as befriending them."

"The major lives in my house, but I never put my foot inside his apartment, nor does he come to me. Sometimes I stop to have a chat with him in front of the bar. He is a very clever and learned man."

"However learned he is, he is a Shvaba." Ratko cut him with a look and went on, "You befriend the Turks too, I hear, a Pasha Bajrovic and some others."

"They are local Turks, their ancestors were Serbs."

"Oh, my son, had we done the same, we would not have lasted all these centuries. Never trust a Shvaba or a Turk. They are all aliens and can easily become enemies."

Janko realized that there was no use contradicting, and said in a conciliatory tone, "I really don't know what you want. How do you expect Jelka and me to behave?"

"Be seen with other people as well, not only with the gentry. Hold on to the middle classes, take your place amongst them, you don't know what the future holds. If tomorrow you lost your footing, these new friends would drop you like dirt, but our old friends won't. Listen to my advice, son. Invite to the christening the whole family of your godfather, his wife and daughter. Simuna will be happy to see them. Come straight from the monastery to us for lunch. Your mother cannot wait to see your son. Thank God we've lived to rejoice in him. Now that the forty days have passed, Jelka can come too. She won't be considered unclean. Let the priest say a prayer for her health. Something is upsetting her as if she were ill. I'm afraid this birth may have damaged her insides. She is not at all her old self, God help us."

Upset by this, Janko got up to go. "All right, Adzo, I'll arrange it with the godfather."

"Wait, let me say one more thing. You have a doctor in the house. Call him to see what is sapping her health. Had we had the doctor for Stevo's first wife, we wouldn't have buried such a beauty. I still cannot forgive myself for letting a lovely woman like her perish before our eyes."

The christening was conducted as Ratko wished. They named the child Nikola, after the saint of the godfather's *slava*, and the festivities lasted three whole days. Jelka began to recover as her son grew strong, but she was not as happy as before. There was a constant emptiness in her heart as if a scar had been left on it, as if she had become numb to all the joys of life. She imagined she could feel no other suffering as deeply as Janko's infidelity.

Less than three months after Nikola's birth, Simuna died. Ratko organized a fine farewell for her. He himself went to order the coffin, choosing seasoned pinewood, without knots, so that it would last longer. To the funeral, he invited all their relatives from the village, and all Simuna's friends from her youth. "This is her day, let everybody see her off," he told his sons. "And after the funeral they can all dine and sleep here. Among so many houses, there will be room for everybody. We can spread mattresses for the old, and if some youngsters have to sleep on carpets, they won't find it too hard, peasant bones are strong."

Soon after Simuna, Ratko, too, died, suddenly from a heart attack.

His sons mourned him and gave him a beautiful funeral, but they knew that since Simuna's death, life had become unbearable for him in its everyday monotony, and that he awaited death as a relief from it. Besides, death is more easily accepted if it comes in due time, and to the old before the young.

6

Life went on as it always does: bitter or sweet, it flows on its relentless course. Time, which insidiously changes both people and things, time and love wore down the barrier that Janko's infidelity had placed between him and Jelka. After that trial for them both, they found new understanding and the unity of being which can only exist between husband and wife when they love one another.

All three Kojics prospered, and Ratko's family branched out. Rosa and Jelka were fertile and bore children at regular intervals of two years at the most. Pava gave birth less frequently, but as her children were healthy and strong despite her delicate health, Petko did not mind because he himself did not desire a large family.

Stevo was ambitious and took part in the social activities that had slowly begun to develop in Plevlje. He became a member of the Church and school councils, helped all cultural undertakings, gave donations of money and in turn was gradually admitted into the ranks of the most respected citizens. Janko remained an admirer of Austrian culture and often traveled to Sarajevo and Vienna to buy stocks for his shop and also for his brothers. He strove to imitate the way of life of the Sarajevo merchants and bought precious and unusual objects in Vienna which were looked after with care and shown to guests as rarities, almost as relics. In time, he also began to help the educational and literary movements in town, contributed large sums of money to Serbia for the Literary Guild and became its benefactor. He had good relations with the Turks too, although some of them resented him either because he mixed with the Shvabas or for his affinity with Serbia, but he was friendly with Pasha Bajrovic and with the mufti and paid no attention to others.

Stevo was concerned about this broadmindedness of Janko's, and his wish to be on good terms with everybody, which the Serbs began to take amiss, and once he came to warn him: "It is not good that you are seeing so much of the Pasha. They say he has signed some agreement with the Shvabas as some of our people did."

"I don't care a bit who has signed what, I'm not interested in politics. Bajrovic is good to the Serbs and lets us get away with many things."

"My God, you must be blind, you don't see that everything is coming to a head. It is rumored that the Shvabas will not stay and that Serbia and Montenegro are getting ready to liberate us. Yet in your bar a picture of Franz Josef still hangs. If we don't dare to put up a picture of the Serbian king, we don't have to keep the other, even if he is a tsar."

"Don't start lecturing me, I'm not an adolescent." Janko got angry. "You think I don't wish to be liberated? But that won't happen soon, nor does anyone ask us what we want. If they said that the Russians will come, I would believe. They are equal to the Turkish and Shvaba strength, but how could Serbia and Montenegro withstand either?"

"I advise you to break away from the Pasha. He is a marked man with the Serbs as well as the Turks. Get more involved with us, come to the meetings when you are invited. It isn't enough to contribute only money. Not everyone is invited, it is a big honor."

Janko continued to befriend whoever he chose, but because of Stevo, he became a member of many councils and began to climb the social ladder. The higher they climbed, the bigger the donations they gave, spending money left and right, but as they also earned well, it was not difficult for them to give it away. Only Petko was thrifty enough not to involve himself either with politics or social activities, nor did he care to be elected to any honorary councils. He resented giving money for anything except, secretly, women. He liked to drink, but in moderation. Some of his fortune he invested in two-story lodging houses, and he also bought more land adjoining the meadows and fields he received when the family separated, so that now all the land from Gypsy Lane to Muratbeg's field belonged to him. He understood farming and made profits from his land besides the income from the rents, his *kafana*, and the trade with the peasants.

While all three brothers maintained their affairs and prospered, Rosa withdrew completely from her sisters-in-law and, after Simuna and Ratko died, no Kojic visited Stevo's house, not even on feast days.

"I don't need them," Rosa used to say. "They only spite me, so what for? Nobody knows how the Kojics really are and what I suffer. Stevo is quick-tempered and rough, he can hit too. I don't mind that, every man beats his wife, but he lives like his godless family, goes to church only for the meetings with other councilors, doesn't say prayers, and also spoils the children, buys them all kinds of nonsense."

Nor did Rosa allow her children to play with the children of her in-laws. The closer Jelka and Pava became, the more she retreated. She nursed her children alone when illnesses spread, didn't let anyone into the house, to prevent ill-will and sorcery being brought in, took no help from strangers and gave none. Her sons and daughters were brought up to be modest and God-fearing; from an early age they all had to fast, receive communion, and go to church every Sunday.

Jelka became even fonder of Pava after Nikola's birth because Pava had noticed that she was suffering and came to see her more often, was tender toward her, but never asked what was upsetting her. After that, they became like sisters, raised their children together, jointly prepared for holidays, and helped each other in difficult times. When Pava gave birth to her second child, she could not get up for a long time as the confinement was difficult and her health sensitive, so for three weeks Jelka did not leave her side.

"Truly, Jelka, but for you I would have been in my grave by now," Pava would often recall later on. "What would have happened to me, alone, without any of my kin and unable to shake off the fever? Without you we would both have died, my child and I."

"Forget it, love, stop thanking me. You have helped me too, after my mother you are the nearest to me. Who do I have? Jula is far away, and our uncles still angry that I chose Janko against their will. They still can't take to the Kojics and seldom come to see us. Were it not for you, I would sometimes go mad with loneliness."

After Nikola, Jelka had borne another four daughters, Marija, Gordana, Sofija, and Nevenka, then two sons, Vaso and Chedo. Until then she did not resent bearing children so often, as she did not have many sons and was glad each time she was pregnant, hoping it would be a boy. But after she had Chedo, she wanted a rest for a while, and one day she asked Pava whether she knew some secret which helped not to conceive.

"My God, Jelka, don't you believe me?" Pava was astonished. "I would love to have more children, they are my only family here. Petko is not affectionate like Janko, nor am I that fond of him. I can't understand why I married him. Father ill, mother in mourning for my brothers, so they let me, young as I was, decide my destiny in a hurry." Her eyes filled with tears and she fell silent.

Jelka had been noticing the change in Pava for some time, but refrained from asking her anything as Pava herself did not wish to confide in her. "Well, if I could I'd stop having more children," she finally said to change the subject. "The Shvaba women must know something. They give birth when they want to, and when they don't wish to have more children, the doctors give them something, I'm sure, to prevent them from conceiving. They don't turn out children as I do, one after another as if they were piglets."

"It isn't that they know something," Pava laughed, "but they are not strong and healthy like you. If it weren't for those fine dresses, they would never tempt the evil eye."

Barely a month later, Pava became pregnant. At first she was very happy, but as time went on, she grew increasingly sad and listless, until finally she fell ill. When Jelka came to visit her she found her deathly pale, with swollen eyes and her head bandaged. A maid was looking after her. Jelka sent her to see to the children and closed the door behind her. "What has happened, my Pava, why are you like this?"

Pava burst into tears. "Oh, Jelka, I can't bear it any longer without getting it off my chest. You have your mother here and can confide in her, but I have no one and I'll tell you, I feel it may help." She lifted herself and leant against the pillow, trembling as if in a fever and wiping away her tears with the back of her hand. "It's a long time since Petko began to stray. I heard that he has now found some prostitute in the town, who keeps a tavern. Many men know her, Serbs and Turks. A woman told me that she was boasting about Petko and his presents. She said he forbade her to entertain others, became jealous being so fond of her, and spends on her regardless. I mentioned this to him last evening, and, sister, he sprang up and hit me across this ear, which hurt me for some time. I saw sparks, as if something burst deep inside my ear, and as if someone had driven an iron pin into my brain. My whole head began to buzz and roar, and stabbing pains pierced like arrows. I fell to the floor."

She sighed deeply and paused a little to collect herself. "You think he came to me? On the contrary, he told me to remember for as long as I live never to ask him what he does and how much he spends. Did I bring him a dowry, by any chance? If I'm not contented in this house where I have everything, I can go back to my mother. As he was saying this, everything began to swim before my eyes. I felt a wind blowing through my head, here at the back of it. My stomach contracted and I started to vomit. I crawled into the next room but even then that dog did not bother to follow. I turned the key in the lock, afraid he might hit me again, and did not dare utter a sound. Some fluid began to drip from my ear, one drop after another . . . I grabbed the tablecloth and wrapped it round my head. There I spent the night. I calmed down a little but the stabbing pains continued. At dawn I came out, washed the carpet where I had been sick, washed myself and changed, then wrapped my head in this shawl and came here to lie down. The maid has looked after me, but he has not come anywhere near. Oh, I tell you, if I were not pregnant I would put a noose around my neck and hang myself, but it would be a sin to do it to this child I am carrying. I have to endure because of my children, but I won't forgive him, not even on my deathbed."

Jelka could hardly keep back her tears. "Don't be upset, my Pava, that's how men are. Who knows what mine does? They soon grow used to their wives and seek a change. But a whore will remain a whore, and you are his wife. You gave him children. Let him roam, he'll get fed up and come back to be near you again."

"You don't know what torture this is, that's why you can talk like that. One cannot understand unless one has experienced it."

Jelka felt like telling her about Zlata to make her feel better, but she refrained from doing so, partly because of Janko, to save his face as he himself had suffered through it, and also because Savka had taught her from an early age not to confide her troubles to anyone. She started coming more often to see Pava, brought her sweets and presents to cheer her up, and nursed her during her confinement. Pava gave birth to a healthy boy, which brought great joy to Petko, and he became much more attentive to her.

Three years had gone by since the birth of Jelka's youngest son, when a dangerous illness spread through Plevlje from which the children fell like ears of wheat under a sharp scythe. Fear invaded every house, and people flocked to the monastery to pray, and began to give money to the poor and to beggars to appease God. Priests blessed the houses with holy water, and sprinkled it over the rooms and courtyards and the streets in front of the gates. Soothsayers scattered through the town to divine with charcoal and molten lead.

Amongst the first children to fall ill was the son of Jelka's relative, Rakila, from Mocevac. As soon as the news reached Jelka, she asked Pava to keep an eye on her house while she visited Rakila to see if she could be of help. Pava grew worried. "Don't go. They say it is a croup, a pest that stalks through houses like a demon and suffocates little children. Rosa has locked her children in and lets no one into the home. She has hung amulets around their necks and every day she scatters charcoal and holy water in front of her door."

"Leave those old wives' tales. I believe in God, not in divining. I must go, she always comes to me when one of my children is ill."

When she was ready, just in case, she tied around her neck an amulet sewn into a piece of cloth, which she hid inside her dress.

She also wore a cross on a gold chain to protect her from evil. Arriving at Rakila's, she found the house full of people. They told her that the illness was very serious and showed her into the room in which the child lay. It was getting dark. The stale air in the room was saturated with the smell of vinegar and raki. She quietly approached Rakila, who was sitting beside a tall cradle, and touched her shoulder. The other turned around and, seeing Jelka, began to cry.

"What am I to do, sister? The boy hasn't opened his eyes since yesterday. He can hardly breathe!"

"Have you got him to sweat?"

"They rubbed him with raki and vinegar, and put warm bricks under his little feet, but nothing helped."

Jelka approached the cradle. "Have you tried ammonia?"

"Yes, a woman blew it through a paper funnel into his throat, but he almost passed away, went blue . . . It took us a long time to bring him around." Saying this, she leaned over the cradle and screamed. "Oh, God, he's dying."

The child was choking, his eyes rolling in agony. Jelka took him in her arms and began to rock him in an effort to give him some relief. "Open the window, it's stuffy in here. He'll feel better in the fresh air."

Rakila opened the window. The child gasped once more, stretched, and the look in his eyes glazed. Terrified, Jelka also began to cry. Rakila's sister came running into the room, took the child, laid it back in the cradle, then, feeling his forehead and his tiny hands said, "Bring the candle." Whilst someone brought in a lit candle, Jelka was trying to subdue Rakila, who was screaming, tearing her hair and writhing like a trampled worm. The other women came in and began to lament softly. The dead child was bathed, dressed, and laid on a table.

Jelka stayed with Rakila all this time, numb with horror and fear for her children. When she realized that night had fallen, she got up and left without saying goodbye to anyone. Petrified, she ran all the way home. As she climbed the stairs, Vaso and Chedo, undressed and only in their scanty nightshirts, rushed into her arms and hung around her neck. Tired and shaken, she took them back to her room and sat on a chair to get her breath back. Chedo climbed on her lap, she picked up Vaso too and began to kiss them anxiously, shedding tears of gratitude because they were so healthy and lively.

Just then Pava came in. "Look at those rascals! And I thought they had fallen asleep long ago."

"Never mind, as long as they are so healthy. My poor Rakila, her child died. He was always so delicate and the illness was too much for him."

"What are you saying?" Pava was flabbergasted. "How did it happen so quickly?"

"He was already dying when I arrived. He was ill only a few days. My, Pava, how terrifying it is to see a child die." She burst into tears, got up and put her sons back into their beds, kissed them once more and went to change. Pava stayed a while longer, they made coffee and drank it, then she left, worried.

Jelka could not sleep all that night. She thought about the misfortune that had befallen Rakila, about Rosa and the way she was spraying the courtyard and the street in front of it with holy water, lye, and charcoal to chase away the illness should it reach her doors, and began to regret her visit to Rakila. The next day, she went early to church, said prayers, gave money to all the beggars in the churchyard, and felt a little more at ease.

During the following few days, she anxiously enquired whether any child in Mocevac had died and whether the illness had reached the Hill. It was said that three children had died in Varosh, two in Golubinja, and a countless number in the Turkish quarter. Pava had seen from her windows the Turks carrying small corpses wrapped in white shrouds to their graveyards.

Just as Jelka was beginning to hope that the illness would bypass the houses on the Hill, Chedo began to ail. He did not have a high fever and she found consolation in the thought that he had caught a cold. She bathed him, changed him into a nightshirt, and took him to bed. He slept restlessly, began to labor for breath and the light disturbed him, so she extinguished the lamp and kept a vigil over his bed all night. When dawn rose, she closed the shutters of the windows, and left the *kandilo* to illuminate the room. In the morning, Janko sent his man to Savka to ask her to come over, and he went to call the doctor.

Pava came running as soon as she heard that Chedo was not well.

She entered the room where Jelka was and quietly, so as not to wake the child, embraced her.

"I'm afraid, Pava, that it could be croup."

"It isn't, don't fret. Not one child from the Hill has contracted it: the air is healthy here and there's no damp."

"He has difficulty in breathing."

"Shall I call Petko to blow ammonia into his throat?"

"Janko won't allow it. He doesn't believe in such things and has gone to call the military doctor."

As she said that, the door opened and Janko appeared with the doctor. Before approaching the child, the doctor said something in German to Janko and he explained to Pava in a low voice that she must leave the room. When she had gone out, the doctor ordered the windows to be opened and the child to be completely undressed, then began to examine him. As he was sounding his chest and back, listening to his breathing, taking his temperature and looking into his throat, Jelka held her breath for fear that Chedo would catch cold, but did not dare utter a word. Finally, the doctor said she could dress the child, but not too warmly, then went to the washstand and, while washing his hands, began to explain something to Janko in German. When he finished, he picked up his bag and left the room accompanied by Janko, who appeared very worried. As soon as Janko returned, Jelka asked anxiously, "What did he say? Don't hide anything from me."

"He says it's diphtheria. We must immediately isolate him from Vaso and the other children. This illness is very contagious."

"Will he prescribe some medicine?"

"Yes, he'll send it from the pharmacy."

"Janko, I'm afraid of what may happen to Chedo."

"Don't be afraid. We have the Austrian doctor to cure him. They don't lose as many children as we do. Chedo will feel better as soon as we give him medicine, you'll see." He took her hand and said gently, "I know how difficult it is for you, but you must keep your wits about you if we are to save Chedo. I too realize the danger but if the doctor says he will recover, that means that he will." Having said that, he went to the washstand, washed his hands thoroughly with soap, and went out.

The medicine arrived in pills which Chedo could not swallow and they had to dissolve them in water and give them to him drop by drop. Jelka was under the impression that the child was getting better and could breathe more easily, but she did not leave his side nor did she allow anyone to take her place.

Savka supervised the house and, with Djana's help, looked after the younger children. Jelka did not allow her to enter the sick room for fear of spreading the illness to the other children, and spoke to her from the doorway. Only Janko came in from time to time to help her with the medicine and to bring her some food, but she could not touch anything except coffee. Around dawn, Janko slept for a few hours, and as soon as it was daylight he came in again to ask how the child was. "Did he get any sleep?"

"Yes, a little," Jelka lied, seeing how worried he was. "And you didn't shut an eye. Why don't you lie down on a *secija* and sleep for a while? I'll stay here until you wake."

"Don't worry about me, I don't feel sleepy at all. Better go and see how the other children are."

As he went out, Savka met him in the corridor and told him in a whisper that Vaso was not feeling well. "He is rubbing his eyes and complaining of a pain in his throat."

Janko stopped, petrified. "Put him in my room so that Jelka doesn't notice anything. I will bring the doctor immediately."

The doctor examined both boys and talked with Janko for a long time. He sent Janko's man for a new medicine in liquid form, and gave instructions to be called if there was any change, then left, also worried. That day Janko did not leave the house and spent all the time with Vaso, gave him the medicine and some linden tisane and tried to keep him amused. He only went to see Chedo and give him the medicine which the child was swallowing with increasing difficulty so that they had to force it down his throat. Jelka was terrified, but did not lose hope. "He'll recover, I'm sure," she tried to console herself. "His little cheeks are rosy and he is not thin. Rakila's child was weak, nothing but skin and bone."

On the third night Chedo began to choke and Janko ran to fetch the doctor. Seeing that the child could not breathe, the doctor wrapped a piece of cotton wool around a small wooden spill, dipped it in a yellow liquid and began to clean his throat with it. Chedo started to gasp: his face turned blue, and his eyes bulged with strain. Jelka started to cry loudly, and Janko tensed and gave a sign to the doctor to stop. The doctor himself realized that the child could endure it no longer, got up, and, without a word, started for the door. Janko followed to see him off and when he came back he embraced Jelka with a deep sigh. "It is up to God now. Try to calm down and watch over his breathing. I'm going to see if Savka needs help." He was now even more afraid for Vaso but did not want Jelka to notice it.

Left alone, Jelka was gripped by fear because she had no one to share her despair with, no one to consult if Chedo's condition deteriorated further still. Just then, the door opened quietly and Pava appeared. "I couldn't come earlier, they wouldn't let me in here."

"In God's name, Pava, what are you doing here? You know the doctor forbade it."

"No one saw me. I came to give you a hand and will leave at dawn."

"I'm frightened you may pass it on to your children."

"Nonsense, dear, doctor's talk."

Jelka gave a sigh of relief that someone would be with her. "All right, but please don't come any nearer and don't touch either me or the child."

Pava took a chair and sat down at some distance from her. She kept quiet.

"How does he look to you?" Jelka asked anxiously.

"He seems better. The medicine has quietened him."

"And I am afraid because he is as if in a trance. If he were hot, I'd say it was the fever."

"Don't be afraid, everything is in God's hands. He will save him."

The door opened again and Savka came in, pale and silent like a ghost.

"Please, Mother, don't come nearer, you mix with other children."

Savka was quite relieved to see that Jelka was not alone. "Can I at least hand you a pot of coffee from the doorway?" she asked in a whisper. "You've had nothing to eat, you will lose your strength."

"All right, then, bring the coffee," Jelka almost snapped back, but, when Savka turned around without a word, she felt sorry and added,

"And afterwards lie down to rest. You are bearing the biggest load."

When Savka returned with the coffee, Pava took the tray from her and thanked her softly, then served Jelka and returned to the chair. They drank the coffee and talked in whispers. The *kandilo* flickered, illuminating the room brightly at times. Jelka got up occasionally to look at the child. The conversation flagged gradually until it finally died out and they both sank into their own thoughts.

Suddenly Jelka rose with a start. "God, he's choking!" She grabbed the child and, pressing it to her chest, ran into the corridor. "He's dying in my arms! Don't let it happen! God, where are you? Save him, oh God!"

Janko rushed out of his room, Savka also came, and the children woke up.

"Bring the candle," Savka cried.

"Not the candle, I won't let him die!" Jelka pulled away, beside herself with grief, and knelt in front of the icons. "Merciful God, help me."

Janko took Chedo from her arms, carried him back into the room, and laid him on the bed. Savka approached, placed the lit candle above the child's head and crossed herself. "God bless his soul, he's gone."

Jelka remained on the floor in front of the icons, numb and dazed, until Janko lifted her and led her into another room.

Savka took Pava aside and whispered to her, "Stay with Jelka and don't let her come out. Vaso is also ill, but she mustn't find out. Janko took him into his room."

Savka bathed Chedo herself, dressed him and laid him on the table in the visitors' room. At sunrise the house filled with relatives and women from the neighborhood who sat around the little corpse and began to lament softly.

As soon as the doctor learned of Chedo's death, he came to suggest to Janko that they should transfer Vaso to the hospital where he could receive better care. Janko agreed immediately, for the child's sake and also to take the strain off Jelka. By the time of the funeral they had already moved Vaso by carriage to the hospital. This was kept secret from Jelka until the funeral was over. Only when she returned from the cemetery did they tell her that Vaso was ill. She stopped crying, went to the icons and began to pray. "Save this child, merciful God, and I won't even mention Chedo. Don't take Vaso from me, dear God." She shed no more tears. Most difficult for her to bear was the fact that no one except Janko was allowed visits to the hospital, but she did not complain.

At first Janko was quite collected, but when he heard that the illness was advancing, he fell into despair. He stayed longer and longer at the hospital because he could not hide his agony from Jelka.

Shortly afterwards, the doctors assembled for consultation. After a long discussion, they called Janko in and suggested that the chief surgeon should open Vaso's throat above the Adam's apple and insert a rubber tube through which the child could breathe. Only in this way could his life be saved. Later, when he recovered, he could be taken to Sarajevo where the tube would be replaced with a metal device.

"Will he breathe through this device all his life?" Janko asked.

"Perhaps, when he is older, it will be possible to rectify this by surgery. By then, surgery will be more advanced. If not, he'll have to live with this device, as many people do in Austria," the chief surgeon explained.

Janko spoke to the doctor who lived in his house and asked whether they could guarantee that the child's life would be saved if this were done. In reply, the surgeon said something in Latin and the doctor interpreted it to Janko, "Mister Primarius says that he is not God and cannot guarantee it, but he believes that the operation would help."

Janko got up and, holding his head in his hands, began to pace the floor. Having crossed the room two or three times, he made a decision and stopped in front of the doctors. "If you cannot be sure that he'll survive, don't do anything, don't make him suffer any more. Let me take the child home," he said in despair.

"I advise you to agree to the operation. If life is at stake, one should try everything. Perhaps we'll save him."

"I cannot take it upon myself to make my son a cripple for life, even if you were sure he'll survive. Therefore, I beg you, let me take him home."

They did not try to persuade him any more but offered him the hospital coach, and he left together with the child's doctor.

Vaso died the next morning.

Jelka collapsed with grief. Afraid that her heart would give out, the doctors fought to keep her alive by injections. As soon as she left the sickbed, she started going to the cemetery every day. She paid no attention to her children, her home, or other members of the family, as if everything around her had grown desolate. Janko too was so shaken by the loss of his children that he changed visibly, lost weight and turned ashen, as if he had aged in these few days.

People could not understand why they so abandoned themselves to sorrow. It was not a rare occurrence for several members of the family to die during an epidemic. Besides, it was considered a sin to grieve for younger children for fear of drawing misfortune to the older ones. Particularly inconceivable was that Janko, a man, should suffer so much.

On top of his sorrow, Janko was oppressed by his conscience because he had not allowed surgery to be performed and was keeping this from Jelka, so one evening he confessed to her.

She was appalled. "Was the operation possible?"

"It was." Janko could hardly utter the words.

Jelka burst into tears. "Why didn't you allow it, for God's sake? Perhaps it would have saved him."

He tried to explain that the doctors were not certain that Vaso could survive the operation, and even the chief surgeon could not give him a guarantee, which was the reason why he had not agreed to have the child's torment prolonged. "And even if he survived, he would have had to breathe through a device in his throat, unlike any normal person, and would have cursed me for not letting him die."

Jelka was sobbing violently. "If only he had lived, for his mother's sake, no matter how different from others. Why didn't you ask me, you murderer? Why did you let him die? It is as if you yourself had condemned him to death."

This especially hurt him because he had hoped that she would understand his decision and help him free his harrowed conscience. "How can you be so heartless? I never reproached you for passing on the illness from Rakila's child."

"Who said that?" She turned on him distraught.

179

Janko became speechless, realizing that it was still too soon for such thoughts, but it was too late now. Jelka beat her breast with clenched fists, looking around with glassy, horrified eyes. "What am I to do, cursed soul? How am I to go on living?"

He approached her, seized her hands and tried to pacify her. "Don't, my Jelka, it's too late, nothing can be amended. If we are guilty, God will punish us. Don't let anyone know what is torturing us. Don't let people turn our misfortune into gossip. Let us hope our other children will stay healthy all their lives, our consolation is in them."

She struggled to get away, sobbing. "Don't talk to me any more and don't pity me. God himself has cursed me. There is no consolation for me, nor can I ever stop grieving for those angels."

Savka came in and began to comfort her, and Janko left the house as if to escape.

After that evening, Jelka seemed completely lost. She lingered at the cemetery for hours, neglected herself, locked her room and did not speak to anyone. Janko, on the other hand, spent more time in the Charshija. He would come to the Hill only to see to the bar, stop briefly at the house, and, seeing Jelka lifeless as she was, go out again. He started meeting Turks in the taverns and returning home late at night drunk.

Savka suffered most. She didn't know how to help Jelka, worried about the children and, when Janko started coming home at dawn, began to fear for him as well. She decided not to return to her home until the grief subsided, and hoped that the time for it would soon come. Women came to visit Jelka, conveyed their condolences and tried to convince her that her children were in paradise and that her sorrow was causing them pain, but she listened to them impassive and unspeaking, until they would eventually get up and leave. One day, Janko's sister Stojana came and told Jelka that Rosa was saying, "She used to go to the monastery only once in a blue moon, but now she can climb to the cemetery there every day. God is great, he bestows what we deserve."

"Leave it, dear, don't bring up Rosa," Savka interrupted in a low voice.

Jelka watched them both indifferently. "Let her talk. Nothing can touch me any more."

When Stojana left, Savka began tentatively, "My child, you see how your enemies are gloating. You mustn't go on like this, because of them, if not for Janko's sake. You have practically driven him out of the house, he no longer wishes to come home. It is an old saying that 'the house doesn't rest on the earth, but on the woman.'"

Jelka sat, rocking from side to side, her cheek leaning on her hand, and listened absentmindedly. Savka went on in a gentler tone, "Turn to your children, my darling, what will happen to them if you and Janko are ruined? Your two eldest daughters cannot dry the tears from their faces. They cry for you as much as for their brothers. Nikola is on the street all day long, fighting with the Turkish children. He'll become a ruffian. The younger girls are neglecting their school work; they don't read and they do no handiwork. I cannot do anything with them."

Eventually Jelka raised her head and gave her mother a questioning look. "And what do you want from me now?"

"I want you to get a grip on your sorrow and stop going to the graveyard. Even if you killed yourself there it wouldn't help you, nor would it raise them from their graves. Don't let these children go to waste and become strangers. Turn to Janko too, help him to pull himself together. It is not good what he does. He spends the night drinking and will destroy himself if he continues so."

"Why don't you tell him?"

"I am his mother-in-law, not his mother. I cannot scold him or advise him," she said, then got up and went to do some work.

Next day, Jelka did not go to the cemetery, mainly because of Rosa. When Pava came to visit her, she told her what Rosa was saying.

"She's vindictive, says that I deserve my misfortune. And what have I done to anyone? She has always been spiteful, toward me and toward others, yet the Lord has not punished her. Her children are alive, is that God's justice?" Afraid of having said that, she quickly crossed herself. "God forgive me."

Pava also crossed herself. "Don't talk like that, it's a sin. You have such lovely children, one cannot tell which is more beautiful or healthier. Why listen to what Rosa says?"

"All girls, except Nikola. I believe I'd have suffered less if I had lost two girls."

"Don't sin, poor dear, they are older. The younger the child, the less the sorrow. God will give you more sons. He will bring you comfort."

Jelka began to cry. "I shall never find any comfort. Janko says I passed on the infection from Rakila's child. My conscience will pursue me for as long as I live."

"That's what the doctor told him, those damned Shvabas. Instead of offering you relief, he poisoned your mind to make it more difficult for you. If it were as he said, all children from Mocevac would be ill. So many women were at Rakila's and not one of their children got sick."

"I held him in my arms and that same evening I was embracing my children without changing my clothes first."

"The others also held him, bathed and laid him out."

"Perhaps their children were not as small. Oh God, what have I done? I killed them, my poor darlings."

Pava put her arms around Jelka and waited until her sobs subsided, then began to comfort her, whispering, "Stop, I beg you, you are torturing yourself and that poor mother of yours. Can't you see how sallow she's become, like a wax candle? Her load's the heaviest. You mustn't go on like this for the sake of Janko too. He is sensitive. He has changed so much one cannot recognize him." She stayed with Jelka for a while, then said goodbye, and Jelka remained alone, deep in thought.

She understood that it was impossible to go on like this. Her sorrow was not relieved by her tears, prayers did not flow from her heart, and it seemed to her that they were lost without response, as they did not bring her any comfort. And she could not take her own life. "The sky is beyond reach and the earth hard," she thought. "There is nowhere one can escape from pain." Finally she got up, combed and plaited her hair, and slowly descended to help her mother with the work.

Savka felt easier when she saw her. She knew that from now on things would get better; her work and looking after her children would help. "Fresh grief is savage, as the saying goes, but even the deepest grief wanes with time. It is sewn into the pattern of life like a thread, and gets ever smaller," she thought.

Jelka gradually resumed the running of the house and the supervision of her children, but she still needed her mother's support in the days when she could not master her sorrow, so Savka decided to stay for as long as she could help. Jelka also tried to be more attentive to Janko, but he continued to go the taverns at night and often returned home drunk. He neglected his business, and his men began to take liberties and did hardly any work. No one knew what the income and what the expenses were, and theft was widespread. When Jelka attempted to remind him tactfully that the reputation of their home would suffer if he continued to ignore his responsibilities and to drink with the Turks, he replied that he could find no peace at night "and the night is the most difficult to endure when one is unhappy." He could not drink with anyone except the Turks because the Serbs did not dare go out at night. "They lock themselves in their houses as soon as it's *aksham*, or get together with neighbors, and where do I fit into such gatherings? As it is, by drinking with the Turks I have found peace and relief from my troubles."

Several more weeks went by. Janko began to pay a little more attention to his business and managed to resume control over his men, but he continued to go out at night and drink, so people talked about it openly. One evening, when he was about to leave, Jelka said worriedly, "It is not good what you are doing, Janko, you will be ruined, keeping bad company."

"My company is not bad. I mix only with reputable people. I spend most time in the men's quarters of Pasha Bajrovic's home, and the best people assemble there. One has only to get to know them."

"This Pasha is disliked by the Serbs and by the Turks. All sorts of things are said about him."

"All lies which someone is spreading around," Janko cut in sharply, but immediately regretted it. He knew well what effort she had to make to overcome her sorrow, and if he could not help her he did not want to add to her worries. He took her hand and sat beside her on the *secija*. "He is an honorable man, from a good family. Many a time he has sent his respects to you and said that you should visit his wife in her quarters. She too has extended an invitation through him and sent her regards."

"I can't go to the Pashinica, especially not while I am in mourning."

"You should go because of your sorrow, to relieve it. I would have gone mad if I didn't have company. Women from good families, Turkish and Serbian, attend her gatherings. Come out with me and we could return home together." He glanced at the clock and rose. "I mustn't tarry, I have arranged to meet with some people this evening." From the door he called to her, "When you decide, let me know and we could leave here together."

Once alone, Jelka reflected on what he had suggested and went to her mother for advice.

"Go on, my dear, go with your man. It is no disgrace. Many of our women are on friendly terms with the Turkish women. Times have changed and our people now mix with theirs. Janko would be coming back with you, and this way you can get him accustomed to returning home earlier. Settle the children and don't worry about anything. You may find some solace there."

Jelka made up her mind to go to the Pashinica, and when they were next invited, she went with Janko. He accompanied her to the women's wing of the Pasha's home, waited until the ringing of the large bell resounded, then left her and went to the other side of the house. Jelka waited a little. She felt embarrassed to enter alone, not knowing anyone. Soon the door opened noiselessly and she saw a woman dressed in clean modest clothes, who bowed to her deeply, holding her hands crossed under her bosom. "That must be their maid," Jelka thought.

"*Bujrum*," the woman greeted her and led the way through the first courtyard, illuminated by large lanterns. That whole area was paved with even white stone slabs and surrounded by high walls. They passed through a narrow gate and entered a spacious garden full of flowers and trees. In the middle of it a fountain sprayed out sparkling drops into a circular stone basin. From its rounded border the water flowed through several openings, murmuring, while the light wind rustled in the treetops, spreading the scent of flowers and the freshness of the evening air. Lanterns hidden amidst the branches of the trees dispersed soft light through the shifting leaves. Peacocks strutted around the fountain, and the birds sang in cages.

When they entered the house, the maid took from the shelf a pair of slippers and helped Jelka to take off her shoes, which she placed next to the others lined up alongside the wall. They climbed the stairs covered by a thick carpet and the maid opened the door of a large room full of women. Through the lacy arabesque of the brass lamps spread a restless reflection of the flames that fell onto the Smyna carpets as pools of light divided by swaying narrow shadows. Seated on the velvet-covered divans were women in multicolored dresses, like a chain of flowers. Ducats, pearls, and precious stones shone around their necks and on their arms. Only a few women wore no jewelry and were dressed in white, their heads covered by scarves. Among the guests were some Serbian women dressed in Austrian fashion and two schoolteachers in their severe outfits.

From the door, Jelka bowed to all and wished them good evening to which each rose a little and responded, "Good fortune to you, Jankovica." They moved aside to make room for her. As she sat down, somewhat surprised that the Turkish women knew who she was, the Pashinica appeared at the door. She had chestnut hair and large dark eyes in an oval face and was of medium height, dressed in light blue clothes embroidered with gold. She bowed and, remaining by the door, began to greet each guest, enquiring for her and for her family's health. When it was Jelka's turn, she only said, "Welcome to my home, Jankovica," but her look lingered on Jelka's face as if examining it gently.

Jelka rose a little and thanked her for the invitation. She followed with interest while the Pashinica greeted other guests, because she knew some of the begums by name but had never seen them. The conversation began. One of the women in white who sat closest to Jelka said to her in a low voice, "We have heard about the death of your children. All of us in white attire are in mourning. Our children also died at the time you lost yours. It was Allah's will. He sends us joy and sorrow, everything is in His power and that is how it must be."

The others also joined in the conversation. Jelka was surprised at the calm with which they had accepted the loss of their children and the confidence with which they were trying to convey to her that they were now in paradise. "They are happier there than with us on earth."

The conversation went on to other children, school, the approaching holidays, Turkish and Serbian dresses and various handiwork. Presently the Pashinica gave a signal by clapping her hands and maids appeared at once with refreshments. They carried on large silver platters filled with oriental pastries—baklavas, *urmashicas, tatlias,* and *kadaifs.* Others followed with glasses of lemonade and sherbet. Before serving, they approached with silver ewers and bowls so that each guest could wash the tips of her fingers. Moving soundlessly, they came up and withdrew, never turning their backs to the guests. After passing the refreshments around a few times, they began to prepare coffee, which was made in the same room on a brazier and poured into small cups. The Pashinica got up then and offered the guests thin cigarettes from a golden box.

Time passed unnoticed. Around midnight, one of the maids came in and whispered something to the Pashinica, who turned to Jelka saying that Janko was waiting for her. Jelka said goodbye to the women nearest to her and bowed from the door to the others, as she had when she came in. The Pashinica accompanied her to the stairs, where the same woman who had received her at the gates was waiting to see her off.

From that evening on, Jelka made friends with the Pashinica, and as well as meeting at the gatherings with other women, they often saw one another on their own so that they could talk more freely.

When the Pashinica called on Jelka for the first time, all wrapped in a *zar*, driving in the Pasha's carriage, people ran into the street from the Barracks to see at which house she would stop. Even the Shvaba women looked out of the windows to see her as she stepped down from the carriage, and immediately sent one of the maids to ask Jelka whether they could join them. Jelka asked whether the Pashinica would mind if they were invited, and laughed. "Do let them come. I, too, would like to see them."

The Austrian women admired her attire without trying to hide their curiosity about every detail of it. They examined the golden tassels of her shawl, the lace blouse, and the silk *dimije* trousers gathered round the ankles into broad, gold-embroidered bands, and were especially enchanted by her jewelry. The Pashinica was beautiful and everything she wore looked even more precious on her. Long diamond earrings threw their reflection on to her silken neck, pearls covered her entire chest, and her white hands with henna-painted nails were adorned with rings and bracelets. They asked her to take off an antique bracelet of fine chain held by an elongated clasp set with precious stones and diamonds. She took it off to let them try it on, but none of them had wrists slim enough to fasten it.

She too was interested in their fashions, but observed them with her calm mysterious smile without betraying her curiosity. Only after they had left did she discuss their dresses with Jelka, pointing out those she liked most and which shoes and hair styles she preferred, astonishing her with the perception of her apparently indifferent eyes.

Plevlje's secret contacts with Serbia and Montenegro were becoming closer all the time and their influence on the people was noticeable. Serbia supported all cultural movements morally and financially, and with the help of the citizens of Plevlje succeeded in expanding the primary school and introducing two higher grades into its program. Prominent Turks such as Pasha Bajrovic and his brother Omerbeg obtained permission for it and secretly donated considerable sums of money to the school council. The teachers came mainly from Serbia, but were being gradually joined by students from Plevlje who had completed higher education in Prizren and Skoplje. While the Turkish schools were attended only by boys, the Serbian schools began to accept girls too.

Janko enrolled his children into the school and was hoping that the higher education would be possible by the time his older children finished the six years of extended primary school. As permission for the high school was being postponed from one year to another, he decided to send Nikola at least to Sarajevo for further education, as he did not wish his daughters to be so far away from home. The very thought of parting from her son was painful to Jelka, but she consented, knowing how much Janko wanted his children to have the opportunity that he himself missed. Nikola was dearer to her than all the other children; he had reconciled her Janko, was better looking and cleverer, full of life yet gentle by nature, and of distinguished bearing, and she neither tried to hide that she loved him most nor did her daughters resent it. Only Janko reproached her for favoring him above the other children, because he was afraid that she would spoil him.

Janko continued to travel to Vienna and to read German books, but he spent less time in his bar and left its management almost entirely in the hands of Jelka's relative. He saw more of the Serbian society but maintained his relationship with Pasha Bajrovic, to which many objected, either out of envy or because they did not know that the Pasha was secretly protecting the Serbian population.

Stevo still could not accept Janko's friendship with the Pasha and the other Turks, but could not openly reproach him, knowing that Janko would take offense. When he learned about the incident with Father Lisica, he immediately seized the opportunity to report it to Janko, hoping in this way to stop him from associating with Turks. He found him in the shop in the Charshija, and when Janko sent his man to fetch coffee for them, Stevo asked, "Did you hear what Father Lisica said?"

Janko shook his head.

"I have only just heard, it is talked about in secret."

They waited until the man returned with the coffee, then they withdrew to the other room behind the shop and closed the door. Once seated, Stevo lit a cigar and began in a low voice, "On Franz Josef's birthday the Shvabas prepared a big celebration and festivities. They invited Pasha Suleiman from the Turkish side and from the Serbian old Father Lisica. He did not want to go and tried to excuse himself, but everybody advised him not to as it would do the Serbs no good if he refused the invitation. And so he went—what else could he do, there was no choice. When they began the toasts, the Pasha got to his feet and raised his glass in a toast to Franz Josef, embroidering his address with choice and beautiful words. Then the Shvaba officer rose and, raising his glass, began to praise not only Frank Josef but also the Sultan, weaving a crown around his name. As the priest listened to it, everything boiled inside him and, when it was his turn, he raised his glass and began his address: 'I am the shepherd of the enslaved people and cannot toast either the emperor or the Sultan.' The Pasha, afraid that the priest might pay with his life for what he intended to say, tugged at his sleeve: 'Be quiet, Father!' Father Lisica pushed him aside and continued, 'I shall therefore toast the Russian Tsar, the head of Slavs wherever we are.' Having said that, he immediately left. God knows what would have happened to him had someone not passed word to the Russian consul in Prizren, who sent a message to the Turks and Austrians that not a hair of Father Lisica's head should be hurt."

Janko knew what Stevo was driving at, although he too was impressed by the priest's gesture, and he said, "The Sultan is not the same as our local Turks, they are of our blood. You see, the Pasha tried to stop Father Lisica and was afraid for him. Blood is thicker than water, we were nursed at the same breast."

"Then why did scaffolds once stood in Varosh, where Serbs had been hanged? Until the Shvabas' arrival they used to impale us too."

"That was long ago. Even our father did not recall it, nor did his father. There are criminals everywhere, every crop has its pests."

Stevo did not insist any further. They drank the coffee and parted as friends, but after that Janko avoided the Turkish tavern, though he continued to be friendly with the Pasha.

Jelka also stopped going to the Pashinica's gatherings, or seeing other Turkish women, so as not to anger Stevo. She would send a message to the Pashinica that she could call on a given day in the afternoon if the other was not going out, to which her friend would send a reply that she was expecting her and would be alone. Thus the two of them became even closer and confided in one another.

Once, as they sat in the garden beside the fountain, Jelka asked her, "Tell me honestly, are you never upset that the Pasha spends evenings without you?"

"Not really. I have my gatherings and he has his. That's much better than if he brought in a second wife. In your law, the man can only have one wife, but in ours he can have as many as he wishes. There are begs whose fortune is not worth the Pasha's little finger, yet they have up to four wives. They would have even more if they could feed and clothe them."

"And what do the men do when they get together?"

"All sorts of things," the Pashinica smiled mischievously. "Sometimes they get women to sing and play tambourines for them whilst they drink. The women dance and sway in front of them, driving the men crazy, so they drink and have fun."

Jelka remembered her despair when she caught Janko with Zlata, and could not comprehend how the Turkish women endured the way of life to which their laws had condemned them. She looked around with great sadness and sighed. At the far end of the garden, among the violet shadows, peacocks strutted; from the low branches of the trees hung cages with rare birds of fiery plumage; water murmured, spreading coolness; the scent of flowers was intoxicating . . . and she could not understand why she was sadder still from such beauty and opulence, why her heart was so heavy.

Just as Savka was intending to return to her house because Jelka had become stronger and reconciled with her sorrow, the news came from Sarajevo that Joka had died. Joka had been middle-aged when Savka married into the Zarkovic home, had lived to a good old age, and had not suffered a painful illness, so Savka was not too upset by her death. She prayed for Joka's soul and quietly shed tears, remembering how Joka had received her, young and inexperienced as she was, introduced her to the customs of the Zarkovic home and taught her how to run the household. Savka's aunts, who had brought her up in the place of her dead parents, had protected her from all hard work. They had only taught her to embroider and crochet fine lace, to welcome and offer hospitality to guests, to cook and make pastry, as well as the noble bearing and behavior befitting the women of the Borisavljevic family. When she married into the Zarkovic family, she had had to learn to run the entire household, instruct the menservants and share the light housework with Joka. She recalled how they nursed the children together, and how Joka used to sing by their cradles lullabies she had learned from the Turkish women with whom she had spent her childhood, having been taken away from her village after the death of her father, a serf. They wanted to turn her into a Muslim when she was thirteen years old, but she ran away one night to the Serbian quarter. There she hid from one house to another, not daring to spend a whole day under the same roof until she was taken by Tane's parents as a servant. Joka had told Savka all about it when, having finished the work, they used to sit under the ash tree and drink coffee.

"Truly, Savka, I was never more contented than I am now. My mother died when I was little and I had to look after the house, believe it or not, since I was six years old. I fed two hens and their chicks, guarded them all day long from being snatched by hawks, lit the fire by myself and put potatoes to bake in the hot ashes so that my father would have something to eat when he returned from the fields. The poor man had to work in the house like a woman. He used to come home exhausted but, unless he made the bread, we had nothing to eat. He washed me, deloused my hair with a comb, did the laundry, until one day he fell ill and died. The Turks came to take me away. I screamed until the whole village gathered around us, but they were all serfs and did not dare to keep me by force. They collected as much money as they could to buy me off, but the beg said my father owed him more. I cried desperately and wanted to run away, but I was afraid to jump off the horse. I remember that, when we arrived, I passed out into a deep sleep. The beg's *hanuma* woke me, beautiful as a picture. 'Come to the *hamam* so I can bathe you and wash your hair,' she told me gently and I stopped being afraid. She fed me fresh bread and milk, and I had never eaten so well.

"They dressed me in *dimije* trousers and a blouse, plaited my hair and adorned it with mother-of-pearl and baubles to protect me from the evil eye. I was ugly, though, they didn't have to fear any evil eye. The *hanuma* cared for me well, chided me gently if I did something wrong and gradually taught me to do the housework. Everything was fine until I grew up. Then the beg began to follow me and always asked me the same question: would I take up the Muslim faith so he could marry me off to a fine beg? I told him that I wouldn't change my faith even if they cut me to pieces, because my parents would turn in their graves if I did. But he said that I was a stupid fool, that they would sing if they could hear that their daughter could become a beg's wife.

"One day I had had enough, so I went to the begum and told her everything. Her face clouded and she said that he was a pig, he wanted the taste of a Serbian chick, to bring her a second wife, but not to worry, she would help me escape that same night. We arranged for the women in the neighborhood to smuggle me from one garden to another until I reached the Serbian quarter. That evening, as I was praying to God, scared, I heard the *hanuma* singing to the beg. She always sang to him in the evenings, stroking his hair until he fell asleep, but that night she also put some herbs that bring sleep into his glass of sherbet. She sang like a nightingale, a song about Jelka, the Serbian girl:

Sweet Jelka, will you change your faith
And become my faithful wife?
Great beg, I will not change my faith
Nor become your faithful wife.
If you want a Serbian maid
You can take the orthodox faith
And the Serbs will find you a bride.

"I was dying of fright because she had chosen that song, and she came in laughing. She told me that he was sleeping like a log but we had better hurry so as not to be seen by her in-laws. That's how I came to Golubinja—and you know the rest. The old mistress was difficult, she was ill and had grown harsh, everything made her angry. When it was decided that I should look after the children and another woman was to nurse her, I breathed more easily. She had suffered a lot, poor soul. Toward the end she did not even ask to see the children. Until one day she died, God save her soul. Afterwards, all the responsibility fell on me until the children grew up, the family separated and I was included in Tane's share. I did not have to do much work for him, but I was afraid of the new mistress, once he got married. When I heard that you came from a rich home, I was quite petrified. They say the worst vipers hatch out of Serbian wealth."

After Joka's death, Savka found it hard to bear the very thought of her empty home full of memories, and she also still worried about Jelka. When Jelka saw that her mother was getting ready to leave, she began to beg her to stay longer or, better still, to move in with them permanently. Janko had suggested it long before, when Jula had married and moved to Sarajevo, but Savka did not wish to be a burden on anyone. Now, however, realizing how much Jelka would miss her and how fond of her the children had become, she made up her mind: she leased out her house, sent all her jewelry to Jula in Sarajevo, and put her land in Zlatibor in Janko's name, so that no one could say that she was eating her son-in-law's bread.

7

Time passed, and the seasons and the years pursued one another. Situated in a valley surrounded by hills and mountains, Plevlje had late summers that lasted three months at the most, of which only one month was really hot. In those times, the change from the heat of day to the cool of evening was sudden: it fell like an icy bluish veil as soon as the sun had set and its long rays withdrew behind the mountains. The autumns were mellower than in many other mountainous regions: light and sunny, they lasted almost until mid-October. As early as November a severe cold would arrive and the snow would cover everything the eye could see. The snow was long-lasting, crisp, and deep, and one walked a long footpath which cut through gardens, lanes, and streets, made by the feet of passersby or horse's hoofs. Nobody cleared it, it was left to dissolve like many other things—God had sent it, God would take it away.

At the beginning of March, sometimes earlier, as soon as the mellower breeze descended from the mountains, the snow began to melt. Mixed with mud, it turned into a yellowish slush that would spread over the entire town, making it hard to get about. In those times even the icicles from the roofs of houses would turn yellow and break off. In the sudden sun, the grass would begin to pierce the thin layers of melting snow and when primroses, snowdrops, and harebells appeared on the banks of the Biserka it meant that spring had arrived. The sun would climb higher, it would rise somewhere above Golubinja and set behind Ljubisnja. Gradually, the sunrise would move northward, somewhere above Galvica, or still further north, and set behind Great Plijesh. Its high extended arch did not last long, only during the hottest summer months, then slowly but insidiously it would return toward the southwest.

With time the way of life in Plevlje was also changing. Furniture was introduced into the houses that had previously been arranged in the Turkish manner, social events were organized in the schools, people danced not only in front of the monastery but also in Citluk or Varosh, and they avoided walking in the park around the Barracks which had been laid out by the Austrians. Serbian women stopped wearing *dimije* trousers, and the younger men as well as the schoolteachers wore suits instead of *shalvare* and *fermen*. Turkish women still seldom went out, and when they did visit each other, or attended gatherings, they walked about in *zars*, their faces covered by veils. In the summer they assembled for picnics beside Cotina on the slopes of the Skakavac and the banks of the Breznica.

The Austrians lived in complete isolation as before. They had their schools, doctors and hospital, their church built of wood, and their graveyard. They did not build private homes only because they were not sure whether they would stay for good. The families of their officers and other military personnel stayed in the newer lodging houses which the Plevlje people had built all around the Barracks and along the Turkish cemetery as far as the Turkish part of the town. But while their women and children did not mix with the town population, the men tried to cultivate both Serbs and Turks, practicing a policy of divide and rule: they stressed to the Serbs that they were the defenders of Christianity, and warned the Turks that Serbia and Montenegro were spreading political propaganda through cultural ties. From 1782 onward, Austria had kept a full garrison in Plevlje, and the military rule was in their hands, although the civilian rule had remained with the Turks. The governor was a pasha, a *cadi* sat in the lawcourt, and the town was policed by *zaptiehs*. In the town hall both the Turks and Serbs were employed, as they were also in the revenue offices where taxes were decreed and paid. In all that time, the Turks did not keep any military units there.

The entire western side of Plevlje was built for the Austrian garrison and many parts there had been named after their arrival. The whole district was called the Barracks, after the first barracks in which the army was installed. The big forested park with its artificial lake was called the Lake, the part where the army bread was baked was Pekara—the Bakery—the ring where the riding horses were exercised was the Trainer. The valley between Bembeg's Hill and Bogishevac was Shvabas' Cemetery and the depression near Glavica was the Dungheap, because all the rubbish and filth from the Shvabas' toilets was deposited there.

The Austrians had laid out the Barracks in such a way that it became the most beautiful part of the town, and anyone arriving in Plevlje from the direction of Metaljka had the impression of entering a modern European town. They had channeled water from several springs and put up bronze fountains from which the water flowed day and night and rippled through the entire park. Rivulets ran along paved concrete channels into the lake and from there the water was distributed through orchards and vegetable gardens which extended all the way to Pekara. In the middle of the lake was an islet with a large pavilion on it where the military brass band played every Sunday. The pavilion was connected to the shore by a wooden bridge built in an arch so that boats could pass underneath. The entire complex was criss-crossed by straight, even paths covered with pebbles, along which benches were placed at regular intervals.

The more the influence of Serbia and Montenegro was felt, the stronger grew the faith in liberation among the Serbian population. On Christmas Day, at dawn, when people from Plevlje climbed the steep path towards the monastery of the Holy Trinity, a song would swell gradually:

The cocks are calling over the hills
God our Savior
Their calls are waking all the slaves,
God our Savior.
Rise high, Serbian slaves,
God our Savior.

Under Stevo's influence, Janko continued his social endeavors with
new enthusiasm and he devoted most time and donated most money
to the Church and the school council. The council succeeded in ob-
taining permission to open four high school classes, which were first
held on the premises of the extended elementary school because the
building permit for it had not yet been issued. Serbia secretly supplied and paid the tutors, but all other costs were borne by the citizens of Plevlje, who also supported the poor pupils from surrounding villages, and bought school books which they often had to smuggle over the frontier hidden among their merchandise. After the fire
that burned down the elementary school buildings and was rumored
to have been caused by Austrian spies, the tuition continued in private houses, until finally the building permit for the high school was
obtained. Omerbeg, the brother of Pasha Bajrovic, helped most in
the matter, not only in the negotiations with the Turkish authorities,
but also with a large cash donation.

When the work on the foundation began, on the day it was blessed,
all the citizens were invited to attend the ceremony and contribute as
much as they could afford. The whole town flocked in, old and young,
rich and poor. There was not a soul that did not give something:
even the destitute old women who earned their bread by spinning
wool had brought all their savings tied in bundles to drop into the
vessel with holy water where donations were being placed. In it were
deposited napoleons, Turkish ducats, *ahmedgias*, *medgedias*, *krajcars*,
earrings, brooches, rings, anything that could be turned into money.

The high school gave greater dignity to all Plevlje, and had especially strong influence on the town's youth, whose education incul-
cated a national pride and desire for freedom. It was forbidden to
teach national history officially—that was one of the conditions under which permission for the high school had been obtained—but

the pupils learned it secretly under the instruction of the teachers, and prepared for liberation. No one knew how and when this would come, but everything indicated that the time was approaching. When the first celebration of St. Sava's Day was held in the hall of the new school, the honorary guests included representatives of the Turkish population, all of them with high-ranking titles. The choir began to sing Saint Sava's anthem without omitting the forbidden verses:

All Serbian lands to be soon united
And the sun of justice and freedom
To shine for us one day.

These verses were spontaneously taken up by the public, who sang the whole anthem on their feet, then waited in a tense silence to see whether the Turks would protest and leave the hall. Standing in the first row were Pasha Selmenovic, the Honorary Pasha Bajrovic, Cadi Celebic, Omerbeg, and several prominent businessmen, all from Plevlje—not one outsider nor any Austrian officers. They listened solemnly and stayed on to attend the rest of the evening's program, then got up and left. None of them ever voiced any complaint.

From his trips to Sarajevo and Vienna, Janko brought dresses, hats, and sunshades for his daughters, especially for Djana, who had developed early into a beautiful young girl and was dressed in the latest Viennese fashion. For Nikola he bought books, a globe, a microscope, a compass, everything he needed for school, everything of the best quality and packed in beautiful boxes. Finding in the education of his children the compensation for his own unfulfilled thirst for knowledge, he took most pride in the progress of Nikola and Marija, who were amongst the best pupils of the high school, and he hoped that his son would go to university. Djana did not continue with high school because she was already fifteen years old when it opened.

Jelka had begun to disguise her sorrow since Djana had reached marriageable age, because she did not wish to cloud her youth with sadness, as Djana was very sensitive and the loss of her brothers had hit her hard. Soon after the opening of the high school Djana had met a priest's son, Rade Oshtric, who belonged to a good and wealthy family from Ilino Hill. He had graduated from the theological seminary and had also been through agricultural college, in order to undertake the running of the vast family estate. All his ancestors were priests, and as their large parish passed from father to son, it had increased the income of each new generation. Thus, the Oshtrics extended their estate over the entire Hill where the church of Saint Elijah was situated. It stretched from Mrzovic to Grevno, and from the valley of the Adza spring along the entire side of the Hill up to the last field behind the Big Grove. Their estate comprised several groves, fields, pastures, and orchards, and the clearing below the pinewoods. Rade's father, Father Kosta, had taught himself from books on farming the modern methods of fertilizing the land, grafting fruit trees, and selecting grain for sowing; he had acquired good animal stock, the latest tools, a still for making raki, and a machine for extracting honey from the fifty beehives he cultivated. They kept shepherds and men for everyday farming, but the heavy work, such as harvesting, reaping, threshing, or picking the gathering fruit, was done by work parties of his own parishioners, mostly those from the surrounding villages.

Rade was good-looking and young. He was very taken with Djana from the day they met, and began to attend every gathering she frequented, so they soon fell in love and became engaged. Janko was pleased with Djana's choice because Rade stood out not only with his good looks and wealth, but with his education and patriotism too, although in these respects he leaned more toward Montenegro than Serbia. As Djana was his eldest daughter, Janko gave her a big dowry and a lavish wedding ceremony which was talked about in Plevlje for months afterwards. Jelka was sorry to marry off such a young daughter into a big family. Besides her parents-in-law, Djana had to cope with two sisters-in-law and her brother-in-law's two motherless children. This reminded Jelka of her own life in the extended family, and the heavy work and responsibility that Djana would have to undertake from her early youth. But, like Jelka, Djana was very much in love with her husband and was happy, although she had to work from morning till night, despite all the maidservants who were kept on the estate.

Soon after Djana's marriage, Jelka became pregnant. Hoping that she would give birth to a boy, she was pleased, although her pregnancy was difficult as she had reached her fortieth year. As time went by, she felt and looked better, as if this new joy had given her new youth. One day, close to her confinement, the Turkish and Serbian children started fighting, as they always did, year in, year out, but this time Nikola took with him a Flober shotgun his father had bought for him in Sarajevo. It was a toy, but so well made that the Turkish children thought he had taken his father's gun, and ran away, horrified. The father of one of the Turkish children heard that Nikola wanted to kill his son, grabbed a knife and ran to find him to cut his throat. The whole of the Charshija was in a ferment, and fortunately someone told Janko what was happening. He caught up with the Turk, restrained him and explained that the Flober was not real but a toy. The Turk finally calmed down and went home, but he bore a grudge against Nikola for frightening him and his child, and threatened to be revenged on him one day.

Jelka heard from the women in the neighborhood what had happened and was so shaken that Janko found her lying unconscious. She gave premature birth to a boy who lived barely six hours. This misfortune did not strike her too hard, as she had not even had time to breast-feed the baby, and she was more concerned that something might happen to Nikola. Janko, too, was afraid for Nikola's safety, so they arranged with a business acquaintance from Sarajevo for Nikola to stay with him. Secretly, for fear that the Turks might learn about this, Janko took him to Sarajevo and enrolled him into the School of Commerce. He left him enough money, and authorization to take more from his account if he needed it, put him up in the respectable home of his friend and stayed with him for a few days until the boy got used to the new environment.

It took Jelka some time to recover from the pain of her parting with Nikola. She also regretted the death of her little son, but did not mourn for him and tried to bear her grief without bitterness, for fear of provoking fate. She reflected at length about her life and her past, prayed more often and endeavored in her prayers not to oppose God's will.

"I am afraid, Mother, that I may be sinful, that in some ways I have caused God's wrath," she said one day to Savka.

"Good heavens, how could you be sinful?"

"Perhaps I have been too proud and have defied fate and people. I hear Rosa was saying that her curses are catching up with me, and that I am sending one son after another to the monastery graveyard."

"Don't listen to what women say, they like to lie and invent. And even if she did curse you, do you think God listens to her curses? He commands the sun and the earth and the stars in the sky, cares for everything that lives and grows, gives us the rain and the sun and the wind and all his other benefices. I don't know, my child, whether he can hear our prayers, let alone people's curses and spitefulness. There are many people in the world, a lot of sorrow and misfortune, he cannot come to everybody's rescue. You make sure that your heart is pure, my dear, and don't wish harm to anybody, not even your enemies, and you will also be forgiven. Let your conscience be at peace. You will endure hardship easier if you know you cannot blame yourself for it."

In her hours of contemplation, Jelka would sometimes remember Zlata. Furious and humiliated by Janko's infidelity, as she had been at the time, it had not occurred to her to wonder how Zlata would endure her shame and what would happen to her, but now, having experienced far greater pain, she could think of her without hatred. Since Janko had married off Zlata to his former servant, Relja, everything was covered up and among the Kojics no one even mentioned her. If any rumors were heard, they were suppressed, because one did not repeat unpleasant things in respectable homes, and all trespasses or quarrels were meticulously concealed.

Relja never revealed from where he had obtained the money for his *kafana*, but implied that he was a landlord from of old. His work went on well, the *kafana* was in a busy place and he tried hard to please every guest: be he Turk or Serb, townsman, villager, or gypsy, he served them all, bowing and scraping, once he saw that they had money and were willing to spend it in his place. He took care that the appearance of his home and his family matched the reputation he imagined he had gained. His house was kept clean and whitewashed both within and without, the courtyard was fenced with new palings, he dressed well, bought better clothes for Zlata and, as he did not have enough money to buy her a new *tepeluk* headdress, he bought her a *kalkan*, worn by the wives of artisans and the landlords of lesser means. When he bought her the *libade* and *kalkan*, her face lit up with joy and she only feared whether she would know how to wear it.

"Don't worry, you'll learn. If God keeps me healthy and the business goes on as well as it has till now, I'll buy you a *tepeluk* one day, so that when you go to church wearing the *tepeluk* and *libade* and start mixing with the wives from the best houses, the riff-raff from our neighborhood will die of envy. We'll show them how well dressed the wife of Master Relja can be."

He tried to mix with the wealthier people, but this was not easy because it was known that he had once been a servant, and there was talk that his wife had been foisted on to him by one of his employers who had dallied with her and then paid to cover it up. This was repeated in the neighborhood as well, especially by Ruza, the old gossipmonger who lived next door and made his life a misery. She was always looking for an excuse to start quarreling so as to smear them. She called Zlata a "Kojic skivvy" and her eldest daughter, Dushanka, a "Kojic bastard." Because of this, blood was almost spilled one day. Relja was cutting some branches on the chopping block when he heard Ruza say "bastard" to Dushanka and, gripping his ax, he ran to hit her with it. Had it not been for Zlata, Ruza's head would have split like a pumpkin. A bitter row ensued in front of the neighbors who came out to listen and savor it, because the poor, being poor, feed on gossip and argument. It is an important part of their life in which there is no other entertainment.

"I know my wife best," Relja shouted, shaking his fist. "She came to me pure as snow."

"Yes? And where did you get your *kafana*?" Ruza shouted back, then ran into her house and turned the key.

Relja started kicking her door. "Shut up, you old whore, if you don't want me to spill your brains. When you were young, the Turks showered your cunt with ducats, and now. . ."

"It was worth it, that's why they showered it," Ruza interrupted from behind the door. "Eat your heart out, I still have those ducats."

"Like hell you have. You haven't two pennies to rub together, never mind ducats. If you had, you wouldn't live on barley bread."

"And what were you raised on if not on barley bread? It's easy to show off white flour now that you have taken a wife with a belly."

"You are lying, Turkish witch, Dushanka is my child!"

"Why is she so white and pretty, then, and all your other children dark like you and your gypsy woman?"

Relja would have continued to threaten Ruza with the ax had Zlata not dragged him into their home.

"Don't argue with that kind. Don't touch shit if you don't want to smell of it."

"The worst of it is that she doesn't leave the child alone. She can say what she likes to you and me so long as she doesn't abuse Dushanka."

Zlata fell silent and began to cry.

"Don't cry, I know that Dushanka is mine and even if she were not, she has brought me good luck and I love her as much as the other children."

The news of the quarrel spread from mouth to mouth until it finally reached Jelka. To cut the gossip short, Jelka decided to visit Zlata. She got ready, brought her sweets and bon-bons for the children and went to Relja's house. Zlata was in the courtyard by the tap, washing. Flabbergasted to see Jelka, she quickly took off her apron and dried her hands on it. She approached timidly and kissed Jelka's hand, then, somewhat confused, led her into the house and asked her to sit down.

"We never get a chance to meet, Zlata, so I decided to call on you at last and see how you live," Jelka said.

"Well, I live well, thank God. How are you? How is Master Janko? I have heard about your bereavement. . ." Perplexed as to whether she should have mentioned this, she fell silent.

"It was God's will. May our children keep well and healthy. One must come to terms with one's fate. I couldn't visit you before, though I kept saying to myself, I ought to call on Zlata, I've heard nothing about her, as if she had vanished from the face of the earth."

"Thank you, thank you very much," Zlata said, and went out to send one of the children to call Relja, then came back, still unable to master her confusion.

"How many children do you have, Zlata?"

"Two girls and one son."

The conversation evolved laboriously, because Zlata was too embarrassed to say anything and would only answer Jelka's questions, standing all the time by the door. Soon Relja arrived, proud and excited as if the bishop himself had entered his home. He brought drinks from the *kafana* and hovered around, not knowing what to offer first to his guest.

"Shall we have raki? Or a beer? I just took it out of the ice box. Come, Zlata, bring some refreshment and I will pour the beer into glasses. It must have a head two fingers deep."

Zlata brought the refreshments and went to change the children before showing them to Jelka. When she had dressed them, smoothed their hair once more and told them how to bow when they entered and to kiss the hand of the lady who had come to visit them, she led all three into the room. They approached Jelka to kiss her hand and lined up next to their mother in order of majority. Dushanka was the most beautiful and the tallest. Jelka looked at her, thinking that she was perhaps Janko's child but had dark eyes like her mother. It surprised her that she did not find the thought upsetting but was, on the contrary, looking with more warmth at her than at the other children. They sat a little longer talking, then Jelka got up to leave. Zlata accompanied her to the street, kissed her hand and glanced proudly at the neighboring women who had gathered to see Master Janko's wife.

As they parted, Jelka said to Zlata, "You must come to see me too. Drop in for a coffee whenever you go to the monastery, it is on your way."

From then on they visited one another as if they were relatives, which put a stop to the gossip about Zlata and her sudden marriage.

Once, when they were alone, Jelka said, "I'm sorry, Zlata, that Janko committed a sin against you."

"We both sinned," Zlata muttered.

"Tell me the truth, did Janko take you into his room by force?"

"No, not by force. He was drunk and I went in to take off his shoes."

"But why didn't you defend yourself?"

"I don't know myself," said Zlata and looked up at Jelka anxiously.

"You see, I forgot myself. Master Janko was very handsome."

Jelka stared silently in front of her. She still found the memory of that night painful, but for the first time now she could feel compassion for Zlata, and understand the fear and shame which she had to endure. Finally, she said, "Listen, we'll forget what happened and will never mention it again. You can come to see me and consider me as an elder relative, turn to me if you need anything and I will always help you if I can and advise you."

Zlata began to cry, knelt in front of her and whispered, "You forgave me once you had entered my home and I shall respect you as one respects a mother."

From then on Zlata addressed Jelka as Dada, as Jelka's children did, and later the whole neighborhood did. In time all Plevlje called her Dada, even the women who were much older than her.

Marija reached marriageable age. She completed four years of high school with excellent results and developed into a great beauty. Golden-haired and blue-eyed like Janko, tall and willowy, with delicate features and a tender nature, her refinement singled her out from all the other girls in Plevlje, and because she dressed in Viennese fashion she acquired the nickname "Jelka's fashion-plate." She met a young teacher from Mocevac, Petronije, a priest's son, when she was still at school, and fell in love with him. He would wait for her in Citluk, where they would exchange a few words, then walk together to the Kojic houses, but neither Janko nor Jelka knew about it.

Petronije was not as wealthy as Father Rade, so his family were afraid that Janko would not approve of him, although their house was older and of greater repute. They did not wish to ask for her hand in person until they found out what the Kojics would say, but sent one of their relatives to enquire and received a reply that Marija was still too young and they would not let her marry anyone yet. They knew this was not the true answer, though they pretended not to suspect anything and waited another year before deciding to ask for her hand again. This time they did not send any messages but made thorough preparations for the betrothal. Petronije's father assembled all the priests of the family, close and distant, and asked his relative the Bishop of Prizren to come. They all responded and assembled. Then, saying nothing to the Kojics, one evening they headed in a procession up the Hill. Meanwhile, somebody learned about it and ran to tell Janko that twelve priests and a bishop were on the way to his home for a betrothal, all of them in cassocks and skull-caps, with only the teacher Petronije in a suit and wearing a fez on his head. When he heard the bishop was calling on him, Janko ordered the best carpet runners to be laid from the stairs across the entire forecourt to the street. He opened wide the gates and waited in front of them to receive the guests, bareheaded. When they drew nearer, he approached the bishop and kissed his hand, saying, "This is the happiest day of my life because your Grace is visiting my home. To me it is as if the Serbian king had come. He is the highest in Serbia, and you amongst us who are not yet liberated."

The bishop blessed him. "My blessings on you, your family, and your home."

The other priests responded in one voice, "Amen," prolonging it as if singing in church.

Jelka waited by the stairs. She bowed and kissed everyone's hand except Petronije's.

When they entered the visitors' room and were seated on the *secijas*, the bishop began without more ado: "You see, Master Janko, we come to ask for the hand of your daughter Marija for our Petronije. Will you give your consent?"

"I leave the decision to my daughter," Janko replied, having no choice. "If she agrees, I shall not object."

Marija agreed and her betrothal was solemnly and quietly performed, without gypsy musicians or *kolo* dancing, without the neighboring women, and without singing.

Because Petronije and his brothers did not have enough money for each to secure a roof over his head, they had divided their father's house into four parts, and on the very day of the engagement the Hill was abuzz with the news that "Jelka's fashion-plate is being married into a quarter of a house."

Jelka was not pleased with the marriage either, as this one too was into a kind of extended family and she was sorry that her daughter had to leave the comfort of her parents' home for such a restricted dwelling. But she knew that nothing could stand in the way of true love, and found consolation in the fact that Marija would be near and could visit her often.

After Marija's marriage, Jelka realized that she was pregnant again. This came as a blow to her because she feared that the child would not be healthy after the death of her prematurely born son, and was worried what people would say, as Djana was close to her confinement and any day now they expected a grandchild.

Janko tried to comfort her. "Don't be upset, it's a sign that we are still young and love each other. Look at Pava, she gave birth a year ago, and she was not sorry."

"Her children are not as old as mine, and besides, she had a son, while I, with my luck, may have a girl, a sixth daughter."

"It could be a boy, and we'll have another son so that Niko is not the only one."

She too began to hope that God would bless her with a male child, and accepted the trouble in which she found herself at her age. As it happened, she bore a girl. She was so unhappy that she could not stop herself from crying every time she fed and changed her. Likewise the other women were sad when they called on her, as if they did not come to rejoice but to mourn. Janko noticed that Jelka was even more upset after their visits and it annoyed him. One day, he entered her room when it was full of women, took from his pocket a handful of napoleons and spilled them around the child's pillow, saying, "At last I've managed to bring a gift for my favorite, I was too busy to do it before. May she be happy and healthy. God has bestowed her on us to give us joy and consolation in our old age. Her father will send her to school to become a teacher and enlighten Serbian children."

The women exchanged glances, picked themselves up, and left to tell in amazement of Janko's joy at having another daughter, though he already had five and only one son. Jelka too was stunned to see so much money. She thought he must have got drunk out of despair and did not know what he was doing. When he came in again, she asked, "For heaven's sake, what came over you to put in so much money? You have never done it before."

"I did it to spite those women. Sitting here with long faces as if it were a wake. They always upset you with their whimpering."

"I thought you were as upset as I am and had got drunk."

"No, dear, I don't mind our girl being born. Good luck to her, let her grow up with our other girls. Every child has its own destiny, its own fortune. If I am still alive, I will send her to study to become a teacher like the daughter of Tane's Stanka." He collected the gold coins from the child's pillow and put them back into his pocket. "I was on my way to pay for the consignment of merchandise which has just arrived."

They christened the girl as soon as Jelka was up, because she was small and weak and they were afraid she might die unchristened. She was named Milena. As time went by everyone grew fond of her, as she was prettier and brighter than Jelka's other children, although she was often ill and for a long time could not walk.

Barely two years had passed since Milena's birth when Pava fell ill. She was given various herbal potions, the priest read prayers for her, she drank the water with which the icons of Our Lady of Cajnice were rinsed, but nothing helped. Finally, Janko persuaded Petko to call the Austrian doctor to see her. He gave her some medicines to take, but told Janko that she had tuberculosis and would not recover. He warned him that the illness was contagious and her children should be separated from her, especially her youngest son, because he had noticed that Pava kept him next to her all the time.

Janko returned home worried, and called Jelka. "Pava is very ill," he said cautiously. "The doctor said that she is suffering from consumption and there is little hope of her recovery. It isn't good that Misho is always with her. We must somehow bring him here and keep him."

Jelka burst into tears. She loved Pava like a sister, and was closer to her than to Jula, whom she had not seen since she left for Sarajevo. She knew Pava was ailing, especially lately, but had become accustomed to the way she looked and was convinced that she would get better. It had never occurred to her that Pava's illness was so dangerous and that she might die.

"Come on, stop that crying and go to her. Convince her she should give you Misho and bring him to our home immediately."

"She won't let him go. He clings to her, doesn't move from her side, and she, too, carries him in her arms everywhere as if afraid to lose sight of him."

"We must save the child at least. Do your best to take him from her."

Jelka withdrew to compose herself, then washed her face, told her daughters to look after Misho if she sent him over, and went to Pava. She found her sitting in bed, holding Misho on her lap. She looked more gaunt than ever, nothing but skin and bone, her face yellowish pale with strangely flushed cheekbones. Jelka's heart contracted but she held back and reproached Pava gently: "Why do you hold that child on your lap as if he were a baby?" She picked up Misho in her arms and jokingly started to tell him off: "You too, why do you hang around her neck like that, almost a young man and still clinging to Mother's skirts? If other children knew, I'm sure they would tease you. What shame, the school won't accept you if anyone knows."

Ashamed, Misho began to cry.

"Don't cry, I'm joking. I won't tell anyone that your mother still holds you on her knee, you can go now and play with Milena." She wiped away his tears and put him down, then called Pava's maid to take him to her house. Seeing him leave obediently, she called after him, "I left two cakes for you and Milena, they're in the pantry. Say that they should give them to you, and afterwards play with Milena in the room and don't go anywhere outside alone."

When Misho left, Pava whispered through tears, "Oh, Jelka, my Misho will be left without a mother. I can see this is a serious illness and I won't get better. My children will be motherless. I feel sorry for them all, but for him most because he'll suffer more, that's why I keep him with me so he'll remember he had a mother. And I am trying to quench my longing too, to feast my eyes on him before I go."

Tears filled Jelka's eyes. "Don't, what's the matter with you? You're making me cry as well. You're run down because you don't look after yourself, don't eat enough." She rearranged Pava's pillows and helped her to lean against them. "You need rest and care, that's why I shall come every day to cook for you especially, and if you don't get better from my food in less than a week, I'm not Jelka. My girls will look after Milena and Misho. He doesn't have to come here until you are stronger." She waited to see whether Pava would protest, and as she said nothing, asked, "Tell me, did you eat anything this morning?"

Pava shook her head and began to cough. Her eyes shone with fever. Jelka went down to the kitchen, prepared a dish of white bread steamed with butter and cream cheese, and took it up with a glass of yogurt.

Pava was in a better mood and more relaxed since Jelka had started nursing her, and the whole family began to hope she would recover. But as the late autumn set in and the weather suddenly became bad and rainy, her illness took a turn for the worse. Jelka did not leave her side, so Janko had to take her home by force to spare her the sight of Pava's final painful hours. The next day Pava died in Petko's arms, bequeathing Misho to Jelka's care.

Jelka was not allowed into Pava's room until the women had laid her out. When it was time for the family to enter and the mourning rites began, Jelka also went in. On a long table covered with a white cloth embroidered in white, Pava lay in a coffin. She appeared to be resting, with a peaceful smile on her bluish lips. Around the bier sat the women from the neighborhood who had laid Pava out, and at the head stood Mara, lamenting:

Sister Pava, my beloved,
Why did you close your eyes
And choose the way of darkness?
You have left for distant lands,
Distant lands of no return.
When you reach the world beyond,
The invisible world beyond,
You will find my husband Mile.
Tell him, dear sister Pava,
That I have been faithful to him,
Did not marry or leave his home.
Alone in it I bear my sorrow
Without confiding in anyone.

"Dear God," Jelka thought, "how much sadness is hidden in Mara, who seems so dry and severe." When Mara stopped lamenting, Jelka approached to kiss Pava's forehead. She had never before kissed a corpse and was horrified at the cold touch on her lips. When her children died, she had been beside herself with grief and was not allowed to see them until the funeral. At the cemetery too she had been kept away from the grave. She remembered only hearing the coffin being nailed, seeing it lowered into the ground, earth falling on it. Those were the worst moments she had known, and she reflected now, "There is nothing, neither my dead children, nor Pava, nor Mara's Mile . . . they have vanished from this or the next world. This that we bury in the earth is something completely different." She could not cry any more and, as she did not know how to lament, she returned home, took Misho on her lap and, only now, succumbed to a flood of tears. She cried for him, for Pava's other children, for herself, for all who are left behind to live in sorrow.

The Kojics waited two days for Pava's family to come to the funeral from Cajnice, but as they did not appear on the second day, they had to bury her. As they returned from the cemetery, at dusk, Pava's mother arrived with her two brothers. She wanted to visit the grave that same evening, but her brothers would not allow her as she could hardly stand upright from sorrow and fatigue. The next day they all went to the cemetery. A light steady rain was falling. When they passed through the gates and started toward the freshly dug mound, Pava's mother left her brother and approached the grave, tall and dignified in black mourning clothes. She stopped beside the cross, bowed and kissed it, then began to lament tearlessly, her hands below her chest, in a Bosnian manner:

Good morning, my daughter.
Why weren't you there to greet me
At the gates of your home?
Why did you leave your children?
Who will nurse and love them now?
Who will teach and advise them?

Here her strength deserted her. She knelt down, laid her head on the wet earth and began to sob.

Immediately after they returned from the graveyard, Pava's family left Plevlje. They were asked to stay one more night at least to rest before their journey, but refused. Although nothing was said, Jelka sensed how upset Pava's mother was to realize how deprived her daughter had been despite Petko's wealth. Now she was seeing the conditions that had cut short Pava's youth and ruined her delicate health.

That evening, when she was alone with Janko, Jelka began bitterly, "It was not Pava's illness that destroyed her, it was Petko. Not only did he burden her with all the work of the house and the children, being too mean to pay for more servants, but he also made her suffer. Only I know what she went through. She confided in me one day, told me that only I and her grave would know about it. She had loved him more than her family, and what did he do in return? When she heard that he had some woman in the Turkish quarter and told him about it, he hit her so that from then on she lost the hearing in her left ear."

Janko listened, appalled. He knew that Petko was mean, but it had never occurred to him that he could be brutal.

"She could not forgive him for it, even in her dying hour," Jelka went on through tears. "She told me, 'There, sister, from then on I began to pine away. There was no joy in my heart and that's when my illness began. He reduced me to this and now I am of no use to either God or people.'"

Janko lowered his head and kept silent.

"How pitiful women are, worse than any living thing. We try to please our man, bear his children, we are faithful, spend all our lives in the house and in work. One would not lay as much on a beast. And our devotion and endeavors are in vain, if we have to endure all sorts of other things, and dare not complain but must be grateful for every mouthful and rag we get."

He looked at her in astonishment, for she had never before reproached him or alluded to anything. Now, enraged because of Pava, she was giving vent to years of accumulated fury.

"I only hope that the time will come for women to retaliate measure for measure, to be protected by law. But for now, let the whores avenge us decent women, and good luck to them!" She threw him a black look, turned around and left, then locked herself in her room to let all her fury and pain pour out in tears.

8

The world was passing through great changes, and various political currents could be felt even in Plevlje. The Austrians had suddenly distanced themselves from the Serbs: they became closer to the Turks, and were seen more often in the Beledija, the Turkish town hall, while in turn the Turks began to frequent the Barracks. The *zaptiehs* patrolled the town more often and the Serbs avoided meeting there. Rumors of unification with Serbia and Montenegro grew, anthologies of national poetry were circulated amongst Serbian homes, poems were learned by heart, especially those from the Kosovo Cycle,[5] while new patriotic songs were being sung in secret. That year at Christmas even the children expressed the national spirit in their own way in *vertep*, nativity scenes performed from house to house. The school had always cultivated this ancient custom in order to collect donations for poor pupils. A procession of school children would go through the town led by several pupils dressed as the kings and wise men, singing Christmas carols: "Your Birth, Christ our Lord" and "Bethlehem, the Old Town." They would visit every Serbian house, and in some of them they recited verses about the birth of Christ and the homage and gifts presented to him. That Christmas, one of the pupils wore a crown similar to that of King Petar of Serbia, and around his shoulders a cloak designed after the king's. After Balthazar's speech ("I am King Balthazar, from the eastern lands . . ."), the boy would step forward and recite, "I am King Petar, flying in the wind, holding a glass of wine to toast everyone."

Merchants who had conducted business with Austria began to be regarded with suspicion, and Janko stopped traveling not only to Vienna but also to Sarajevo. The Kojics stayed out of the public eye and were seldom seen in their *kafanas* and bars. Had they not been afraid of the Shvabas, they would have shut them down altogether to avoid becoming the target of the people's wrath.

The Austrians grew increasingly anxious each day, more so than the Turks. One evening von Ries came to Janko and asked to speak to him alone. As he was deathly pale and trembling, Janko led him into the visitors' room and locked the door behind them. He did not wish anyone to see an Austrian officer in his home now, as they had never visited him before nor did he call on them. After a while, Janko emerged, called Jelka and took her into the room where the money was kept in a chest, under lock and key.

"The Major has asked me to lend him one hundred golden napoleons," he said in a whisper. "His accounts are to be audited tomorrow, and there is a deficit. He has written home to Vienna for money to be sent to him immediately, and as soon as it arrives he will repay me."

"Don't lend him anything at all. Say you haven't got it. I don't trust him, he's a real fox. He persuaded you to put money into the Shvaba bank, which neither Stevo nor Petko have done."

"He says he'll kill himself if I don't agree. He won't live to face the dishonor of being stripped of his rank."

"Let him kill himself, it isn't your fault. Why didn't he look after the money that was entrusted to him? Why is it missing?"

"He say he lost it one night playing cards."

When she heard that, Jelka became even more angry. "He gambled with money that was placed in his trust! That's sacrilege. You know the saying—'The house may burn down but the pledge must be kept.'" Seeing that Janko was still wavering, her tone mellowed. "Don't upset yourself, dear, you can see he is unreliable."

"Why unreliable? The man made a mistake, and thought he'd get the money from home."

"What do you care what he thought, my Janko? Nor is it your worry that he gambled. He should have known better. He shouldn't have courted trouble, especially as the money was not his own!"

"How can you say it isn't my worry? How could I let the man kill himself in my house if I can help him, save him? If he does kill himself, where would my conscience be? It would torture me for as long as I live."

Jelka knew that Janko was sensitive and was shaken by the thought that a man's life depended on his decision, so she tried to force him somehow to think rationally. "I wouldn't be tortured by anything. With all those officers, hasn't he got anyone else to turn to? Why should you care for the Shvabas, or try to save them? I wouldn't trust him if he took a gun now and put it to his forehead."

"I cannot allow that. I'd feel as if I had killed him with my own hand."

"Do as you like, but I tell you I wouldn't give him a penny, never mind a hundred napoleons. That's a small fortune, for heaven's sake!"

"He'll pay it back. He's an aristocrat, honor is more important to him than life."

"Then why did he gamble the money away if he cared so much for his honor? You can give him twice as much if you want, but I wouldn't lift a finger, and that's that. And I don't believe you'll get anything back."

"Well, I'll let him have it, even if he never returns it," Janko decided. "Life is more important than money." So saying, he went to the large chest, unlocked it, took out an iron box and unlocked that too, then counted out a hundred golden napoleons. Putting them into the deep pockets of his *shalvare* trousers, he leveled out the rest of the gold coins, stroked them and said, "There, it doesn't even show that much. We have enough for what we need." Not daring to look at Jelka, he stole out of the room like a thief.

After a while, there was a sound of von Ries taking his leave and Janko locking the entrance door.

Less than two days later, news arrived of the annexation of Bosnia and Hercegovina. There was talk that the Austrians would withdraw their garrison from Plevlje and that the frontier between Austria and Turkey would be at Metaljka. An order was issued forbidding any travel out of Plevlje.

Janko immediately went to the Baron to ask about his money. The other convinced him that he would send him all of it from Vienna as soon as postal services were resumed. He gave him a receipt and told him not to worry because communications with Vienna would soon be restored.

The families of the Shvaba officers left first, then the brothel, and the Viennese merchants Julchik and Goldberg. The Kojics' houses became vacant, the entire garrison was evacuated, and the Barracks were deserted.

Pasha Bajrovic left at the same time as the Shvabas.

The Kojics closed their *kafanas* and bars, and their trade also dwindled. Janko and Stevo did not even go to the Charshija but sat at home and waited to see what would happen. Petko kept his store open but he sold no goods because the peasants were staying in their villages and they were his main customers. The Kojics' business was in total collapse. With the houses untenanted, there was no income from them either. Janko fell into a state of worry and anxiety. He boiled at the very thought of Baron von Ries, not only because he had extracted a hundred napoleons from him but also because, on von Ries's advice, his money had been deposited in the Shvaba bank. He became nervous, withdrew to his room and forbade anyone to disturb him. He could no longer sit down with a book and read, as he used to, but paced the room all day long in despair.

When Jelka saw how depressed he was, she urged him to go out a little. "I hear people are showing their faces in the Charshija and in the *kafanas*. Go out and meet people. You'll feel better."

He took her advice and went to the Charshija, but came back in a worse mood. The local Turks had the upper hand, and some of them had mobbed him, shouting, "You're finished, chief, the Shvabas have gone, your time is up."

Jelka suggested that he should go to Ilino Hill and stay for a while with Djana, but even there he could not find peace. Used to work, and to planning for the future, he now felt like a leper, confined to isolation and inner torment. He could not think of any serious work that would keep him busy. Not yet fifty years old, at the peak of his strength, he didn't know how to spend the days and nights in idleness and uncertainty. He remembered that Ratko had always regretted not having let them learn some craft beside the business. "If I were an artisan, I'd still have my work and would remain what I was before, regardless of circumstances. Stevo doesn't know what to do either. He's taken to drink, the same shrewd Stevo whose wisdom everybody admired, who was respected more than anyone else. Now he drinks like a fish, it's a shameful sight. Petko still holds on somehow. He always did potter around the garden, patch up woodwork, knock nails into loose fences, repair casks and barrels, so he is not idle now. I see him every day doing something, weeding the vegetable beds, cutting the grass, guarding the wheat fields, chasing sparrows and jackdaws, cleaning the cowsheds, spreading manure . . . always something. And what am I to do? If I go on like this, all the capital will be spent, everything sold, and what then?"

Suddenly, he became infuriated by his own despondency. "No, I won't sell up and give my enemies cause to rejoice. I'll live on the capital until circumstances change and I feel I can resume my business again, right to the last penny. And afterwards, if things continue as they are now, a bullet in the head. Jelka can sell the shop and lease the houses. She'll receive the crops from the land in Podpec, and she can manage with the children until Niko returns from his studies. He'll be able to keep her and Milena, and the other three I'll marry off at the first good opportunity. Savka can live on the income from her land and the rent from her house. As for me, to start some other business now, and to fall off my high horse—I can't. I won't pick up a shovel or a pick, nor will I spread manure like Petko. I was a businessman and a businessman I'll stay—while I live I'll stay true to myself."

This attitude gave him courage, his former confidence returned, and he went to the Charshija in a good mood. Deliberately, he stopped at a *kafana* where some Turks were sitting, and joined a company of friends at a table where the Turks could see them. He chatted and laughed as if he hadn't a care in the world. The Turks exchanged glances, winked at one another and began to speak louder so that Janko's group could hear them.

"The pasha ran. He took his entire entourage, male and female, and slipped away without any trouble. But what are we going to do with the people here who were hand in glove with the Shvabas, like the pasha?"

"Not just the Shvabas, they flirted with Serbia too. They were bringing in books from there secretly, and plotting against the Turks."

"Perhaps they've also been smuggling guns and gunpowder from Montenegro, as it's nearer, and are waiting for the right moment to light the fuse for the Turks. This has been brewing for a long time."

"We should throw them all in jail, toss a torch into their houses, and banish their wives and children."

As they went on talking in this way, Janko's company listened, pretending not to hear. Then finally they began to rise and leave, one by one, until he too, realizing that he would be left there alone, got up and went out with the last few.

He returned home upset.

"Why in such a black mood?" Jelka asked him.

He shrugged his shoulders. "Don't ask."

"Is it because of the money and the business? Don't let it get you down, dear. It isn't as though death has struck. Thank God we've enough of everything, money and the rest. We can live even if you don't do any work. You can sell my jewelry, I don't wear it, nor do I need it. The *tepeluk* alone is worth a lot with so much gold and all those pearls on it, and then there's the necklace of thirty-five large gold ducats, and the land in Podpec and in Nova Varosh. Mother says you should sell it, as we won't be getting anything from there now. She has given it to you, you can do what you like with it. All the papers are in your name, registered in the Beledija."

He told her what the Turks had said in the *kafana*. Now she too became afraid.

"Escape to Sarajevo. Niko is there, your money is there in the bank."

"If I had wanted to go with the Shvabas I would have gone when the pasha did, and taken you all with me in time. I wasn't at all involved with them. All I did was trade, and my hands are clean as far as the Serbs and Turks are concerned. If I ran away now, I'd only draw suspicion upon myself. The Turks would burn everything and banish you to God knows where."

"Escape to Serbia."

"That would be all the Turks needed to raise hell. They hate Serbia now more than ever, and would destroy it if they could. They'd say I was a spy, that I spied for Serbia."

"Let them, what do you care?"

"What do I care? Do you realize what a spy is? He is worse than a whore, she sells her body and a spy sells his soul. God forbid that I should bear such a name. And what would happen to you then? The Turks would cut your throat. I have done nothing dishonest that I should have to run away. I sometimes brought back history books from Rudo for the high school, hidden in my merchandise. The Turks banned the teaching of history so that our children wouldn't learn who we were before Kosovo—we had kings and tsars, like Dushan the Mighty and Tsar Lazar, who fell at Kosovo. That's not politics, that's the truth about us and our heritage. We want our children to know that we are not slaves, 'plant without roots' as the Turks call us, but are Serbs and have remained Serbs."

Jelka closed the door and said in a whisper, "I am afraid for you, my Janko, they may kill you."

"Let them kill me. I'd die an honest man, and you won't be dishonored. Nothing frightens me now, not even death. I'll neither run away nor hide, but I'll stay here, come what may. 'A brave man dies once, a coward every day,' as the old saying goes." He lit a cigar and began to pace the floor. "Right now I feel sorry for all Serbs who are still enslaved, wherever they are. We hoped that help would come from somewhere but they all abandoned us. Can't you see what those shitty Europeans are doing? They are using us as a bribe. First they allowed Austria to keep its army in Plevlje, pretending to be protecting the Christians from the Turks, and now it washes its hands of us and leaves us to the mercy of the Turks, to massacre us if they wish. God! What they are doing to our people! Bosnia and Hercegovina are given as presents to Austria, as if we were in no-man's-land, to be robbed at will. 'Let those in Plevlje go to the Turks, and the rest to the Shvabas, and everyone will be pleased.' No one consults us, or takes us into consideration. They share us out like sheep, some to be left in Turkish pens, others to be passed on to Austria. Russia is mighty and could defend us, but she doesn't give a damn that we are suffering, though she prides herself on representing all Slav peoples. It is easy to talk from afar and never shift your ass . . . Well, let them know that we are ready to die first, since we have lived for five hundred years in slavery without renouncing our Serbian origin, and preserved our language and creeds and customs."

Jelka let him talk, hoping that it would relieve his soul, but seeing him ready for the worst made her afraid. "Leave it, for heaven's sake. Worrying about the Serbian cause as if you can help anyone, yet you don't even know what might happen to us."

"Nothing. We'll stay in our homes and won't go anywhere."

"How can we stop mixing with people? That's not good either. I'm very scared."

Janko noticed the pallor of her frightened face and began to comfort her. "I'm only saying that we won't go out until this mob rule is over, until some order is established. The worst times are when a government changes. Then all sorts of people emerge in search of gain and every parasite tries to attach himself to the new masters. It is like when a flood occurs and carries away everything, stones, wood, and all kinds of rubbish and mud, but when it subsides the rubbish rots away, the water clears, and beneath it only clean stones and pebbles remain. Don't worry because those Turks in the *kafana* were showing off, as if they have some say. They are nobodies, a rabble, no one pays any attention to them. I have friends among the Turks whose word matters. They will protect me—they are all of our blood, after all. They have looked after us Serbs who live in Plevlje and the surrounding villages until now, and saved us from the Osmanli Turks. We have always lived with them in peace and harmony, we have the same language, the same heritage, same blood, they have only changed their religion. And, as they say, it is not important how one worships, but whose milk one has suckled. They don't dislike any of our holidays, that's why we can still celebrate them. The pasha showed me a secret recess in the wall of the men's quarters where his ancestors used to hide their icons. If he were here, I would have no trouble." He sighed deeply, took another puff and put out his cigar. "I hope that all this will calm down and Pasha Bajrovic will come back. People will be allowed to cross the frontier and I'll have access to my money. Money cannot be lost in the bank. I'll also find that renegade, that sly fox Major von Ries. If I have to, I'll go to the Austrian Tsar himself, to Franz Josef, to complain and tell him what his officers have been doing, his aristocrats and shits. I have the receipt. As for the banks, the Austrian Empire is responsible, unless it's like their officers were. When order is restored here, there will be more work too and I'll start doing business again. It doesn't matter who rules, whether the Turks or the Shvabas, everybody needs trade. I will lease the houses also, it doesn't matter to whom, even to the gypsies, as long as they don't stand empty."

"And you will bring back Niko, even if he has not finished his schooling."

"No, under no circumstances should we bring him here now. That Turk may try to revenge himself, the one who wanted to cut his throat when the Turkish children ran about shouting that our children had guns. Although I showed him that it was a toy gun, a Flober, which I bought in Sarajevo to shoot the birds with, he went away angry and bore a grudge. Now we must avoid any Turks with whom we had some quarrel, however small. Niko is better off than we are. I have left him in a good Serbian home, and Jula is near and will look after him." Seeing how upset she was, having lost the hope that her son would soon return, he took her hand into both of his and whispered, "Difficult times are upon us, but there is no way of avoiding them."

When the Austrians withdrew, they left everything in such good order that it was as if they hoped to return soon. It was rumored that one of the first Turkish officers to reach Plevlje had said when he inspected the Barracks, "I say, what these Shvabas have built in thirty years, we won't be able to demolish in fifty."

The Turkish *asker* arrived and spread out all over the Barracks, the big park around the lake where the bronze fountain flowed murmuring day and night, across the flower beds, orchards, and white paths, and also over the Hill and around the Krstata Barracks. The inhabitants of Plevlje had never seen such an unruly army, such disarray. All the soldiers were from the Asian part of Turkey, and among them were many Arabs.

The Kojics locked their gates and covered the windows facing the Barracks with thick curtains.

Dirty and disheveled, the soldiers roamed like noisy savages around the Barracks and the gypsy graveyard. They spent all day out of doors except when it was raining, and even then they would crowd inside like a flock of sheep and continue to shout and make a noise. On sunny days they would strip to the waist, lie on the grass, and hunt for lice in their shirts. They lit open-air fires and cooked lamb and rice in enormous cauldrons; sometimes they made halva with flour and suet. They killed sheep in the gypsy graveyard, hung them there to be cut up and skinned, sold the skins to the gypsies, and threw the entrails all over the place. Beggars, vagrants, and dogs would rush in and fight over the entrails, while the *asker* would look on and laugh. The whole place stank with their refuse. They ate with their fingers, seated on the ground, ten or so of them around the big tin cauldrons. In these same cauldrons they washed their underwear and shirts, then spread them over the grass and shrubs to dry. If they saw a female, whether a young girl or an old woman, they would howl, call after them in Turkish or an Arab language, and point at their crotch.

The population became even more terrified and locked themselves in their houses. No one ventured into the street. Makeshift gates were made in the courtyard and garden fences, so that neighbors could communicate without going into the street, or they could get to the fields and from there to Mocevac and other parts of the town.

After the army came the families of the officers. The Kojic houses were occupied again, but by tenants who could do as they pleased with them. They altered the apartments at will, without asking anyone's permission. On each floor they built washrooms, and they would knock holes in the walls and insert short pipes through which dirty water ran down the outside walls, across the courtyards and on to the street. They build lavatories next to the houses and screened the outer staircases with planks that reached all the way to the roof, so that no one could see their *hanumas* when they went to the lavatory. They set the amount of the rent, and paid when they wished and as much as they wished. Later, officers arrived from Istanbul, and there was more order in the army. The new tenants were tidier and behaved more decently, but no one mixed with them either, since not even the local Turks could understand their language, let alone the Serbs. Those who spoke Turkish could be counted on one hand, and they too found it difficult to accept the behavior and way of life of the newcomers, so they avoided them.

The frontier to Bosnia was closed, and all trade and road traffic ceased, not only in the direction of Sarajevo and further to Dubrovnik and Trieste, but also towards Salonika. Hardly anybody was allowed to travel even as far as Prijepolje, Nova Varosh, and Bijelo Polje, and all business stopped dead, both trade and crafts. Silversmiths, weavers, and skin and leather craftsmen were left without work. Life came to a total halt.

Janko locked himself in his house with his family and did not go out even when other people began to meet secretly and visit one another. He isolated himself, withdrew to his room, and never left it. He read, his brothers visited him and they talked, played cards, discussed politics, and so the days went by. At first the children too would go in and see him, but in accordance with his wishes, they did not stay long. Their presence always upset him, especially when Milena was taken in. She, more than the other children, made him feel sad because she was much younger than they and the very thought of her future pained and worried him. As time went by, he was more and more convinced that everybody would benefit when he was gone. He did not expect, and was no longer afraid, that the Turks would kill him, but he did not wish to go on living because it appeared to him that all his avenues were closed and there was no way out. Sorrow and indolence gradually took over, he relapsed into lethargy, stopped reading and talking, and refused to see even his brothers when they called.

Jelka was very worried by his frame of mind, but did not confide her concern to anyone. As Savka had weakened with age, she refrained from burdening her without grave necessity, and she did not wish to talk about Janko with anyone else. Hoping that he would recover once the conditions in Plevlje changed, she prayed to God to preserve his spirit until such time, and tried to drown her anxiety in work. There was a lot to do, as it was difficult to obtain servants because of the *asker*, and her only help was Dzema, who had been coming for years to weed the garden, clean the courtyard, fetch the water, sweep the street in front of the house, or scrub floors. Dzema was a small stocky woman with a face marked by smallpox, which she had contracted in childhood. Always in a good mood, she never asked for anything, but was content with whatever she was given. She was honest—if ducats were left about she would never take them— but she liked to boast or make things up, which sometimes annoyed Jelka, although Dzema meant no harm. Once, for instance, Jelka heard from a woman next door that Dzema was boasting in Mocevac how she had been baking baklava and pita for Jelka. This made Jelka angry, and next day, when Dzema came, she told her off.

"Why were you saying that you make my baklava, as if I were a cripple? And as if you knew how, when you have never seen a baklava in your home."

"Why do you mind that I said it, dear? Let them think that I did know how to make a baklava."

Jelka felt sorry, remembering that Dzema did not have much to show off about in her destitution. Her husband had become paralyzed years ago and she had to support him and the children with whatever she could earn in service and from what people gave her. Dzema always felt like a part of Jelka's family because Jelka helped and protected her, although she often gave her a good telling off if she did something stupid, like one time when Dzema told her she was pregnant.

"How can you be pregnant when your Huso has been paralyzed for so many years?"

"And how would you know whether a paralyzed man can make children or not? Yours was never paralyzed."

"You really are silly, poor soul, but everyone knows that. Unless someone has taken advantage of your stupidity."

Dzema blushed violently and said, "Really, Dada, you are doing me an injustice. Do you really think I would trample on my honor? Nobody's hand except Huso's has ever touched me, nor ever will."

"All right, Dzema, don't be angry, because it's your own fault. Pregnant, and your husband paralyzed! Don't talk so silly ever again. What else will people think but that you went astray with someone?"

"That had never occurred to me, God help me. I felt ashamed not having more children, and my youngest son is eight years old. All my friends, as soon as it's summer—here comes another child. That's why I wrapped something around my waist, pretending to be pregnant, and later I was going to say that I had had a miscarriage."

"My poor Dzema, what do you want more children for when you can hardly feed the ones you have, as your man is ill and doesn't work?"

"Still, however difficult it is for me to make ends meet, I would like more children. Every child has its own destiny and God is happy when more are being born. They say, when Muhammad was writing the Quran, he watched children playing, rolling and frolicking in the grass, and would sometimes leave the Quran to play with them, that's how much he loved children."

One day during those difficult times of the *asker*, when Dzema was doing the laundry, Jelka brought her coffee to the kitchen quarters and sat down to drink it with her. Worried and depressed, she smoked her cigarettes, and as she observed Dzema's sweating, pockmarked face, sloping shoulders, breasts that hung unsupported to her stomach, legs like trunks, fat and shapeless, and bare feet wide and square, with swollen toes, almost without nails, she asked herself how Dzema accepted her destiny with such grace. She never complained because her illness had disfigured her from childhood, her Huso was paralyzed, and she had to take on all the cares of feeding him and the children, keeping the house, and nursing him. Her children were beautiful and healthy, but Jelka had never seen Huso, so she asked, "Was your Huso handsome?"

"Yes, like a picture. Dark hair and neat, clipped black mustache. As a young man, he used to be all spruced up, fez at an angle, slender and spruce like a real gent."

"And were you pretty?"

"I don't know. I wasn't fat then, but my face was always pockmarked and my whole youth bitter. When I was young, I shed more tears than I drank water. All night long I used to cry, my pillow was wet with tears. They talked about love and I thought about it all the time, longed for it, but I couldn't hope, poor soul, that anyone would fall in love with me."

"Were you courting?"

"I did, but we covered our faces and I made sure to hide mine behind the veil. Young men used to come to our doors, but we stood behind them and so we chatted and amused ourselves. They begged us to open the shutters a little so they could see us, and we did. Some girls uncovered their eyes and face slightly, but I didn't dare do it and instead would bend down pretending to pick up a slipper or kerchief I had dropped, to show off my waist and my figure. What else could I do? That at least was beautiful."

"Did you marry Huso for love?"

"Yes, I fell so much in love with him that I could hear and recognize the sound of his footsteps from afar. My heart would always tell me, 'Here comes your Huso,' and it would start beating so wildly when I heard him approaching as if about to burst."

"So you did court and romance a lot with one another?"

"Oh, yes, I loved him more than my own mother, yet I fretted at the thought that he didn't know what my face looked like and imagined perhaps that I was a beauty, but once he saw it, if I married him, he would cool off and send me away. I thought of not marrying ever. Better to be an old spinster than to marry and slave for someone who did not desire me."

"Go on, Dzema, tell me about your wedding."

"I haven't got time, dear, gossiping away and all this washing waiting. You will say afterwards that I am lazy."

"How can I say you are lazy if I hold you up? Do tell me about it, let the washing wait."

Dzema made herself more comfortable, wiped the corners of her mouth with her hand and began: "Huso seems more and more persistent, always in front of my door and annoyed if other young men stop here. His cronies noticed this and because of him do not turn up any more; only he comes every evening. My friends tease me, but instead of being happy I fall only deeper into worry and sadness. I long for him more than ever, can't sleep all night long. As I work, he is always in front of my eyes. His words ring in my ears and if he says something especially nice to me, I hold on to it in my thoughts, repeat every word to myself again and again from beginning to end. I lose all my senses and my mother scolds me. 'What's the matter with you, you don't hear anything you are told. Someone has turned your head. Don't be like that, it isn't good to fall for any man. They hang around until they marry you and, having got what they wanted, start thinking about others, while the poor women die in fear and unhappiness. Don't let anyone steal your heart to wound it afterwards. Better be always wooden.' And I am thinking it is too late telling me now, my heart has flown away to Huso long ago, it seems to me I don't have it any more. I only hear its beating when he comes. Huso started begging me to lift the veil so he could see my eyes, but I pretend to be shy, to hide it because of our faith. My mother taught me so. 'If you don't like it,' I told him, 'go to those who unveil when begged.' That night I cried until dawn. I reproached Allah for disfiguring me so that I couldn't rejoice in my youth like my friends did. The next day Huso said, 'I am going to betroth you.' I stood still as if turned to stone. He went on, 'Will you take me? Do you love me a little at least?' I said that I would, and, overcome by tears, I quickly ran away. From then on until the marriage I despaired and worried about how to show him my face."

"But how did you go to the wedding? You must have had to unveil in front of the *hodja*."

"We don't attend the wedding service. Huso went to the *hodja* like everyone else does, told him that he was taking such and such a girl for a wife, paid him, and the *hodja* entered it in his book, gave Huso the marriage certificate and all was done. At the wedding feast the bride does not even see her man. He is in a separate room with the men and the bride with the women, that much you must know."

"How could I know when I never was at a Turkish wedding? What I am asking is how did he see your face?"

"Well, to tell you the truth, that moment when I unveiled my face was the most difficult for me." Dzema sighed. "As I sat with the women, I couldn't think of anything else. They joke, tease me, talk about the bridal chamber, but I am silent as if mute. Not a word, not even a sound. 'Look at her, she's in a trance, cannot wait to get to the mattress,' says one brazen hussy. She married a short while ago and became cheeky, doesn't know how wretched I am at the very thought of it. I am afraid, as a lamb is of the knife, that Huso may say when he sees me, 'Go away, freak, your face is like the bark of the oak tree,' and send me away. How could I face my friends afterwards? When the guests finally left, and the bridesmaids led me to Huso, I stopped by the door in the corner, petrified. What will happen now?

"The bridesmaids went out, Huso approached and took off my veil. I quickly covered my face with my hands, my heart bursting. Huso moved my hands aside, looked at me and said, 'Don't be bashful, love, you are my wife now.' I told him I was not bashful but afraid that he should see me, pockmarked as I am. He laughed and said gently, 'You think I didn't see you without a veil before? Once I was spying through your fence as you were weeding the vegetable bed in the garden and I saw your face as clearly as I see it now.' He holds my hand, draws closer, and my whole body is quivering, on fire so that I am burning, all the blood rushes to my heart as if it too is listening and stops me from breathing. As Huso goes on speaking, joy overwhelms me because he has found me pretty even then and wanted me as I am, pockmarked. 'You wore brightly patterned *dimije* trousers, a shirt, and a small jerkin. The tassels on your kerchief and the curls on your hair fell over your forehead, you leaned across the vegetable bed to reach some weeds and your jerkin opened, bursting under the fullness of your breast. You looked to me like a forest nymph. I fell in love with everything about you, your hair and eyes and neck and waist, and your face too became dear to me. You are beautiful to your Huso and no other can equal you, never mind better you.' He started kissing me, not even my mother had kissed me so, all over."

Dzema paused and sighed again deeply. "We were poor, but we had good times when we were young. He never said anything offensive to me, nor did he ever abuse me. And our children are healthy and good-looking like him. I was happier than any woman. Now he is ill and has become harsh. Keeps shouting at me, nothing is good enough for him, but I don't say anything. I feel sorry for him, poor soul. Day and night unable to move, and has had enough of the whole world. What can I do? Such is our *kismet*."

"Is he still good-looking?"

"No, dear, he has become thin as a rake, a far cry from the old

Huso. And I too have changed, I was not always such a hag. A hard life changes a person, not only in looks but one's nature too. Still, he is dear to me, he is my man, without him there'd be no children either. Thank Allah that I am healthy and can work. As long as I can last until we have set the children on the right path. I arranged for my eldest son to be apprenticed as a craftsman, and I'll do the same with the other two as soon as they finish the first four grades at school. I could do it before then, but I'd like the school to give them just a little education. I am fortunate there, learning comes easy to them." Having said that, she rose with a start. "I am wasting time, my dear, and will never be finished." As she turned to the trough to resume the washing, Jelka collected the cups, got up, and went out.

Janko was retreating further and further into himself and getting lost in his thoughts. He no longer talked with Jelka nor answered her questions, grew increasingly unaware of his surroundings and resigned himself to deep depression. This went on for days on end. Months went by, until finally his mind clouded.

Jelka had noticed this, but did not tell anyone. She hid it from her children and her mother, did not allow anyone to see him, and looked after him alone, bringing him food, tidying and cleaning the room, making the bed, dressing him, bathing and shaving him, and cutting his hair. For a while she hoped that he would return to his senses, but even when she realized that there was no change in him whatsover, she could not decide what to do for a long time. Finally, she asked Stevo to call. She took him to Janko's room, and left them alone to see whether he would notice anything, then waited by the door, shaking like a leaf. When Stevo came out, she said nothing, only looked at him searchingly. Stevo was worried and depressed. Both remained silent for a while, then she asked, "What do you think of Janko? How does he look to you?"

"Not well at all. He is not of sound mind. His brain has turned and that's a fact. He didn't even recognize me."

"What are we to do?"

"Cure him. It is an illness like any other, but we can't do anything now, nor can we take him anywhere. Say nothing and bear with him. Don't tell anyone because no one can help you. If you need anything, I am here. As long as my children are cared for, yours will be too."

"That won't be necessary, brother Stevo. I still have everything we need. But what am I to do about the way he is, for God's sake?"

"As I told you, keep quiet and wait. Something is brewing in Serbia and Montenegro, it could lead to a fight with the Turks."

"If only it would, God willing. Life can't go on as it is."

Stevo only sighed deeply and left. She saw him off, then, wretched and embittered, went to her mother to confide in her.

Savka was dumbfounded when she heard of Janko's condition. She sat, staring in front of her and swaying to and fro. Silence filled the room. After a long pause, Savka began, as if talking to herself, "My child, your misfortune is great and all my wisdom too small to advise you. I feel sorry for him, poor soul, more than for you. You are clever and sensible, your spirit is strong, and as long as God keeps your children well, you will be able to manage better than some men. But for him, God would do more good by taking his life if already he has taken his mind. There is no cure for such affliction. They used to take those who suffered from it to the Ostrog and Mileshevo monasteries, and the priests would anoint them and read prayers, but I never heard that they cured anyone." Tears ran down her face, but she continued as if lamenting, as if unaware of them and of Jelka's presence: "How could this happen to him who was like a father to the poor? He bought those huts in the gypsy quarter, next to the ground where he wanted to build the hotel, but couldn't throw the gypsies on to the street and pull the huts down. He let them stay there for nothing and kept giving them things. They know he is kindhearted and keep taking advantage. If a child is born, they come running. 'Master Janko, I've got a new baby and the wife has nothing to eat, how is she going to feed it?' So he gives. Another one comes, his father died and he has no means to bury him, so Janko gives again. And how generous he was to the prisoners at Easter and Christmas. His men would take loaded baskets to the jail. He overlooked no one, but remembered each, either with a bottle of *mastika*, some meat, buns, a packet of cigarettes, or money. And how he looked after me, if I'd had a son of my own he couldn't have done as much. I kept blessing him always, yet look what has befallen him." She wiped away her tears absentmindedly as she went on lamenting, "Dear God, what has happened and how can this be? I haven't laid eyes on a cleverer man in my whole life, and that his mind should turn. Still, God's ways are mysterious, who are we to interfere with His design?"

This infuriated Jelka. Exasperated by the fears and pain she had managed to endure until now, she snapped at her mother, "Leave it, for heaven's sake. I have enough trouble to bear, and you keep mentioning things that stick in my heart like knives. On top of that, you now start on about God and His mysterious ways. What were His mysterious ways when He took Vaso and Chedo from me? What are His ways now, that He should let this misfortune descend on me? God forgive me, but He doesn't know what He is doing."

"Don't, my dearest, don't sin. God alone knows what He is doing. If He doesn't, there would be no sun, or stars, or this beautiful earth we are on, and we would live forever in senseless darkness. He also sends us happiness and consolation for the sorrow we have to bear."

"All my suffering is from Him too! Stop it, Mother, if you can't help, don't add to my troubles. Since you have grown old you appear to have become senile."

"Don't, my child, you are upset so you offend even me. I won't be here forever and you will be sorry." With a resigned gesture Savka went to her room.

Jelka would have regretted it before if she had said this to her mother, but now she felt no remorse; life had become hateful to her and she grew coarse and insensitive.

Until that time, Savka had accepted her fate humbly. "It was so preordained," she thought, and put up with everything, but this last blow to Jelka killed her. She languished, and became gaunt and shrunken, until one day she took to her bed. Her illness was brief. She neither moaned nor complained, but silently endured her suffering. She died quietly, as she had lived. They dressed her in her blue wedding dress and buried her modestly, because the *asker* oppressed Plevlje like a plague.

Jelka did not mourn her mother too much, although she knew that with her death she had lost her best friend. Janko's misfortune obsessed her to the point that she no longer expected anything good from life, and it seemed to her that death had freed Savka from some long and hopeless suffering. And troubles gathered on every side. She fretted for Niko because she had heard nothing from him for a long time, as letters were not getting through any more, nor could anyone cross the frontier. The income from the houses was meager, not even sufficient to cover the cost of repairs, and their capital was dwindling.

Djana was well off but burdened with worries and hard work, she could not leave Ilino Hill for months. Marija lived nearby but had small children, born in close succession. Her responsibilities were great and her husband, Petronije, was so jealous that she was only allowed out to attend Savka's funeral. Otherwise he forbade her to visit Jelka because of the Turkish officers who lived in her houses. The three other daughters had reached marriageable age, and Jelka had to prepare them, assemble their trousseau, think about suitors— yet she did not dare let them out of the house. Locked in like captives, they could not go to the gate or into the courtyard without being accosted by Turkish officers who would start to wink at them and misbehave. Milena was not enrolled in school. She had been raised in the shadow of sorrow and uncertainty. Since birth, her health had been frail. During the first few months she cried day and night, so that the servants had to keep rocking her cradle continually because she would not sleep otherwise. Jelka had thought that she would die, and was resigned to this, as the child would have been relieved from torment. When she quietened down a little and it became clear that she would survive, they started worrying because she was so tiny and unable to walk for a long time, so they called a doctor to examine her. He said that the child was underdeveloped and needed more care, having been born when Jelka was no longer young, but as her constitution was basically strong, she would recover if they gave her the food he prescribed and plenty of exposure to the sun. After that, probably because her conscience reproached her for having in her distress neglected Milena, Jelka began to devote more time to her, despite all her worries. She bathed her in infusions of walnut leaves, laid her naked in the sun, prepared special food for her, and taught her to stand. Milena gained strength quickly and began to walk, but remained small and sensitive. She was prettier than the other children of the family, bright and lively.

Her sisters loved her, looked after her and dressed her well; they braided her hair into plaits before putting her to bed, and in the morning combed it out so that it fell in waves down her back, held in place by a ribbon. As she could not go to school because of the *asker*, her sisters taught her to write and do sums, read fairy tales and recited poetry to her. She was mainly with grownups, except when they took her to Mocevac or sent her to Ilino Hill to play with her older sister's children. They seldom let her out into the court-yard or on the street, to stop her from mixing with the children of the Turkish officers, but she sometimes escaped, longing for the company of her own age, and learned to say a few words in their language.

In those bleak times of hopelessness, it seemed to Jelka that any-thing at all would be better, no matter what, as long as there was some change. Before, she had been young and strong, and was pro-pelled forward by nature itself, but now she was afraid of being over-taken by hard events. As she was sitting in the garden and reflecting on this, Ahmet, their former servant, appeared at the gates. Jelka was pleased to see him because he had worked for Janko for a long time and all the family looked upon him as a kind of relative.

"I hear the master is ill," he began from the gateway, "and that you have no man working for you. So I came to help out if you need me."

"You've come at a time when we need you most. Thank you for remembering us."

"Of course I do, mistress. I earned good money in your home and had I not married, I'd never have left."

Jelka led him into the house and asked him to sit down. "Well, how are you? How is your wife?"

"She is dead, may she rest in peace. We have had a good life to-gether and since she died I feel as if the whole world had died with her. I'm left alone like a withered branch."

"Did you have any children?"

"No, we were each other's only family, that's why I find it so diffi-cult. When one is young, one can easily replace a wife, but there is no greater sorrow than losing your wife in old age. I can't find peace at home, that's why I come to offer my services, if only for food, and if there is a space for me to sleep, to have a roof over my head."

"Of course there is, in a house of this size. You will have everything you need and we'll pay you what you ask."

"Whatever you can spare will be enough for me. I am not able to work as I used to any more. One gets older and strength runs out."

"It is enough if you run an occasional errand to the Charshija, chop some wood, and lend a hand in the garden and courtyard, or clean the cowshed and take the cows to the cowherd. Everything would help."

"That much I can do."

"You'll work as much as you feel able, Ahmet, you're welcome here." She got up to show him the small house in the backyard where the servants used to live.

Soon after she had seen to Ahmet, Stevo arrived in a whirl of excitement and told her that the war had started. Serbia and Montenegro had risen against the Turks. Jelka lit up with delight, even though she was afraid that the Turks might now retaliate against the population.

"Let something happen, if only for the worse," she whispered, crossing herself. "This life is not worth living."

Stevo warned her not to talk to anyone and advised her to stockpile as much food as she could, because it might be impossible to leave the house if it should come to a battle for Plevlje. He refused to stop for a drink and went to call at a few more houses before dark.

By the following day the news that the Balkan war had broken out was all over the town. Everybody was relieved at the thought that freedom was close, even if it meant dying for it. The whole town stirred and was transformed by expectation. People began to call on each other at night through the network of garden passages, spreading the news. Jelka's daughters, Gordana, Sofija, and Nevenka, assembled all the young girls from the Hill at their home and arranged for them to make national flags for the day of liberation, and then distribute them secretly through the town, to be hidden in various houses in case the Turks should notice anything.

Jelka hoped that the tidings of freedom might raise Janko's spirits and she tried to talk to him every time she entered his room, but he just stared absently at her, lost in his world. Seeing him like that, she too was unable to rejoice, because she knew how much he had suffered from their enslavement and that, only a few months earlier, the news of the liberation would have prevented his illness. She tried to occupy her thoughts by preparing stocks of food, should the fighting be prolonged, and quenched her sorrow in work.

Less than a week had gone by when, just before sunset, a neighbor rushed in to announce the arrival of Jelka's daughter from Ilino Hill. Jelka went to the gate and saw Djana approaching on a horse, holding her newborn son on her lap. Behind her, on a horse led by a servant, were her two daughters. Jelka felt more frightened than pleased to see them. She took the child from Djana and helped her dismount. They took the girls down too but sent the man back with the horses so that he should reach home in daylight.

When they went in and had locked the door behind them, Jelka asked, "Where is the priest?"

"He has escaped to join the rebellion in Montenegro, and taken with him the villagers from Greb and Mrzovic."

"And your mother-in-law?"

"I sent her with one of the godparents to my sister-in-law in Dzevair."

"Will the servants look after your house?"

"They are too afraid of the Turks, so I told them to run if they see any danger, and leave everything."

"What will happen to the livestock?"

"Never mind the livestock, let it all perish as long as we save our heads and Rade reaches Montenegro alive. I worry about him most."

By then Nevenka had come down. She embraced Djana and the children and said that her sisters had gone to Stevo to hear if there was any more news. Milena too ran in, overjoyed by the arrival of her cousins. They all helped Djana to make herself and the children more comfortable, Jelka sent Nevenka to get Ahmet and prepare the rooms for the guests with him, and she went to bring refreshments. Gordana and Sofija arrived before dinner, bubbling with excitement and bringing word that there would be no fighting for Plevlje. Stevo had told them in confidence that the *askers* and the Osmanli Turks would leave the town without any resistance and the local Turks would take over power and protect the Serbs should the *askers* intend to commit reprisals before leaving.

Fear and hopes merged in those turbulent times and every day brought changes. Secret donations were being collected for welcoming the liberators, and there was talk that the money came not only from the Serbs but also from the Turks, and that Omerbeg had promised to contribute three hundred sheep to be slaughtered on the arrival of the Serbian troops. The families of the Turkish officers departed and the Kojic houses were vacated. Jelka locked the gates of the upper houses and Ahmet nailed them up; they also secured the lower gates with iron hinges. No one left the house, not even as far as the fountain, and water from the well was drunk instead, although it was hard and used for cooking and washing too. Fear reigned until the *asker* left. They could be heard preparing and finally departing, but no one dared to go out of the house. A deathy silence spread over the town: not a soul stirred.

A day later, at midnight, Janko's sister Stojana somehow crept up to the house to tell them the rumor that Father Rade had been killed. Some Turk was boasting all over the town that he had killed him and that he was wearing the priest's habit to prove it.

"The lying dog!" Jelka cut her short angrily. "They plundered their home and he stole the habit and put it on."

Djana turned pale and burst into tears.

Jelka did not invite Stojana to sit down, and as soon as she had seen her off began to scold Djana in whispers. "Why do you cry and mourn for a living person? Don't listen to what the Turks have made up, they are feeling vindictive because he slipped away, and on top of that he took so many villagers with him. Calm yourself and look after your children. Don't you see that something is afoot tonight? Who knows what happens to us all?"

That night neither of them could close an eye. Djana did not stop crying, though softly so as not to disturb the children. And Jelka, unable to hide her anxiety, kept going out to look around, on the pretext of being afraid that someone might start a fire.

And the night was long, as if dawn would never come.

9

Before sunrise, footsteps were heard on the street. Jelka stole to the gate in her stockinged feet and looked through a knot-hole in the shutters. She listened. She could hear voices but they were faint and growing fainter. She waited a little, and then a man passed by on the other side of the street. She could not see him but she heard a voice calling, "A Serbian army has entered Prijepolje and is heading towards Plevlje." She ran into the house, beside herself with joy. "Get up everybody! Freedom is coming, thank merciful God, the Serbian army is arriving!"

They all rushed out and began to embrace one another. Only Djana burst out crying.

"My Rade is not coming. I know now that he has been killed. If he were alive he would have found a way of sending me a message."

Jelka took her aside. "How could he send you word when no one dared to leave the village? And who knows where he is in Montenegro? Don't be upset, my dear, this day has been awaited for five hundred years." She turned to the others, and said excitedly, "Let's tidy up and get ready. People will be pouring out to celebrate with one another."

Just then a loud knocking was heard at the gates, and she hurried to open them. The youth who stood there was panting and covered in perspiration.

"Welcome with good tidings," Jelka greeted him. "Are you announcing the arrival of our army? Blessed be their way."

"Yes, I came to say that the reception will be on Trlica Hill. Everybody should come, especially young folk, pupils, and all the other children."

"Wait, let me get you a gift for the good news, and some flowers."

"I have no time," the youth smiled, and went on to spread his news from door to door.

Jelka and her daughters hurriedly put on their festive clothes and started dressing Milena and Djana's daughters so that they too could go to welcome the army. Only Djana was still crying. When she saw that her children were about to leave with Milena, she tried to stop them. "Mine won't go, their father is dead."

Jelka became annoyed. "Don't upset the children, in God's name. Don't tempt providence when you don't know whether he has been killed. If it is true, there will be time enough for crying, for you and for them. Don't mar this day, and spoil other people's joy." A sigh escaped her as she spoke. "If only my husband had been fortunate enough to fall in this war instead of being tormented as he is." That morning, carried away by the good news, she had gone to his room and said, "Get up, Janko, our freedom has come, you always longed for it and have lived to see it," but he remained silent. As she remembered this, tears flooded her eyes, but she stopped herself from crying and addressed Djana in a milder voice. "I have told you to relax and hope. You should dress and go out among the people, it would help. If Janko were not in such a condition, I would go too. Look out of the window. Everybody is on the move, old and young. Why don't you go too, my dear? Put yourself in God's hands."

Joyous voices and songs reached them from everywhere. The day was sunny and warm, mellow with autumn. Jelka went from one room to another, opening wide all the windows so that the new bliss and new fortune would enter with the sunshine. She was once more gripped by the irresistible feeling of hope and joy which she had experienced only in her youth, and she kept telling herself, "Niko will come back to me now and everything will be well again. With God's help Janko will recover soon. There'll be no more fear, no more oppression."

Milena went out with her cousins Magda and Dobrila. The entrance gates were wide open and people were coming into their garden and stepping over the circular flower bed to pick armfuls of flowers. She could not understand why Mother allowed it, and instead of telling them off, laughed and called out of the window, "Good day and good luck to you."

When she went into the street, she was stunned: never before had she seen so many people, such a crowd. They were shouting to one another, embracing and kissing as if in a trance. Near her an old man was crawling, dragging his paralyzed legs and supporting himself on his arms. From time to time he would stop to make a sign of the cross and kiss the ground, repeating all along, "Thank you, Lord, for letting me live to see this day." He cried with joy as he continued to crawl down the rocky side of Dubure.

In this heaving multitude, Milena could not find her bearings and work out which way to go with her cousins, as none of them knew Trlica or where it was situated. Eventually they headed for the Barracks, following the people going in that direction. When they reached the Barracks, they continued alongside the Turkish cemetery toward Jalija. Suddenly someone shouted, "Here they come!" Everybody moved out of the way, to the other side of the ditch, next to the cemetery fence. By then, the thunder of horses' hoofs had reached them. Some fifty riders approached at a gallop, dressed in tan uniforms, with cartridge belts across their chests and shotguns on their shoulders. On their heads were Montenegro-style caps. The man at the head carried a tricolor flag.

People began to cheer. "Long live the heroes! Long live the liberators!"

The riders joyously responded, "Happy freedom to you, brothers!" and hurtled by like a gust of wind.

People stared after them with admiration and someone said, "I saw Father Rade from Ilino Hill."

"I recognized him too," added another.

238

"Some of our villagers from across the river are with them."

"Yes, they got away to join the Montenegro uprising. Those are the guerrillas, then! Well done, they entered first!"

"The Montenegro army may be close behind them and could arrive before the Serbians. They are nearer and can cut across the Hill while the Serbs march in formation. Good luck to them both!"

Only now did people seem fully to comprehend the actuality of the day; everyone was even more overwhelmed by joy, caught in a wave of excitement and hurry.

Magda and Dobrila wanted to return home to tell Mother that someone had seen their father, but they changed their minds and went after the riders to look for him. Milena continued with the crowd. Every living soul seemed to be racing towards the Charshija. From every house, street, and lane, people appeared and merged into a multitude which flowed like a broad river through the Charshija towards Varosh and Trlica. They stopped at the foot of Trlica and began to line up on both sides of the road. In the front row stood the schoolchildren, with teachers from the elementary and high schools; beside them young girls dressed all in white and with big bouquets of flowers in their arms; opposite them Serbian and Turkish representatives of the town; and next to them priests with tall headdresses and turbaned *hodjas*. Behind the organized line-up, people spread over the fields and pastures on one side and climbed the steep incline to Trlica on the other.

Milena stepped onto a large flat rock and looked around her, mesmerized, over the sea of heads. They waited for a long time and she grew impatient—her legs ached and she felt tired. She wanted to return home, but did not know how she would make her way through such a crowd. Before her the empty road wound upwards like a white snake climbing Trlica. Suddenly from behind a bend appeared a gray line of soldiers. Everything stirred. People began to shout and cheer, a song burst out, all order disappeared. The teachers and supervisors shouted and pleaded, and somehow, with great effort, they managed to restore the line-up. Milena could not take her eyes off the gray mass that flooded down the road while from around the bend a new contingent emerged, forming a new line. As the army drew nearer, the individual soldiers could be singled out.

Everybody went mad with joy. People were kissing one another, or throwing their caps in the air. Many burst into tears. The songs intermingled: "A Serb is a willing soldier . . ." beamed from one side of the road and "Wounded on the battlefield . . ." from the other. Milena knew the first song and she too started singing, shouting at the top of her voice as if she would thus express all the excitement she felt, the immeasurable joy and elation. From all sides flowers fell on the soldiers, as if the sky had shed a rain of petals. The air resounded with "Long live the Serbian army! Long live King Petar!"

As they reached the crowd, the officers dismounted and greeted the teachers and the town representatives in the first row. Young girls ran to their horses to adorn them with flowers and stroke their necks. Milena spotted the old man she had seen in front of her house as he crawled by the side of the road, avoiding the horses' hoofs and raising his hands to bless the soldiers. Intoxicating mirth flooded the entire crowd. Only on the faces of the soldiers did not one feature move, as the sweat ran down their stern countenaces. Sunburnt and covered by white dust, they marched several to a row, erect under their full military equipment, with rucksacks on their backs and guns at their shoulders. From their hips hung short shovels. The sound of their boots resounded on the stone-paved road, and it seemed to Milena that it echoed in her chest. People set off together with the soldiers. Milena joined them and instinctively began to march to the rhythm of the drums. Her ears rang with the songs, cheers, and drumbeats. She was heady with a strange, all-embracing happiness that she had not known before. They proceeded down the Charshija, then along Jalija and behind the Turkish cemetery to Pekara. Then the people were told to turn back, while the soldiers continued towards Bogishevac.

Milena, together with the other children, followed the army. At the foot of Bogishevac the soldiers were ordered to fall out. They relaxed, lowered and stacked their rifles, took the knapsacks off their backs and laid them on the ground, unstrapped their shovels and sat down on the grass exhausted. Someone said that the Montenegrin army had already pitched camp at the top of Bogishevac. All the children, Milena amongst them, set off to see them. On their way they encountered groups of Montenegrin officers walking down toward the Serbian army. They too wore gray uniforms but their caps were of Montenegro style, though made of the same material, and with metal badges of a winged eagle. Milena saw Magda and Dobrila as they slowly headed for home, and she ran to catch up with them. Tired and disappointed because they could not find their father, they told her that they were going back to let their mother know that he was alive. As they talked, they heard someone calling them by name and turned round. Father Rade was coming towards them, dressed in officer's uniform, except that instead of the eagle he wore a cross on his cap. Magda and Dobrila ran to embrace him, crying with joy. He picked them both up in his arms and started kissing them.

"Mother thinks that you were killed and she cries all the time," Magda whispered through tears.

He put them down, kissed Milena too and said joyfully, "Go quickly and tell her you saw me and that I will be coming this evening. I am on duty now."

The three of them flew down the hill as if on wings, racing with one another to reach the house first, and from the gates began to shout that they had seen Father Rade.

Djana came down the stairs. Her legs gave way and she sat on the lowest step, holding on to the banister. "Perhaps you just imagined it. Did you speak with him?"

"Yes, Mama, he kissed us and said he'll be coming this evening."

Milena was overcome by exhaustion and happiness. To her, the first day of liberation, as she had experienced it, represented the absence of fear and sorrow, freedom to mix with people and go wherever she liked, crowds and song and excitement. Now she only wished to lie down, no matter where. She could not wait for dinner, nor was she feeling hungry, although she had had nothing to eat all day. Drunk with joy, she fell asleep the moment her head touched the pillow.

She was awakened by the rays of the morning sun, which pierced the foliage of the quince tree in front of her window and spilled over the arabesques of the carpet. A murmur of voices filled the house. Magda and Dobrila, already dressed, rushed in to tell her that a dinner reception was being arranged in their house for the Serbian and Montenegrin officers. She too dressed and they went down for breakfast. Old Marta, the celebrated cook, was already in the kitchen preparing the dishes. The children had always found her amusing because she would allow them to hang around and ask questions while she rolled out the dough, or told them stories in a way no one else did, in riddles, as it were, posing questions and answering them herself. Milena enjoyed watching her as she worked, quick and skillful despite her stoutness. She wore a shirt held in at the waist by the belt of her ample *dimije* trousers, and a jerkin fastened under her breasts, which sprawled all over it like masses of dough. Around her graying hair was tied a fine thin kerchief. Her ears were large and flattened to the head, torn open at the lobes from the long wear of heavy earrings.

As there was great commotion in the house, the children headed for the town, where the celebrations continued, *kolos* were being danced, and songs and music resounded throughout the day. When evening came and the sun began to sink behind the mountaintops, they returned home, tired and hungry.

In the visitors' room stood tables covered with starched cloths and already set for dinner. Everybody was festively dressed, even the maids who were there to help serve. The guests were expected at any time and Milena and her cousins were immediately sent to the room facing the garden, with a warning that they would be locked in if they peeped through the door or ran into the corridor. The girls sat on the broad sill of the window that overlooked the flight of steps, lifted the curtain and watched the guests arriving. They were being welcomed by Father Rade and Djana, who stood on the landing, and in the entrance hall by Jelka. Sounds of men's voices and laughter reached them from the visitors' room.

When it was time to sit at table, the maids began to carry full tureens, bowls, and platters into the small room next door where Sofija, Nevenka, and Gordana supervised the serving round the table. Everything went smoothly. Only the children were forgotten and did not get even their usual dinner. The first to rebel was Dobrila, being freer and more independent than the other children. "What cheek is this? For us nothing, and they are having a feast in there!" Seeing that Milena and Magda did not dare do anything about it, she shot out like a cannonball, ran into the small room and emptied a platter of *burek* into her pinafore. All three sat on the carpet and ate the whole lot, then, full up and contented, wiped their hands on their pinafores, undressed and squeezed into the same bed. They listened to the distant sound of voices mixed with songs and the music of a *gusle* until they fell fast asleep.

For Jelka this was a sad evening, although it was considered a great honor that her home had been chosen as one of the first to give a reception for the liberators. It hurt her that Janko, the head of the family, was not present, and she felt that she had somehow done him an injury by allowing others to be entertained in his home while he dwelt in timeless sorrow. Several times during the evening she went to his room, offered him various dishes and tried to start some conversation, but he remained remote as always. Only for an instant, when he heard the sound of the *gusle*, did he smile and say the one word "*gusle* . . .," but then he retreated again into his desolate world. Father Rade and Marija's husband, Petronije, were acting as hosts and she had not refused the honor shown to her for fear of upsetting them, because she was hoping to send Janko for treatment as soon as possible and to establish contact with Niko through them. They were now more influential than Stevo even. New times belong to the new generation and she set store by the folk proverb, "Anger not those you have to beg for favors."

The day after the reception, Jelka asked her sons-in-law to bring the army doctor to see Janko, which they did straight away. The doctor established that the patient needed hospital care and should be sent to the specialist in Belgrade. Petronije took him there, entered him into the hospital as a war victim, and stayed for a few days to see how he was being treated. Everyone began to hope that Janko would be cured, as he was now under the supervision of doctors, especially as Jelka started receiving regular reports of his slow recovery. They informed her that he was regaining his sanity from time to time, although the cure was hampered by his lack of desire to live and his continued refusal of food.

Father Rade was demobilized immediately after the liberation and went to Ilino Hill to see what was left of the house and the estate and whether he could take his family there. When the villagers and the servants heard that he was back, they gathered around him, bringing the horses and cattle they had managed to save for him, and some of the furniture, carpets, and bedding which they had hidden in their own homes. The rest had been plundered, the granary emptied, the hay set on fire, and the house ruined but not burnt down. He found among the villagers a few builders who could repair some of the rooms well enough to provide sleeping and cooking facilities, then went to collect Djana and their children. Before their departure they christened their son in the monastery and named him Slobodan, from the Serbian word for freedom.

Milena pined when her cousins left, as she was once more alone with grown-up sisters, but after a short time the school reopened and she entered the first grade. This was a big event: in her eyes it introduced change into the entire home, and made her suddenly the most important member of the family. Petronije bought her a satchel, an alphabet, and a black slate, their shoemaker Pajic made her a new pair of lace-up shoes, and her sisters a new dress. On the eve of her first day at school, she could not eat dinner for excitement and asked to be bathed and put to bed earlier in order to get more quickly through the night. But she could not fall asleep for fear of oversleeping and being late for school. "Better if I say a prayer for God to wake me early," she thought, and got up, lifted the curtain and tucked it behind her sister's bed on the other side of the window, then began to cross herself. It occurred to her that God might still not see her properly in the semi-darkness, so she turned up the flame of the lamp, knelt beside it, asked Him not to let her be late, and went to bed. Still she could not fall asleep, and she reached for the satchel which was propped up against the foot of the bed. Although that day she had looked again at everything that had been bought for her to put inside it, she once more took out the slate, black with red lines and framed in white wood, with a yellow porous sponge attached. Having glanced through the alphabet book with colored pictures, she became interested in the pencil box, with its separate compartment and a real lock with a small key. Inside it were two sticks of chalk wrapped in colored paper. Carefully, she put everything in the satchel and placed it beside the bed. Still she was afraid of being late. She imagined that God would be coming from Trlica, because the sun rose behind it, and by the time He woke up all the children He might be late in reaching her house. "Just in case, I'd better get dressed now," she thought and got up, put on her dress, her new stockings and shoes, and returned to bed.

When they found her next morning, they had to take off her clothes and iron her dress, but instead of telling her off they teased her until they realized she was in tears, partly because of hurt pride, but also from excitement and anxiety. They had to force her to eat some breakfast, combed out the many plaits of her hair and let it tumble from a big bow tied at the nape of her neck, all the way down to her waist, then they let her go. Ahmet waited for her in the courtyard and accompanied her to the school, which lay at the other end of Mocevac. As soon as she heard children's voices and shrieks in the distance, she tried to pull her hand out of Ahmet's rough hold, but he did not release her until they entered the school playground.

Pupils from all grades were waiting in the playground for the teachers to order them into their allotted classrooms. Not knowing anyone, Milena stood by the steps not far from a fair-haired girl in a black satin pinafore with frills piped with blue ribbon. The girl approached and asked Milena what her name was, then told her that she was called Svetlana and that she lived in School Lane next to the high school. They liked each other and decided to sit at the same desk. When the bell rang, the teacher of the first year came out, took them away from the other pupils, lined them up two by two and led them to the classroom. She was tall and young, with her hair combed into a bun, dressed in a white blouse and long black skirt reaching all the way to the ground. Her black shoes, buttoned on the side, could only be seen when she walked. During the first lesson she told them how to behave now that they had become pupils, to speak softly when in school and only when they asked them to, not to run, jump, or chase one another in the corridors and, when they were out in the street, to make way for grownups and greet them. She then taught them a prayer which they all repeated after her like a choir. During break, she led them to the playground, arranged them in a circle and showed them how to dance a *kolo*, two steps right, one left, then afterwards played with them the "cat and mouse" game. One of the pupils was a cat and had to chase the mouse, but all the others formed a ring round them, holding hands and letting the mouse through whilst they blocked the way for the cat. The teacher changed places in the ring and when she stopped next to her, Milena thought she was holding the hand of someone holy.

From the first day Milena loved school, her teacher, and Svetlana. She enjoyed all her lessons, but was most interested in learning folk stories, poetry, and Bible stories. The Bible seemed too sad to her, however, and she could not understand some of it, so she often interrupted her teacher with questions. "Why did God have to drown so many people in the flood? Why did He not teach them to be good?" When she heard that Christ was a Jew, she burst into tears. "Please, Miss, you made a mistake, he was a Serb." The more she thought about religion, the more difficult it was for her to believe that God was merciful and omnipotent, as He could not save His own son but had allowed him to be crucified. She participated widely in other subjects too, and suggested easier solutions for some problems. It appeared to her unnecessary to learn geography by naming all the hills and mountains around Plevlje. "Why not write its name in white stones on every hill? Then everyone would know what the hill is called." She did all her homework easily and quickly, except that she had no patience for some, and her sisters would secretly finish her needlework or copy for her pages of straight and diagonal lines, as her arm ached all the way to her shoulder from such efforts, which she considered to be just a waste of time.

That year Milena looked forward with trepidation to the feast of St. John the Evangelist, because it was believed that on the eve of his day the Saint called on all good schoolchildren and tied around their wrists the red and gold thread with which embroidery was done, to encourage them in their learning and help them to become as good a storyteller as he. Those children who were lazy or had soiled their mouths with curses or bad words, the Saint did not mark with gold and silk. Milena spent a sleepless night in tense expectation, determined to see St. John with her own eyes, continually drifting into sleep and waking up in fear of not hearing him come, or being missed out. Before dawn she heard footsteps approaching up the stairs. Her heart fluttered as she frantically listened to the footsteps coming along the corridor, the door of her room opening . . . Not daring to see the Saint eye to eye, she pulled the cover over her head and froze. The footsteps approached her bed and someone carefully lifted the cover. Before her stood her mother holding the box in which she kept the threads and the gold for embroidery.

Milena began to cry with disappointment. "I don't want you to tie my wrist if St. John did not come."

Her mother was upset too that Milena had seen her and began to comfort her. "Listen, my love, you are clever and I can tell you that it is the mothers who tie the wrists of all children. We only say that the Saint does it."

"Why do you deceive us? I'll tell all the other children."

"Let them go on believing, but if you don't want me to, I won't do it for you any more, as you already know."

From then on this custom was not kept in their home, and Milena, although she never mentioned it to anyone, began to doubt the mysterious power of the saints.

After she started school, Milena's relations with her sisters also changed, and she became more independent. They continued to look after her and spoil her, but they would sometimes ask her to run an errand for them, unknown to Jelka, who was so strict that everyone except Milena was a little afraid of her. On St. George's Day, the following spring, they sent her without Jelka's knowledge to bring them *omaya*, magic water, because they would have been embarrassed if anyone knew that they, educated girls, believed in magic of such a kind.

St. George's Day was a holiday celebrated by everybody, Serbs, Turks, and gypsies. The whole town looked festive, clean, almost bathed, as if the houses, gardens, and streets had been washed. Young people especially celebrated it, as it was the day of spring, love, and health. Milena liked it most because of *omaya*, the ancient custom in which everybody participated and which added a mystical, fairy-tale quality to this holiday. St. George's Day falls on May 6, when everything is in flower, and the sun shines warmer, rises higher and throws more light on the town and the hills that surround it.[7] On the eve of the holiday the slaughtered lambs and various pastries were taken to the Pekara to be cooked, the flower gardens were weeded and tidied, the courtyards swept, the grass growing between the cobblestones in front of each house pulled up, and everyone cleaned his part of the street with a birch broom. Walls were whitewashed, carpets beaten, new dresses made or old ones remade. Everything was ready, clean, and tidy, with the fresh scent that nature has in spring. In the evening, around *aksham*, people went to the watermills by Citluk, where the water was drawn from under the big wheel of the first mill, and various herbs and flowers put in it before it was taken home to be placed under a rose bush, where it stayed overnight. At dawn, before sunrise, young girls washed their faces or bathed in it to gain health, beauty, or good fortune in love. People believed that during the night *omaya* acquired a magic power from the plants and herbs that had been soaked in it: the new shoots of the flowering willow to give a girl a willow waist; a slip of dogwood for good health; a piece of yule log for firmness; leaves of agrimony for the tenderness and sweetness of its flower; a few roses to color her cheeks; leaves of elecampane to turn the heads of her young men; violets for the scent; and many other plants and various herbs. Milena's sisters gave her a pitcher and explained where to go and what she should bring back, so she set off, flattered and proud to have been entrusted with such an important task. She caught up with some Mocevac women who were going towards the river carrying jugs and asked them to show her which plants she should get.

"Who are you getting *omaya* for? What family are you from?"

"I'm the daughter of Janko Kojic and I want the *omaya* for my sisters."

"And why didn't they come for it, those fine ladies? Too educated, I suppose."

"No, it's just that they have too much to do."

The women gave her a few plants and directed her towards the monastery plum orchard where several willows grew by the fence. There was already a crowd of people there, pushing, shouting to each other, arguing and fighting for the willow shoots which some youths were cutting off the trees and throwing down. Milena did not manage to get through, but she begged the women around her for a few shoots. They also gave her various herbs, flowers, and chips of wood, so she collected in her pinafore everything she needed for *omaya*. She now had to cross a long narrow plank over the river and give her pitcher to the men who stood waist-deep in the water and filled the vessels from under the very wheel of the watermill. Gingerly she made a few steps. Under her roared and surged the green waters of the mountain river. The plank began to flex under her feet, fear gripped her, and she turned back. She watched the river rush past her, the water under the wheel raging and foaming, and, not knowing what to do next, sat down on the bank.

After a while a tall boy came up. "Do you want me to fetch *omaya* for you?"

"Yes, I do." She cheered up. "If you can take it from under the wheel, otherwise it is no good."

"Don't you worry," said the boy, took her pitcher and disappeared into the crowd.

He returned soon after with a full pitcher. "Here, I fetched it from the foaming stream at the bottom of the wheel, it is real *omaya*," he said and was gone.

Milena carefully put all the plants, leaves, flowers, and pieces of wood inside and started for home. The tips of the long willow shoots reached above her shoulder as she walked cautiously, trying not to spill the water or lose any plants, feeling grown up and impatient to reach home.

On the way she met her cousin Misho, the son of her late aunt Pava. "Whose pitcher is that?" he asked, alarmed.

"Mine, I am taking *omaya* to my sisters."

"You poor thing, why did you give it to Rakura? He pissed into it, I saw it with my own eyes."

Milena's heart sank as if someone had hit her over the head, as if something holy had been desecrated. She had lost face in front of her sisters, in front of everybody. In a fit of rage, she poured everything out of the pitcher and started banging it against the stony ground. When she realized how scratched and dented it had become, she sat down in the middle of the road and began to cry and pull her hair.

People gathered around, asking her whose child she was, but she was ashamed to say for fear of dishonoring her mother. Just then some of their neighbors approached. They lifted her, wiped the tears from her face, and smoothed her disheveled hair. "Don't cry," they comforted her, "we'll give your sisters some of our own *omaya*. We carry two jugs each." She went with them, and all along the way tears came to her eyes at the thought of the dented pitcher and her disgrace. When she reached the gates of her home, she started crying at the top of her voice. Jelka ran out, and when Milena told her what had happened, she took her in her arms, trying to calm her. "You fool, why didn't you bring those fine ladies the *omaya*, piss and all? Pretending to be educated and sending a child into such a commotion."

The enthusiasm of the liberation began to fade with time. Life in freedom continued with many problems and difficulties. The frontiers with Austria and Turkey were closed and the only communication was with Serbia. Trade was at a standstill, merchants were gradually going downhill, many crafts had died out and nothing was being built, so that poverty increased as it did during the *asker* times. At first the power was held by the State representatives of Serbia and Montenegro, but the Serbs soon left and Plevlje became part of Montenegro.

The Kojics leased their houses to the newly arrived families of the Montenegrin officers and clerks. Jelka had assumed all the worry and responsibility of negotiating rents, repairing, and decorating, as she still could not get in touch with Niko, and the hope of Janko's early recovery was gradually fading. Regular reports were arriving about Janko's treatment and she continued to hope that the doctors in Belgrade would save him, but by now she had come to accept the possibility that his stay in hospital might last longer than had been first anticipated. One day, as she was getting ready to go with Milena to Dzevair on a visit to a relative with a new-born baby, Marija and Petronije arrived with a telegram from Belgrade. Milena, already dressed for the visit, was waiting for her mother in the courtyard. She was not pleased to see her sister and brother-in-law because she was afraid that they might stay and the visit to Dzevair would be postponed. Impatiently she hung around the entrance door.

Suddenly a wave of crying spread through the house. Petrified, she ran into the visiting room. Her mother was seated on the *secija*, ghostly pale, and softly lamenting. Gathered around her were all Milena's sisters, crying loudly, and in the middle of the room stood Petronije with his head bowed, holding a telegram in his hand. Milena was told that her father had died. She too burst into tears, caught up in the general sorrow, although she could hardly remember her father. During the last few years she had never entered his room, because Jelka had not allowed anyone to see him once his illness had worsened, as if this would have humiliated him, distorted his image. All Milena's memories of her father were connected with two incidents from her early childhood, when he was well. After his death she often recalled them in her thoughts and tried to conjure up his presence.

Her first memory was like a dream, unformed, and only isolated details had stayed clear in her dim recollections. They were all dressed up, ready to go to Ilino Hill on Saint Elijah's Day, waiting for the carriage to arrive. It came, and they got in and left. The morning was cool and sunny. Her father had sat her on his knee and she clung tight to his encircling arms. She was a little bit apprehensive when the carriage drove off and she heard the rattle of the wheels and the beating of the horses' hoofs against the cobbled street. At first she thought the coach was flying, and later that houses, gardens, trees, and everything round were hurtling towards them. The drive to the Charshija went with lightning speed, then the coachman hauled on the reins and the horses slowed down. Milena looked at the vivid colors of the carpets and rugs hung over the *cepenaks* in front of the shops, at the rows of bowls and copper dishes which glittered in the sun, and the baskets of various fruits and strings of walnuts and hazelnuts embellished with wool of various colors, and she was sorry when the shops were behind them. As soon as they came to the highway, the coachmen started cracking the whip again and the horses began to trot. They crossed the wooden bridge over the Cotina under which blue-green water swirled and roared, continued on the highway a little longer, then swerved onto a field. The wheels sank into the soft grass and the carriage swayed under them as they slowly drove up to the steep side of Ilino Hill. There they got down and began to climb the path towards the church. Father lifted her in his arms.

She could see below her, at the foot of the hill, the spring from which the water flowed to form a brook. Around it, on the grass under the brush and the trees, people had spread colored rugs and blankets and lit small fires. Not far from them stalls had been erected, around which the vendors' cries competed, and a group of gypsies stood in a semicircle with violins in their hands, waiting for people to gather round them.

When they entered the church, she was met by a breath of cold air and the smell of incense. Candles were burning in the shadows and their flickering flames threw restless light over the golden frames of the icons. Milena was bored by the service, and after a while she began to beg her father to take her out. He angrily told her to be patient but she wrapped her arms around his neck and whispered in his ear that she wanted to go. Finally, he carried her out and asked irritably, "What do you want to do now?"

"I want to go to Djana."

Her father pointed at a grove behind which Djana's house could be seen. "Do you see that house behind the tree?"

She was looking at the clearing on the other side, where the granaries were, and answered, "Yes, I do."

"Will you be afraid to go there alone?"

"No."

"All right, follow this path down to the glen, then along the plum orchard and straight across the field to the house. I must return to the church."

She started down the narrow path and reached the plum orchard, as her father had explained. From the orchard she headed through some tall grass towards the granary shed. The sun was at its zenith, like a flaming ball, the hot air shimmered and vibrated above the wheat fields that surrounded the pasture. The song of the crickets rose from the grass and the wheat, defeaning her ears. Swarms of shiny blue flies circled around her head and she had to keep her eyelids lowered to stop them flying into her eyes. She lost her way and wandered into the tall grass which reached above her shoulders. From the grass she could hear the singing of the birds, dominated by the cuckoo, whose cries frightened her. She ran toward the shed, the sight of which she had never lost, but when she pushed the door open and saw nothing but a layer of gray dust and bits of straw, she began to scream.

Her cries were heard at the house, from where she was spotted through a window, and they came to pick her up. She must have wandered for a long time because her family arrived from the church soon after. Her father held her in his arms until she stopped sobbing and, placing her on his knee, began to comfort her. "My precious little ladybird got lost. What would her daddy do if they hadn't found her?" he whispered tenderly, stroking her hair and her hot forehead. Those words of his, his warm voice, his embrace and the security of his lap, after all the fear of being lost, had remained in her memory clearer than any other event from her early childhood.

The other recollection of her father was more recent, and she could visualize his tall figure, his broad straight forehead and fair wavy hair.

It was Christmas Eve, snowing, wintry, festive. Everything was being hurriedly prepared for tomorrow's holiday. They had promised her that her father would take her to the church service at dawn and she was hopping with excitement. She ran around her mother and sisters, asking questions and disturbing them in their work until they chased her off to the upstairs rooms and forbade her to come down. All the rooms on the upper floors were covered by new carpets which on ordinary days were removed and kept rolled up in trunks. The walls and furniture had been dusted, and the air was full of the smell of incense. In front of every icon a *kandilo* was burning. It was warm everywhere because in all rooms the built-in white stoves were lit, with their shiny green ceramic rings. She ran from one room to the other, rolled on the *secija* seats, and listened to the wall clocks as they chimed the hours. The mahogany clock in the visitors' room had the loudest sound and was bigger and more beautiful than the others, bought in Vienna, with gleaming weights and a pendulum suspended from a thin rod that swayed from left to right, and shone as if made of gold. They all chimed at the same time, but not in the same rhythm, some faster, others slower, the big clock resounding longest of all. She was bored being alone, and now and then she would go to the balcony to watch the snow fall. It seemed to come from every side, swirling and turning as if emerging out of the sky, the walls of the houses, the ground. From the roofs hung long slender icicles which glistened like crystal. The dense cover of snow was piled in thick drifts on the ground, criss-crossed by paths; it hung from the fences in ragged chunks and capped the posts, and the glare of its whiteness blinded her.

Against the wall of their other house leaned the three yule logs, cut from the young oak tree. It seemed to her that everything was filled with expectation which could be felt even in the evening twilight. It only remained for Father to come from the Charshija and the yule logs would be brought into the house. Unable to control her impatience, she went down to her sisters, who had already dressed for the evening and had started to set the Christmas Eve dinner. They told her off, afraid that she might catch cold, and sent her back to the heated upper rooms.

She began to look at the icons. The Mother of God appeared to her very sad, the Christ on the Cross emaciated, all his ribs showing, the pallor of his face almost gray, and the crown of thorns reminded her of a Turkish turban. Saint Nikola was old, with a beard, and looked like a priest. Best of all she liked Saint Stevan, in the visitor's room, a large icon painted in vivid colors and set in a heavy gilded frame. He was young and handsome, his fair hair fell in curls over his forehead and on to his shoulders, and his face was white and rosy like that of painted angels. A long red robe, edged with gold braid around the sleeves and the hem, fell in folds to his small narrow feet. His hands were also narrow, like a girl's, with long slender fingers. A thought crossed her mind. "He must have been a girl dressed in prophet's clothes." She too intended to put on men's clothes when she grew up because she was desolate at a being girl, especially since she had heard how unhappy everyone had been when she was born. In her prayers she asked God to change her into a boy, and whenever a rainbow appeared she ran, hoping to pass beneath it, as it was believed that this would transform a girl's gender.

While she was immersed in these thoughts, they came to tell her that her father had arrived and to take her to the kitchen quarters. A large fire burned in the hearth and all the members of the family were already standing around it waiting, while cold air with the tang of snow wafted in through the open door. Her father appeared, tall, dressed in a Hercegovinian outfit trimmed with gold braid. He was bareheaded, with fresh snowflakes on his hair, smiling and carrying a yule log. "Good evening and Happy Christmas Eve," he said in a deep full voice. They showered him with wheat grain and replied, "Good fortune to you." He approached the fire, stirred the embers and, placing the yule log on them, began his blessings. He spoke about happiness, health, and love in the family, and to Milena no other prayer sounded as holy and close to her heart, so exquisite. When he finished, he went for the second log, then for the third. The fire blazed, sparks flew everywhere as the crackling flames enveloped the logs, heat poured from the fireplace and, from the wide-open doors, icy air blew in. A song rang out from the neighboring houses: "Christmas, our joy . . ." They all joined in. The song spread throughout the town, it could be heard in Mocevac and up in Golubinja. Milena began to shiver from too many emotions, felt drained and sleepy and could not wait to return to the warm rooms.

In accordance with the custom, the dinner was served on white cloth laid on the floor and made up of fasting dishes. In the middle were bowls and platters of fish garnished with rice, mashed beans with oil and spices, pickled cabbage, cucumbers and peppers, pies of rice and spinach, dried fruit and fasting cake, but Milena could hardly eat anything. She fell asleep during dinner and did not remember being carried to bed.

She was woken before dawn. Lamps and candles lit the rooms, as it was still dark outside. Dressed warmly and wrapped in a large shawl, she waited for the yuleman to arrive and rekindle the logs, as was the custom, then they all left for the monastery.

The path in the snow was broad, trodden by the people who went before them. Her father held her hand, while someone carried a lantern in front of them. When they began to climb Mount Glavica, her father lifted her in his arms. Day was breaking. Milena could see the columns of people converging on the monastery from several directions. She embraced her father's neck, leaned her head against his, and watched the dark rows winding across the white vastness, the flickering lights of lanterns swaying in the distance and dissolving into the mystical twilight. She felt warm and secure against his chest.

Somewhere in the distance above them, a song began and spread in waves down the sides of Glavica:

The cocks are calling over the hills,
God, our savior.
Their loud calls are waking all the slaves,
God, our Savior . . .

Janko was mourned quietly and with dignity by his family. As they could not all attend his funeral in Belgrade, a service was held in the monastery for the peaceful rest of his soul, which was attended by all relatives and friends and by the prominent citizens of Plevlje. Father Rade gave the sermon, in which he mentioned Janko's patriotism and the greatness of his spirit, his help to the church and the school councils, and his generosity to the poor.

After the sharp pain which the suddenness of Janko's death had inflicted, Jelka began to find consolation in the fact that he was free from torment and that his unhappy soul had finally found peace, since he himself did not wish to live. She shed more tears over the last years of his life, which had condemned him to solitude and helplessness, than she did over her own loss. Remembering their youth, their great love, the happiness and understanding they had, she felt as divorced from that world of the past which they had shared as he now was.

The house seemed deserted without the head of the family, although Janko had not been able to rule it for some years.

10

A few months after Janko's death came the news that contacts with Sarajevo had been re-established. Less than a week later, a coach stopped in front of Jelka's house and from it stepped Niko. He was tall and distinguished, with an oval face and large dark eyes. Milena was astonished how quickly all the members of the family managed to gather around him—even Ahmet, who immediately started to take the suitcases out of the coach. She looked at Niko with admiration from a distance; he was elegant, clean, and perfumed. Somehow extraordinarily clean, more so than anyone else she knew. Jelka cried with happiness as she embraced him. His sisters seemed rather confused; overwhelmed by joy, they timidly approached to kiss his hand, as he was now the head of the family. He did not allow this, but kissed them instead, and just then noticed Milena, who was standing in the background as if she did not belong to the gathering in front of the gates.

"Come, Milena, come to your brother, why are you so shy?" He came to her, picked her up in his arms and kissed her, looking at her with delighted fascination because she had been born after his departure. "How tiny you are. I thought you would be much bigger."

This perplexed her even more; she felt guilty that she had not grown faster and, trying to wriggle out of his embrace, she wanted to run away, to hide from everybody and to have a good cry.

"Why are you so timid? Don't be afraid of Niko, you are his youngest sister. I brought you a doll, bigger than any you have ever seen before. She can shut her eyes."

Without letting her out of his arms, he started towards the house, followed by his mother and sisters.

Ahmet was standing by the stairs and, to show his displeasure that no one had paid him any attention, he asked somewhat angrily, "Well, tell me at least where I should take my master's suitcases."

Jelka's face lit up because Ahmet addressed her son as his master, and she said to Niko, "For heaven's sake, didn't you recognize Ahmet? Why didn't you greet him?"

Niko put Milena down and approached Ahmet. "Forgive me, my friend, I didn't recognize you, it's a long time since I left," and putting his hand on the old man's shoulder, he asked, "How are you, Ahmet?"

Ahmet began to blink with satisfaction. "Well, thanks be to Allah. I came back, as you can see, to retire under the old roof. I decided to die in your home, even if you bury me in the Serbian graveyard."

"You'll live with us for a while yet," smiled Niko. "But when the time for dying comes, we'll make sure you are buried by your own people according to Turkish custom."

Ahmet was told to take the suitcases to Janko's room. After his death, it had been prepared for Niko as the new head of the family. The sisters scattered to prepare refreshments, and Jelka went to the street to send messengers to all their relatives with the news that her son had arrived. Children gathered and joyously ran to give the message, knowing that they would be generously rewarded for such important news.

Niko was going through all the visitors' and living rooms, absorbing everything around him eagerly, as if collecting distant memories, and Milena followed close behind, partly because of the promised doll, but also because she was enchanted by all his movements, his well groomed face and hair, his unusual clothes.

Niko's arrival brought indescribable joy into the house. Jelka could hardly restrain the tears of bliss and pride, the sisters competed as to who would serve him better, the guests and relatives came hurrying to celebrate the traveler's return. It seemed to Milena that this day was, for everyone, the biggest holiday ever.

After dinner, Niko went to his father's room, where Jelka joined him, as in the press of guests she had hardly been able to exchange more than a few words with him alone all day. Niko gave her a chair and he sat on the bed facing her. While waiting for him to speak first, she caressed with her look every feature of his face. For years she had been trying to envisage this moment. Tears flooded her eyes at the thought that Janko had not lived to see him again. Niko, too, looking at Janko's desk and his books, was thinking of his father.

"The news of Father's death was a heavy blow. I am sorry I was not with you at the time and that I did not see him for so many years. All my longings for him remain unfulfilled."

"Perhaps it is better that you did not see him when he was ill. He'll always stay in your memory as he was when his health and his mind served him well," said Jelka, and she began to cry.

"Don't, Mama, don't cry. It is better for him that his torment is ended."

"For him, yes, he found peace," Jelka whispered, wiping her tears away with a handkerchief. "Thank God that you are back. When I saw you, I saw daylight again."

He got up, put his arms round her shoulders, then, taking her hand, asked her to sit beside him on the bed. "I know how difficult it must have been for you, my poor Mother. All the responsibility lay on your shoulders for so many years. But we are free now and everything will change for the better."

"As long as you are here, may God in His mercy look after you." She crossed herself and tried to smile, then she asked, "Did you finish school?"

"Not yet. I gave up business academy because I don't intend to become a businessman, and with that training one could only be that or a clerk. I continued with high school and have passed the matriculation exams, but I want to go on to study law. As soon as I have rested a little and feasted my eyes on you all, I will go to Belgrade to enter the university."

"Then you'll leave us again. I thought I would be able to hand over the running of the house to you and see you married."

"I must finish my studies first. There's plenty of time for marriage. As for the house, don't worry, I will help you. Belgrade is not on the other side of the world, and Serbia is not a foreign country. I will be able to spend all my vacations here," he said confidently, and got up to look around the room. "I will leave everything as it was when Father was here, except that we'll buy a cupboard for my books and bring in the piano. He wrote to me that he had bought one from the Austrians, as they were leaving a piano of good Viennese make. Where is it now?"

"In the bar next door. It is big, and takes up a lot of space, and no one knows how to play it."

"I will play it for you. I took lessons for six years. I learned German too, as I thought of going to Vienna to study."

"You can have it brought in, but don't play it yet, as we are still in mourning."

Niko consented without a word and, with a deep sigh, went to his father's desk. "You did not lease the bar?"

"No, I can't bear seeing anyone there where he used to work. The shop and the warehouse I leased because I don't go to the Charshija often and it hurt me less."

"I'm glad you didn't lease the bar. We'll never lease it to anyone."

They fell silent for a time, immersed in their own thoughts.

"How did you manage with money for so many years? Was what Janko left you sufficient?" Jelka asked.

"More than sufficient. When I turned eighteen, I was able to withdraw everything that was left in my name from the bank—two hundred florins. I also tried, before leaving, to withdraw Father's capital, but they told me that no one except you has any right to it. That's how Father arranged it."

"It's well that you could get those two hundred florins, that's a lot of money. How much did you bring back?"

"Not much. I lived on it, and bought several suits and presents . . . I don't know myself how I spent so much. Ready money goes fast."

"Is life so expensive in Sarajevo?"

"No, the living is not expensive, but I spent on other things. I paid for my piano and German lessons, learned to ride, helped some of my poorer friends, gave donations for Young Bosnia. I became a member of it, but don't tell anyone."

"What is Young Bosnia?"

"It is a secret society which many students join, mainly young people fighting against the Austrian occupation."

Jelka thought, "Soft-hearted and spendthrift like his father. He too was always giving donations and helping everyone, but when he was in trouble, no one was there to help. I won't tell him what savings I still have, he doesn't know how to manage money."

To him she said, "As long as you are alive and healthy, we'll live somehow, frugally, from the rents and produce of our land. We'll keep the capital I have left to marry off your sisters and for Milena's education. That was Janko's wish."

"Don't worry, Mother, I can always get a job as a clerk—I have my matriculation. We are liberated, and as soon as the war with the Turks is over, everything will improve. I can work and study in Belgrade, that's how many students live. By the time Milena is old enough for higher education, I will be an established judge."

"You won't manage both," Jelka said gently, looking at his suit, cut from the most expensive cloth, and his silk shirt and tie. "You are used to having everything and are easy with money. I will keep sending you a little money at a time, and later I will collect Janko's capital from the Sarajevo bank. He also had an account in Vienna."

"I will take you there too. We can't do it now, the whole world is at boiling point. If Bosnia becomes free, we'll go first to Sarajevo. We'll see."

"Could war still break out?"

"Who knows? In these circumstances anything is possible."

"God forbid it, even if we never recover our money."

"Don't you be afraid of anything, I am here to care for you and Milena," Niko said, and embraced her. Seeing how worried she had become, he switched the conversation to Milena. "How many grades has she finished?"

"Only one. She started school a little late because of the *asker*. But she learns well, and has excellent marks."

"She'll catch up, she's still small. Looks a bit pale though. We must get her to play outside in the sun more."

"I haven't allowed her to because there is no one of her own age, and besides, she's a tomboy, only likes to play with boys."

"Let her play with whoever she chooses. Times have changed and girls too mustn't always be kept indoors." He looked at his watch and was astonished to see that it was after midnight. "How quickly the time has gone. It is wonderful to be home. There is nothing like being with one's own mother." He approached again and kissed her cheek.

This made her feel sad, reminding her of Janko. "Don't kiss me so much, it frightens me that you are so gentle. And it's not the custom here. My daughters kiss my hand when I go out and when I return. I too did not kiss my mother, nor she me, although we loved one another."

Niko laughed and embraced her once more. "But I will go on kissing you, I pined for you long enough. Now go to sleep, we are both tired."

The following day Niko's things were unpacked: suits, shirts, shoes, everything expensively elegant, in the latest fashion, even his underwear and fine socks. The piano was brought into the room and a carpenter made him shelves which reached all the way to the ceiling. Niko arranged on them all the books he had brought and those that Janko had received from Serbia before the *asker* and had kept in the blind store-room, as well as all the series from the Literary Guild, which had arrived from Belgrade after the liberation.

Niko's arrival inspired the whole family with a sense of security. Brought up in the cult of regarding a man as the head of the family, and attached to him, the only son and heir, by a different kind of love, stronger than toward any other member of the household, they felt that a new life had begun for them all, full of new dignity and the hope of continuing the family line through Niko. Jelka passed authority to him and, when the Plevlje notables came to convey condolences for Janko's death, he would receive them in the visitor's room as host.

As soon as he had settled down, he began to enquire about work. Although he did not have a university degree, he had gained enough knowledge for his age, being only twenty-one years old, spoke excellent German, was well traveled, and everyone considered him to be a clever and cultured man. He was honest, he came from a good family which had influential friends and contacts, and there were immediate prospects of a high-ranking clerk's position for him. He also intended to demand repayment of all loans from his father's debtors, unless in the meantime they themselves returned the money, which should have been given back to Jelka long ago.

Soon after Niko's return, Jelka's three daughters became engaged, all of them to Montenegrins, and into big houses; two of the men were judges, the other the director of the postal service. The daughters were now doing voluntary work as nurses, attending first aid courses and sewing sheets for the army.

Milena was endlessly happy. Instead of sorrow and tears, joy dominated their home, and Niko, who was waited on and indulged by everyone, spoiled her, brought her presents, took her for walks and allowed her to go wherever she wished, secretly gave her money for candy and bon-bons, chose books for her to read, and treated her tenderly because she could least remember her father. She loved him more than her sisters, more perhaps than she loved her mother, and with a joyful love. She was closer to him and felt more secure in his presence, more free and independent.

That summer, during the school vacation, Milena would spend almost the whole day playing outside. She tried to join the war games of the boys from the neighborhood, and brought with her the wooden sabers and guns which Niko made for her, but they would not accept her because she was a girl. She wandered around the parks and the lake, having learned early to enjoy the beauty of nature, as she had been raised with sisters much older than herself and was often forced to find amusements on her own. Through Niko's influence, her mother too allowed her out of the house so that she could spend more time in the sun and fresh air. She was only forbidden to go to the gypsy quarter, and yet this interested her most, because one of her school friends, Dobrinka, lived in that neighborhood and told her about gypsy feasts and fighting, their clandestine brothels, and the inns run by former whores. Milena was curious about it all and, although feeling a little ashamed, she started meeting Dobrinka secretly and roaming through the gypsy quarter.

There she discovered a world she had not known before. She saw what poverty was and where the poor lived, learned what was being done in the brothels, how cruel people can be, and how bewildering their destiny. Out of the low dilapidated hovels the half-naked children peered, pale and dirty, with spindly legs and big stomachs. They stared at her with starved eyes, curiously, and she at them, neither with revulsion nor compassion. In front of these gypsy huts were the drinking houses, *mehanas*, which had mushroomed since the Shvaba brothel had left, strung out next to one another toward the Turkish cemetery all the way to Jalija and the first blacksmiths' workshops. Both Turks and Serbs came there to drink. Best known was the *mehana* belonging to a middle-aged woman called Hatidza, who hired young girls to serve drinks. She had once been respectable, the wife of a Turkish officer, but when her husband died she had become involved in this business. In her youth she had been beautiful, which could still be detected in her features, and had entertained the guests herself, but later her girls had replaced her. She did not cover her face, and would go into the street in *dimije* trousers and a blouse, her hair held by a fine kerchief, with locks escaping around her temples and cheeks. Only when she went to the Charshija would she put on a black silk *zar* with green stripes which she had kept from her married days. No other woman had a *zar* like that, and she was easily recognized, although her face was covered by a veil through which it was just possible to perceive the eyes and eyebrows accentuated by mascara.

Milena and Dobrinka would sometimes go to the Turkish cemetery, climb on some of the larger stones and look through the windows of the upper floor of the Hatizda *mehana*. From there they could see a bed surrounded on three sides by frilled lace drapes which fell from the ceiling and which were attached to the bedposts by a red ribbon. If the windows were closed, they knew that there was someone in the room.

Not all the *mehanas* in that row were brothels. Some were kept by respectable women, and these they greeted, while they passed the others without looking up. There were also two or three shops there with *cepenaks*, where they used to buy sweets, pastries, pears, plums, and cooking apples, as it was nearer and cheaper for them than going to the Charshija.

Milena accepted everything as a matter of fact, and did not ask herself why the shops were dirty and stocked little merchandise, why the gypsy houses were like hovels, why the dubious *cafanas* existed. That was how things were: gypsies were gypsies, poor people poor, and whores were whores. No one told her that it could be any different.

At the beginning of the gypsy quarter stood a spacious one-story house which had once been an inn where peasants and other travelers would spend the night when they were delayed at the market or were passing through on their journey. Now it was abandoned and forgotten, with a sagging roof of rotten wooden planks, and bulging brick walls, damp and cracked from seeping rain, so that the dark filthy interior could be seen through the gaps. The doorway gaped empty, and the posts to which double doors had once been fastened were now standing awry, mildewy and worm-eaten. Only the broad threshold remained whole and straight. There, in some mildewed corner of this lair, lived Rista Musabejdzija, a fat old woman who spoke in a man's hoarse voice and terrified Milena. When children teased her or stole her firewood, she emerged to throw at them whatever she could lay her hands on, stones, bricks, or her old clogs. If it was a fine day, she sat on the threshold or the stone paving in front of the house, sunning herself and smoking. She wore *dimije* trousers of dyed cotton, a white blouse with wide sleeves, which had turned gray with dirt, and a padded jerkin of brown cloth. Her hennaed hair was covered with a thin scarf and she always wore a flower tucked behind her ears, from which hung large golden earrings, thick and round, reaching almost to her shoulders as she had hardly any neck. Her bare feet were swollen and dirty, the color of clay, with thick yellowing nails. She lived on charity and fortune telling. She divined for the peasant women, throwing beans or looking at cards.

Once, when Milena went with her mother to the Charshija, Rista was sitting in the sun on the threshold, fingering the long strings of her amber rosary beads. Jelka greeted her, and laboriously she lifted her large body, pressed her right hand under her chest and bowed.

"Why are you getting up, Rista dear?"

"You're right, Jankovica, it's hard for me to get up after sitting around for so long." She lowered herself on the threshold and went on, "God knows, all I do is sit or lie, can't move anywhere."

"Are you ill? Is something hurting you?"

"Yes, I'm quite ill. Everything hurts me. I've got shooting pains in my back and, as you see, have to wear a padded vest even in the sun, but I've got to struggle on until I die. I've become a proper hag, it's time for me to go. My legs don't support me any more, I'm all swollen and one day I'll croak—the sooner the better, God willing."

"Hold on, Rista, life is still before you. Old age is not easy for anybody."

"But nobody's is like mine. May God spare even my enemies from it."

When they were out of earshot, Milena asked her mother, "How is it that you know that woman?"

"My child, it is true what they say—'Young whore, old beggar.' That's Rista for you. It's sad that she was once a great beauty and was the mistress of Musabejdzija. He was the head of road taxes and had a lot of money. She used to be all in silks and velvet, with strings of gold ducats down to her waist, covering all her chest. He showered her with presents, bought her pearl necklaces, bracelets, earrings, and rings encrusted with precious stones. They said she wore around her waist a belt of pure gold, fashioned like the most beautiful lace. She ate from silver bowls and with silver spoons. And look what's become of her now. More hungry than fed, gives everything, poor soul, for tobacco because she can't live without it. She still keeps those earrings and the rosary beads, dyes her hair with henna and wears make-up, to remind herself of the good old days when Musabejdzija was alive."

"Why do you greet her when she was a whore, and a Turkish one too?"

"She was only his, and no one else's. She loved him and he wanted to marry her, but she wouldn't change her religion and spurn her Serbian name. She used to help Serbs, and saved many lives from the very gallows, so they say. Musabejdzija did not mind giving bribes to save the men she pleaded for. He was crazy about her, never got married himself. The Turks began to hate him because of her, plotted against him, and finally someone killed him. She has been no one's mistress since. At first she lived on the ducats he had left her. Afterwards she sold her jewelry and the rest until finally everything went. If you don't learn to work and save, you soon lose everything, even though you had pots of gold. There's an old saying that one's last tooth can eat the whole of Istanbul."

"Then why didn't you give her something, if she helped the Serbs?"

"I always send her gifts at Christmas and Easter, and other times I let her take sackfuls from the garden, beans, potatoes, pumpkins, and the rest. Now that she can't go anywhere, I'll have to get someone to take it to her. God help those who have to wait for others to give to them. Everybody forgets the poor unless they put out their hands and beg."

"Are there many poor?"

"Yes, my child, more than there are others."

"Will they, now that we're free, be given something to stop them being poor?"

"They can never be given enough. God himself seems to have forgotten them. The poor have always been with us and always will be."

It was also in the gypsy quarter that Milena had first seen Krckalo, a half-crazed beggar of indeterminate age, without a home or family. He used to sleep not far from Rista's inn, on a big heap of rubbish collected over the years. No one knew his real name, so they called him Krckalo because he shook incessantly. He begged only when he was hungry. During the winter he would sneak into some cowshed or under the steps of a house to spend the night, and then run away at dawn like a wild animal, because people would chase him away if they found him. During the summer he dwelt mostly on the rubbish heap, scratching around as if looking for something. Dressed in rags, dirty and always barefooted, even in winter, he roamed the gypsy quarter talking to himself. He was quiet except when children teased him about the ruptured hernia that sometimes showed through his torn breeches: "You'll lose your hernia, Krckalo!" Then he would fly into a rage and throw stones at them until they dispersed, and then bend down to put back the purple hernia, the size of a squash. Milena felt sorry for him, and one day she asked her mother whether she knew him and whether he could be helped.

267

"My child, he is a proper martyr, a sorrowful sight. There is no helping him except by giving him food. If he was in his right mind, somebody would take him to look after the cows, fetch water, or cut wood, and he would have food to eat and a roof over his head, but as it is he struggles on . . . a dog is better off than he is. I am surprised he is still alive. It would be better if he found peace at last—rest for that pitiful body and freedom for that poor human soul."

"If he died?"

"That's the only way, for there is no other help or salvation for him," Jelka said, and crossed herself, then she asked, "Where did you see Krckalo?"

Milena was suddenly overcome with guilt about wandering through the gypsy quarter and she timidly admitted that she went there secretly.

"Don't do it any more," Jelka reproached her gently. "All kinds of things happen there, that's why I forbade you to go, to save you seeing all that misery. There is also much filth there and all sorts of illnesses. Play in our garden or around the Barracks."

"Can I bring Dobrinka? She lives there and she's my school friend."

"If you like her, bring her over. It would be better for her too if she plays here."

From then on, Milena asked Dobrinka to her home. They played in the garden or roved around her uncle's field and the surrounding hills. When the harvest and threshing began, they enjoyed sitting nearby watching the women as they deftly gathered up armfuls of wheat, cut it and laid it into neat rows, for the men to tie into sheaves and set up in stacks. Milena reveled in the summer sunshine, and its bright yellow color which was reflected in the ripe wheat, the stubble, the haystacks, the fallen leaves, the buttercups, primroses, dandelions, in everything that absorbed the color of the sun's rays. They made trips to the water mills, to Skakavac, and to the Abyss. There was more freedom now and people went for a stroll to these places as they used to go to Citluk before, even the *bulas*, although they still covered their faces. The *bulas* picnicked there in groups and could be seen sitting beside their little fires, drinking coffee, smoking and watching the sunset.

For the Abyss they had to start early in the afternoon, as they needed time to climb all the way to the crater. They would sit on the planks that covered it and look at the surrounding hills. Beneath them, under the rocks, was the source of the Breznica. It was said that the Abyss was bottomless, and that in the past, before the crater was covered with planks and nailed down, the suicides used to throw themselves into it, those who did not want their bodies to be found. Milena often thought about it, imagining them still falling, and she argued with Dobrinka, who could not picture such a scene and maintained that the Abyss must have an end somewhere. They peered through the gaps between the planks, but only dark depths yawned below, and nothing could be perceived. Dropping a stone into the Abyss, they listened as it hit the rocks, bounced off them and fell further away until at last all sound died away. When the shadows of twilight gathered around them and began to crawl across Chitluk, the sun still illuminated the Ljubisnja and Plijesh mountains. It descended gradually behind the peaks and, when it had sunk completely, its purple reflection remained in the sky. The outlines of the mountains shone golden like a flame for a while, then faded away into the deepening blue. Then the children hurried homeward, gripped by fear of the mysterious shadows and of the darkness which gradually pervaded everything around them.

Just as life in Plevlje was settling down a little, and people were starting to think about the future, war broke out with Bulgaria and mobilization began. The whole town was on the move. Jelka fretted about Niko at first, but was relieved when it became known that where there was only one son in the family he would not be mobilized. Hardly a few days had passed when Misho, Pava's son, told Milena that the new army would be passing through the Charshija and she ran with him to see it. The volunteers appeared first, in squads of ten, with a leader marching in front of each, carrying a flag. The Montenegrins and the young men from the surrounding villages went by, still without uniforms, wearing their best clothes.

Suddenly a voice cried, "Here come the Plevlje men." From afar Milena sighted Niko marching resolutely at the head of his formation with a flag in his hands. Her heart began to beat with pride and emotion, he appeared to her taller and more handsome than his companions. From the ranks a song resounded: "The warriors' bugle is sounding, a great battle awaits us . . ." The people around her began to cheer. "Long live the volunteers, long live our heroes! Down with the Bulgars, treacherous brothers." Too exhilarated to wait for the whole procession to pass, Milena ran to convey the wonderful news to her mother, as Niko had not told them that he was enlisting as a volunteer.

Jelka was petrified. She turned pale and said in a whisper, "Did they have to take an only son?"

"No, Mama, they did not force him to join, he enlisted himself. He's a volunteer, carries a flag! They are the brave ones!" She could not understand why her mother listened as if in terror of what she was saying, why she did not receive the news with the admiration that she herself felt, and which others were expressing. Trying to control her fear and pain at parting with her son again, Jelka knelt in front of th icons and began to pray aloud, "Merciful God, save the only sons of all mothers. Dear Lord, look after Niko, take my life, take any other of my children, but protect my only son."

Jelka did not wish to show her fear in front of her son, nor did she utter a word of reproach because he had not consulted her before enlisting as a volunteer. Niko was bright and elated as if embarking on some extraordinary journey full of adventure, danger, and conquest, in which he would be able to express his courage and patriotism. He awaited the day of departure with impatience, parted joyfully from mother and sisters, and left with the rest of the forces.

Jelka's home seemed deserted without Niko. The older daughters spent the whole day on their voluntary duties, she was constantly busy with housework to stop her from thinking, and Milena was left on her own. She was no longer interested in outings with Dobrinka and besides, she felt sorry that no one stayed with Mother in the house, so she looked for amusement there. She climbed into the attic where old clothes were stored—her sisters' hats, Savka's trousseau and needlework, everything neatly placed in trunks—or she crept into the blind store-room and looked through the piles of papers, periodicals, and books that Niko had not taken to his room. There she found a dusty book without its cover but full of unusual pictures. She wiped off the dust, straightened the creased pages, and began to read it. Through the adventures of Robinson Crusoe she could conjure up visions of the sea she had never seen, the ship, the storm and the shipwreck, and then she found herself alone on the desert island. This book awoke in her such interest in reading that it became her greatest pleasure. There was a large choice of books in the house and she no longer went out at all.

Jelka became worried that Milena was spending all her time bent over a book. She tried to forbid it, but when it was found that Milena was hiding in the cowshed, under the stairs or under her bed, where they once discovered her asleep with the book, she told her, "All right, if you like reading so much, take a book as you go for a walk and when you get tired sit down and read, but if you continue to sit here for hours bent over it, I'll throw all those books on the fire."

So Milena started to go out into the open air again. She went mostly to the Barracks, and sat beside the lake or lay on the grass to read. Sometimes she went to the Shvabas' cemetery, in between Bogishevac and Bembeg's Hill. Shadowy, almost dark under the dense branches of the trees, the cemetery was well kept. In the middle of it was a wooden cross with a crucified Christ in bronze. The headstones were of white or black marble, the mounds surrounded by iron fences, and the small graves of children were embellished with statues of cherubs who held wreaths above the marble slabs. Everything had been kept tidy and looked after, but no one from the families of the dead came to visit them.

One day, on her way home, Milena noticed in front of the Great Mosque a group of visitors going to see its interior, as it was said that this was one of the oldest and most beautiful mosques in the Balkans. She joined them, although she knew that her mother would not have allowed it, despite the fact that after the liberation Serbs had been permitted to enter the Great Mosque on given days, to look at it as a famous historical sight.

"A sacred place is a sacred place, whether Serbian or Turkish," Jelka had once said, when she heard that there were some who climbed the minaret. These she considered no better than heathens. "As no one except the priest can enter beyond the altar in our sanctuary, so no one should desecrate the minaret."

In front of the entrance was a notice: "This temple is a holy place. Do not bring in the filth of the streets and the refuse heaps." Abashed and afraid of being seen by someone who knew her, Milena was not sure whether this applied to the Serbs too, and as no one else took off their shoes, she did not either. When she entered the broad hexagonal interior, its floor covered by a Persian carpet woven to reflect the design of the vault, she pressed against the wall with the other visitors and breathlessly waited for the service to end. All the walls were decorated with reliefs and monumental Turkish calligraphy, without a single icon. Clusters of rich stone carvings projected in each corner. On the small balcony, which could be reached by a narrow flight of steps against the wall, stood the *hodja*, who read aloud in a language she did not understand. The balcony was also of very finely chiseled stone, as if floating above the ground. The faithful were kneeling and bowing on the carpet, barefooted and with turned up sleeves, having just washed reverently under the fountain in front of the entrance. From time to time they would lower their faces to the carpet and remain still with their backs bent, then they would straighten up, turn the palms of their hands towards the *hodja* and whisper their prayers. The mosque was filled with hushed praying which inspired fear in Milena, and she tried not to look at the faithful. She raised her eyes to the harmonious arabesques on the vault, painted in soft colors dominated by blue tints.

When the service was over, those who wanted to do so climbed the minaret. Although at first she wavered, Milena was unable to resist the urge to climb to the top of the slender tower, taller than any other building in Plevlje. She avoided treading on the carpet as she approached the tall steps that led to a side entrance where it was so dark that she could only grope her way as she began to climb. She had the impression of climbing up a chimney. At times bright sunlight would blaze through a sizeable and unprotected rectangular opening. Blinded by the dazzle, she would stop, afraid that someone might accidentally push her, as the staircase was very narrow and a child could easily fall through the openings. Her legs ached and it was becoming increasingly difficult to climb on to the next high step. Somehow she reached the top on all fours.

Coming out on to the balcony that circled the minaret, she almost fainted, so violently was she engulfed by the blazing sunshine. She had to close her eyes, her head felt giddy from the spiral climb, and the people from behind had caught up with her and were pushing her toward the parapet. When she had collected herself somewhat, she looked at the town below. It seemed to her that she was looking at it from the sky and had never experienced anything so majestic. The parapet was tall and she could not see the Charshija and the shops below her, even when she stood on tiptoe. She begged for someone to lift her up, but no one paid any attention to her. Finally, she took off and folded her coat, and stood on top of it. When she glanced down, she had a sensation that the whole minaret was swinging, falling to one side, and she quickly crouched down, burying her face in her hands. Losing all desire to observe anything further, she grabbed her coat and began to descend.

The descent was also difficult. She was even more frightened when passing the openings through which the light poured in, because she might trip, roll down, and disappear in a flash, as if she had never existed. She hardly had the strength to reach her home and went to bed immediately. Afraid of telling her mother where she had been, she could not complain of the pains in her thighs which persisted for days after the climb. Several times she dreamed she was standing at the top of the minaret which started swaying and slowly falling, and would wake up in great fear.

Very soon after Niko's departure came the news that the Bulgars were defeated. The soldiers from Plevlje did not even reach the front line and never tasted gun smoke, but they were nevertheless received on their return with great honor. The very fact that the town was in a position to send its soldiers to war, that it had so many volunteers, and had been among the first to spring to the defense of the country, was a significant historical event after some five hundred years of slavery.

The joy in Jelka's home was now greater still because her son had returned from the war as a hero, a volunteer. All the relatives assembled to share her happiness in greeting the soldier's return, which was celebrated for days. Niko immediately obtained a post as a high-ranking military clerk at the town's headquarters, and he enjoyed his duties. His plans to study law in Belgrade had to be postponed until the political situation in Europe became more settled.

Jelka devoted herself to running the house and to receiving guests, in keeping with her custom in the years before Janko's illness, and it was once more evident that their home had a family head. Before dark, when Niko returned from work, she would go to the gates to welcome him. She strove to please him, attended to his every wish, and even allowed him to play the piano when the young people gathered in their home, because she did not wish the sorrow for Janko to overshadow the gladness that Niko had brought into the family. This, she was convinced, would have been Janko's wish too.

When a whole year had passed since Janko's death, Jelka's daughters married, one after another. The weddings were festive, as befitted the Kojic home, but without many people and excessive celebration.

Milena felt that the whole house had been opened up to life again, to light and youth. She enjoyed the visits by Niko's friends, the music and songs, the comings and goings of guests, the wedding celebrations, the holiday feeling that reigned in the house, and especially the company of Magda and Dobrila, who stayed with them for several days at the time of the weddings.

The news of the Sarajevo assassination struck Plevlje like a thunderbolt from a clear sky. It was announced in *The Voice of Montenegro* and was the sole subject of all conversation. Every day fresh reports reached them about the cruelty of the Austrian government toward the Serbian population in Sarajevo, the reprisals that Austria intended to carry out against Serbia, and the ultimatums she had issued. As Jelka's house was opposite the Krstata Barracks, Niko's friends and her sons-in-law assembled there and their talks sometimes continued late into the night. Milena was sent to Djana's estate, because they could no longer allow her to wander about alone and she had been staying all day long with the adults.

At that time, the wife of Rade's brother, Father Oshtric, escaped with her six children to Ilino Hill, after her husband was killed by the Austrians for his connection with Young Bosnia.

Immediately after the assassination of Franz Ferdinand, when Gavrilo Princip and his companions were caught, several young men, members of Young Bosnia, had gone to their teacher Jovanka Oshtric, who was sympathetic to their cause. Straight away, while confusion still reigned, she had put them on the train at Bistrik station and sent them to her brother, Father Oshtric, in Rudo, and he had transported them to Serbia. She was not caught, but someone betrayed the priest to the Austrians. They tortured him, and when they could not force him to talk, sentenced him to a horrible death: they placed the gallows on the bank of the River Lin and hung him in such a way that he was immersed to his waist in water. Even after he died, they did not allow the family to bury him, but let the river decompose his body.

Amidst the grief that gripped Rade's home, no one paid much attention to the children because there were so many of them and they could make their own amusement. They spent the whole day playing outdoors, roaming the groves and orchards, the pastures and plains of Ilino Hill. It was early autumn, sunny and mild, and the children forgot their sorrows in the freedom they discovered on the estate and in each other's company. In the morning they would get up before the others and, still undressed, run to the orchards to eat the apples and pears that had fallen from the trees during the night, then return to their beds and stay there until someone came to wake them. Then the washing, combing, and dressing would begin, everything according to the established rules, as in the army. They received their breakfast upstairs, not with the grownups. A tablecloth of thickly woven cotton would be spread over the carpet in one of the upper rooms, and laid with large green bowls of cornmeal steamed with cream cheese, and yogurt mixed with the cream skimmed from shallow wooden containers. Each child would get a spoon, metal or wooden, and the rowdy meal would start.

Food never tasted as good to Milena as it did there, especially from the wooden spoons, which Jelka did not keep in the house. She would join in heartily with the other children although they had to force her to eat at home. After breakfast, play would begin. They rolled down the slopes, climbed trees, went to Grevno to build watermills in the brook, picked hazelnuts, ran races, divided into groups and organized competitions or played war games. They had something small for lunch, whatever was at hand—a piece of bread with cheese or ham, hard-boiled eggs, a glass of milk, or fruit.

Before sunset, they often went to a field some way away from the house where there was a sheep pen, and while they waited for the sheep and goats to be brought back from pasture, they would catch the insects that at twilight began to buzz above the grass, and chase around trying to put them down each other's necks. The pen was fenced with rough wooden planks, and it was built in two parts, connected by a gate. When the shepherds started to arrive with their flocks, the dairy women who did the milking and made the cream and cheese came down from the main buildings carrying wooden pails. They would sit on the logs on each side of the gate and begin to milk. The children joined in to help separate the sheep from the goats and pass them one by one to be milked. From the udders sharp jets of milk would spurt into white foam, and the aroma of fresh milk mixed with the smell of the flocks and the dried trodden grass. When the pails were full, the lambs and kids were let to suckle what was left after milking. Everything was in an uproar of bleating until the young found their mothers' udders, buried their heads in them and became quiet, gulping and wagging their tails with satisfaction. The children would then return to the house while twilight veiled the woods and the fireflies lit up like precious stones. After washing, they would go to the upstairs rooms to change into nightshirts and sit down on the carpet to wait for dinner. Then the storytelling would begin: "The Tower That Was Neither in Heaven nor on Earth," "Bashchelik," "The Hill of Glass," and many others that Milena had discovered in the books. She enjoyed those evening moments especially, because she lagged behind the other children in running, climbing, and fighting, yet as she knew the most interesting stories, they all listened to her breathlessly and scrambled to get a seat beside her. She conveyed to them images of deserts and jungles, faraway cities, oceans and desert islands, birds of paradise, castles, three-headed monsters and giants.

For dinner they used to get meat and potato stew, or lamb with french beans, or mutton with beans or spinach, and for dessert fresh or boiled fruit, rice pudding and honey. Starved after frolicking in the fresh air, they would fight over food, sometimes jokingly using their spoons as weapons. The tureens and bowls would be collected empty, almost licked clean. After the meal they were sent to bed, and only then was the dinner served for the adult members of the family, on the floor below. One night, Milena had discovered by accident that the food prepared for the grownups was more plentiful and varied. She woke up around midnight to go to the toilet downstairs, and through the half open door of the dining room she spotted Magda, standing half asleep by the table and eating a big slice of meat pie. She joined her and started choosing amongst the leftovers of various pies, roasts, salads, and cakes. The following night Magda woke her up at about the same time, and so the two of them continued with their clandestine feasts until one of the maids caught them in the act. They were not scolded, but from then on the dining room table was cleared as soon as the dinner was over.

Djana noticed that Milena was thinner than the other children and she began bringing her a bun between meals, or a freshly baked roll with cream cheese, which she used to hide in her apron, ordering her to eat it secretly from the other children. "Run away where they can't see you, they always grab more food than you do." Milena would steal down the narrow path to the Grove, sit on some boulder and eat, watching the play of shadows on the sparse grass. Sometimes she would lift a pile of fallen leaves and watch the insects scatter from beneath it. They were of various colors, blue and green with a satin sheen, red with black dots, dark brown like roasted coffee beans, yellow and transparent like pine resin. Some were in black hard armor and had antlers like a deer. She grew to like those moments of solitude, listened to the songs of birds and learned to distinguish that of the nightingale, the lark, the blackbird, thrush, and starling. There she could also give rein to her fantasies, and imagine long-haired wood nymphs wrapped in their floating veils, green as the mountain stream, winged white horses, wizards and fairy tale princes.

For the children, the merriest and most exciting event at Ilino Hill was the hay-making. All the young people from the surrounding villages would assemble then, and the young men would mow with scythes and the girls turn over the hay with pitchforks and pile it into hayricks. The reapers lined up at equal intervals and swung their arms rhythmically as the scythes whizzed and flashed in the sun. Effortlessly and evenly, they cut through the grass, which fell in heady-smelling swathes. In front of the reapers, crickets and quails escaped, sometimes leaving behind their nests full of eggs, while the larks soared and sang in the air above the men's heads. The sun burned, but it was not hot because the constant breeze that came from the Grove or from the glen cooled the air. When one glade was finished, everybody would move on to another one, and only Milena would sometimes remain for a little while longer to observe the wavy rows of cut grass and listen as the stillness, which for a while reigned around her, was gradually invaded by a furtive rustle in the stubble, the buzzing of insects and the sudden deafening twittering of birds.

Lunch was brought for the reapers: a cauldron of stew, lambs on the roasting spit, thick yogurt in wooden containers, rye bread, and baskets of apples, pears, and white plums as big as eggs, grafted by Rade's father himself. The reapers, sweaty and with flushed faces, would then sit in the shade to be served by the maids from the estate. The mowing stopped in the evening and the grass, already dry, was piled into stacks. Afterwards the mowers, more than thirty in all, would assemble in the paved courtyard between the old and the new house. The men would take a seat on the stone bench that ran along the whole length of the house, and the women sat on the ground or on the stone slabs around the bleached sheet of thickly woven cotton. The raki was served first, the same glass passed around from one man to another. The girls did not drink, and if any of the married women were persuaded to take a sip, they would hold the glass in one hand and with the other modestly screen their mouths. After dinner, folk songs were sung and, still singing, the mowers would rise and leave for home. Illuminated by moonlight, they set out along the steep path towards Grevno, and their songs, mostly touching and melancholy like a distant sorrow, faded across the glades and groves.

Milena was saddened most by a song about a woman whose only brother was captured by the Turks and condemned to death. When, in despair, she offered to sacrifice one of her sons for him, the Turks agreed to the exchange. The song described further how, on the night of the execution, she went from one son to the other, tortured by her indecision as to which one she should wake at dawn and send to the Turks. She could not choose the first son because he was married, the second was betrothed, and the third not yet old enough to shave. Finally, she decided to wake the youngest and said that she was sending him to be her brother's best man at his wedding, "to escort him to his bride," and after every stanza came the refrain: "To uncle's wedding—to be betrayed."

There were also funny and joyous songs but Milena preferred the

sad, yearning ones, reflecting secret, unrequited love, or those that
described the hard life in the village, especially for women who, after their marriage, had to be subservient to every member of the
family, from the oldest to the youngest:

Sing, Jela, sing, Jela,
My snow-white lamb,
You will remember, you will remember,
The freedom of your youth.
You will remember, you will remember,
Once you are mine.

I was a queen, I was a queen,
Before I was married,
Royally fell asleep,
Royally woke.
Neither a queen nor a girl
Am I now,
But a bride, but a bride,
Newly wed.

On the eve of Mitrovday, the weather suddenly became cold and
it drizzled from early morning. At this time of year the plums were
picked and, as the plum orchard in the glade was not yet finished,
the children had to help collect the fruit while it was still fresh. The
men from the estate climbed the trees and shook the branches while
the maids and the children removed their shoes in the wet grass,
spread out in a row and collected the plums which fell like massive
rain, hitting their heads and their bent backs and rolling around their
feet. Milena was cold, the wet plums escaped from her frozen hands,
her lacerated feet hurt, but she did not drop behind the others and
tried to keep in line. Evening was drawing by the time the picking
was done, so that they all rushed home. In front of the entrance door
a butt of rainwater was put out for the children. They washed their
muddy feet there, slipped on their clogs, and ran to bathe and change
as their clothes were completely drenched. Afterwards, they went to
the room opposite the kitchen, which had already been prepared

for the holiday. The walls were white-washed, everything clean and dusted, the fire burned in the polished tin stove, and in front of the icon of the Mother of God the *kandilo* flickered. The icon was small, and set in a plate of silver and gold, behind which only the faces and hands of Christ and the Mother of God could be seen, painted in somber colors. Milena felt pleasantly exhausted, the room was warm, the fire crackled and drummed in the thin stove, and the twilight gathered round the blue-red undulating flame of the *kandilo*.

The following day Jelka came to take Milena home, as the weather had changed and the end of the school holiday was approaching. Milena regretted parting with the jolly company of children, the woods, fields, and pastures, the wide open spaces and the freedom she had experienced on the estate, but she did not dare oppose her mother's word, and also she had missed Niko very much and was happy to see him again. As they descended Ilino Hill, Milena noticed that her mother looked sad and worried, and she was afraid that she might somehow have upset her.

"Why are you being like this? You were not alone. Niko took my place."

"The mobilization has begun, my child, and I feel anxious."

"Is Niko going to volunteer again?"

"No, I made him swear on my life that he would not volunteer, but still I am afraid. They are mobilizing all the young men. Rosa's three elder sons have been called up, she is left with only Vojo. Rosa has him at least, but if they take Niko, I'll be left only with daughters."

"They won't take only sons," Milena tried to reassure her.

"I hope not, but a mother can't help worrying. There is nothing worse than to be a mother in time of war."

Great excitement reigned in Plevlje. Large numbers of soldiers were mustered at the Barracks, a new hospital was opened, and the Allied Mission arrived, consisting of doctors and nurses from Russia, France, and England. Milena was mainly interested in the nurses, who wore white overalls with long sleeves and a high-collared jerkin belted tight at the waist. On their heads were large scarves resembling a nun's headdress, which fell down to their shoulders and had a red cross above the forehead. The same red cross was sewn on to a broad armband. The children again played war games, though they no longer divided into Serbs and Turks, but into allies and enemies. When Milena tried to join them once more, they wanted to send her away.

"Women don't go to war."

"Why not? I saw a woman officer in the Mission."

"Ah, but she is English and wears trousers. How can you carry a sword or a gun wearing a skirt?"

"I can be a doctor or a nurse—they are in skirts."

The boys exchanged looks, as the idea had not occurred to them before, and moved aside to talk it over. "All right," they finally agreed. "If you wear a scarf like theirs and put a red cross on your sleeve. You must also have a white shoulder bag."

Milena ran home all excited and pleaded with her mother to make her all the things she needed. Into the bag she put bandages cut from old sheets and various medicinal herbs she found in the pantry.

The children played mostly around the Barracks, because the park was covered by fallen leaves which no one had swept up or collected for years, especially in the side lanes, which people seldom used, and where the layer of leaves was knee-deep. It served them in all sorts of ways: they would clear a bigger space for the hospital and make beds of dead leaves in it, dig trenches through the deeper piles, and use them to cover the soldiers who fell in battle, placing on the mounds crosses made of two sticks tied with string. Milena would attend to all the wounded regardless of which side they were on, dress their wounds and pass them on to the boys who carried them on a plank to the hospital. Those who lay motionless were covered with leaves, and as none of the boys wanted to play the priest because priests wore cassocks, Milena had to take off her nurse's scarf, put a Montenegrin cap on her head instead, and conduct the funeral rites, over the graves. Soon other girls joined in, and the games became even more entertaining for Milena. She was now a doctor, and decided which of the fallen warriors was dead and must be buried, and which was to be carried to the hospital. When they went on playing longer, they brought some food and prepared meals for the patients as well as the other soldiers, fetched water from the fountain in old jugs and served it instead of wine, or used it as medicine and to wash the wounds.

One day, they went to play on Glavica not far from a flock of sheep that were grazing there. Some of the children suggested milking one of the sheep in secret, then lighting a fire between two stones and boiling the milk on it. All agreed enthusiastically—not that they were short of milk, since almost every house kept a cow, but for the fun of lighting a fire, stealing up to the flock, and braving their fears of the shepherd. They crept up amid suppressed laughter and squeals, and began to argue in whispers who would have the courage to do it. Milena decided to try, as she had learned to milk while at the estate. She inched her way to the ewe that had lagged behind the others and stealthily felt her udders. When the streams of milk began to ring at the bottom of the copper jug, her heart started beating faster from the thrill and pride she felt for being braver and more capable than the other children. The milk had hardly covered the bottom of the jug when somebody grabbed her fast by the shoulder. Petrified, she turned around and saw the shepherd, who had noiselessly crept up on her. All the children scattered and she burst into tears, pushed the jug into his hands and tried to struggle free, but he held on to her arm roughly and threatened to take her home and tell her mother that he had caught her stealing. When she heard that this was considered theft, she began to scream and begged him to let her go without telling anyone about her disgrace, and she would bring him the money tomorrow to pay for the milk. The very thought of him leading her up the Hill so that everyone would see her being brought to her mother as a thief was worse for her than if he had killed her there and then. When the shepherd saw how sorry she was, he released her, poured away the milk and gave her the jug, saying, "I don't want your money, but I'm telling you, if you do it once more I'll drag you through all the streets and show everyone you've been stealing milk, and I'll take you to your mother so that she finds out what sort of daughter she has borne." Too ashamed to thank him properly, she tore down the mountain, threw away the jug and went straight home, where she hid under the stairs and had a good cry because of the fear and dishonor she had experienced, her guilty conscience and the disappointment of being abandoned by her friends. From then on, she no longer mixed with the same children, nor did she care for the war games and, as it was soon time to return to school, new impressions overshadowed the painful memory of this event.

11

The new mobilization claimed Niko and he went to fight on the Drina. Jelka was hurt by the injustice of sending her only son to the front while none of her five sons-in-law, Montenegrins, was mobilized. She was the more embittered when three of them visited her and read with enthusiasm from *The Voice of Montenegro*, talking about the great battles in Serbia, on the Cer and Rudnik mountains, about the advances of the Serbian army at the Drina River, the capture of Cajnice, Gorazde, Focha, and Rogatica, and the plans to march on Sarajevo. She could not wait for them to leave. "They pride themselves on the army's conquests," she thought, "but they still cling on to their wives' skirts. Out of the five of them, not one has gone to fight. It's easy to read the papers and boast about someone else's victory, when you never get a whiff of gunpowder, and spare no thought for those who find the bullets whizzing around their ears."

Throughout that long winter, they had no news from Niko, and Jelka succumbed to great anxiety, so Milena did not leave her side, not knowing how else to console her. At long last, someone arrived from the front and brought the news that Niko was wounded and had been transferred to the hospital in Rudo. Jelka was only told that his wounds were light, but it was rumored in the town that shrapnel from a grenade had severed all the fingers on Niko's right hand and most of the palm, though everyone concealed this from her, even Milena. Soon after, Niko's letter came, telling them that he was in Rudo hospital because he was wounded, but not seriously. He had almost completely recovered and would not be sent back to the front as he would be working in the hospital administration. Jelka was relieved and pleased by these tidings. "As long as he doesn't go to where he might get killed," she would say, convinced that Niko was out of danger.

A second letter, from the head of the hospital, informed them that Niko was very ill. That same day, Jelka hired horses from a neighboring village and arranged with the owner to leave immediately for Rudo. There the doctors gave her permission to transport her son home, because the Allied mission was in Plevlje and could offer him better care.

The return journey was difficult and dangerous, as Niko could hardly sit in the saddle because of exhaustion and a high temperature, which caused him at times to lose consciousness. The snow in the mountains around the Sutjeska had not yet melted and the surface of the steep path alongside the ridges of the precipice was slippery and covered with slush. Jelka gave her horse to the owner and she herself led Niko's in an effort to find a safer footing in the snow. Dark clouds swirled above them, around the somber peaks of the crags, icy winds tore through the mountain pass, over the swollen river, but Jelka felt neither cold nor fatigue, only her anxiety as to whether her son would endure through such a wilderness.

As soon as they arrived in Plevlje, a consortium of doctors was summoned and it was established that Niko was suffering from typhus. Little was known about this illness and nobody in the family was aware that it could be fatal, so all hoped he would recover soon because they had confidence in foreign doctors, especially English.

Milena continued to go to school, and when her teacher enquired about her brother's health, she answered confidently, "He feels better and will be well again soon." She was more hurt by Niko's having lost all the fingers on his right hand, except for the thumb and index finger. It seemed to her that this would have upset her less if he was not so handsome, as if the sanctity of his perfection had been desecrated.

Despite the exceptional care devoted to him, Niko's illness worsened. More doctors came to see him and stayed longer in his room. Everybody fell into despair; the sisters no longer left Jelka's house, and Milena was not allowed to go to school. One day they took her to the small room by the entrance, and told her to stay there and not disturb anyone by coming out. She quietly left the door ajar and from time to time peered out. Everywhere there was some hidden anguish, an oppressive silence as before a storm. The sisters passed through the corridor soundlessly and fearfully. Mother did not leave Niko's bedside. Still more doctors arrived, whom she had not seen before. Later, the sisters did not leave the sick room either.

Then a dreadful scream broke the silence. The entire house resounded with lamentations. The doctors left, perplexed, their heads bowed, and behind them Milena's two sisters were led away by their husbands, who tried in whispers to restrain them. They struggled, tore their hair and lamented at the top of their voices, "Niko! Beloved brother!"

Jelka was carried out unconscious and laid on the divan in the adjoining room. Milena followed, sobbing. Her mother lay as if dead, while they sprayed her with water and placed cold towels on her bared chest. Strands of damp hair stuck to her forehead and sunken cheeks, her face was white and quite still, as if petrified. At times, she would regain consciousness for a moment, and dart a bewildered glance at them. Then remembering what had happened, she gasped, "Niko, my only son," and blacked out again.

Milena was racked with sobs, grieving for her mother as much as for her brother. When her sisters saw how much Niko's death pained her and how distressed she was because of Jelka's agony, they took her out of the room.

All the relatives gathered to offer help, and other people started to arrive. One of Jelka's daughters spotted Rosa among some women and, incensed by grief, went to her, grabbed her by the shoulders and pushed her down the stairs. "Go in peace now, your curses have caught up with this son too." Rosa managed somehow to avoid falling headlong down the stairs and, without looking up, she silently disappeared. Milena cried so much for her brother that in order to calm her a little they took her to her Uncle Petko's house and left her with Misho, who was gentle and whom she loved. He tried to cheer her up: he showed her his penknives, books, a set of miniature tools for woodwork, and did not leave her side.

As Niko was the first war victim in Plevlje, the town organized a funeral fit for a hero, and all the inhabitants mourned him. The funeral procession did not take the short cut over Glavica, but went from the Charshija, across Mocevac and Piskavac, to the cemetery. All the shops in the Charshija were shut, and the whole population, Serbian and Turkish, stood bareheaded in front of their houses, waiting for the procession to pass by. The service in the monastery was held by several priests, and speeches were made expressing sorrow and bitterness for the great sacrifices the small countries must endure to stop the big powers from enslaving them unjustly. The throng of people covered the entire ground around the monastery, and those who could not get inside the church stood in and around the courtyard. The mayor made a speech over the open grave and when he addressed Niko as "our hero!", Jelka struggled free, as if demented, embraced the coffin and began to cry, "Rise up, if you are a hero rise up for your mother's sake!" They pulled her forcibly away from the coffin and led her aside. The speaker did not continue, the priest conducted the last rites, and the people dispersed, silent and dispirited.

When they brought Milena back home, her mother was laid up like a ghost. Her sunken face, the color of clay, was lifeless and tearless. She had ordered black curtains to be drawn over the windows of the visitor's room, the table and *secijas* draped in black, and a black flag placed above the gates. No fires were lit in the house, everyone spoke in whispers and moved around in silence, all order was lost, the nights were sleepless, and Jelka was tended as if gravely ill. They cried secretly, and secretly ate the food that had been brought from their uncle's house. Jelka refused to eat or drink, so they had to force her to swallow a few drops of tea and moistened her dry parched lips with lemon. One day she suffered a nervous seizure. Distraught, she got out of bed, grabbed Niko's walking stick and began to smash all the *kandilos* and the glass on the icons. Milena was frozen with fear, while her sisters tried to restrain their mother and anxiously shut the doors and windows to conceal her sacrilege from others. They sent for Petko and Petronije. Father Rade had also arrived and started pleading with her not to court damnation, to stop being blasphemous and offending God.

"Offend whom? My tormentor?" She became more enraged. "I could hardly endure it when He took Vaso and Chedo from me, but I will never stop grieving for my only son. If He is the Almighty, why does He do it? I don't acknowledge Him! Let Him destroy everything, kill us all, I am not afraid! Nothing matters now."

They managed somehow to subdue her and she sank into listlessness. People were notified not to come to bring condolences until Jelka recovered, and no one was received. The family tried to reason with her and give her some solace, but she could not come to terms with life. Finally they advised her to go to the monastery of High Dechani and venerate the holy remains of St. Stevan, hoping that this pilgrimage would help to relieve the torment of her soul and convince her that holiness and God existed. She agreed out of despair and went with her son-in-law, the priest. The journey was long because they went on horses and in a difficult and dangerous time of war. There was no inn along the way where they could spend the night and rest the horses, so they had to leave the main road and search through the villages for shelter in private houses.

Three weeks later they returned.

Jelka was more composed and stronger after her journey, so people began calling in to offer condolences. She always kept Milena at her side and often one of her married daughters too. They took turns in staying at her home to help her with the visitors and with running the house. She received in the visitors' room. When the callers entered, Jelka would rise from the *secija* and, in reply to their greeting, "Peace and good health on your head," she would say, "Good health to all brothers and neighbors." She talked about the High Dechani, the casket of St. Stevan and his power to cure the sick and the bereaved. She appeared dignified and calm in the presence of the visitors, but when they left she sank into an imperious silence and remained thus immobile for hours. Life in the house regained its order in time, but the dense, oppressive silence still reigned over it. Jelka now spoke with Milena as if with a grownup, and they became closer. One day Milena summoned the courage to ask, "Dada, did you really see the saint, or do you only say so?"

Jelka looked at her hopelessly and began to talk as if to herself. "God help us, there is nothing, neither the saint nor any power from him. They dried the bones, put a metal plate in the place of his stomach, and his eye sockets are empty. It was all covered by a silk shroud, but I felt with my own hands what was under it. Bones, like all bones, don't rot when dried. I don't believe any more, either in saints or in the church of the priests. I only believe in God, though I don't know about Him, either. He must exist, for how otherwise could the world exist? But there is more suffering in the world than there is goodness. I saw the desolation and destruction of our poor country. Houses burned down and in ruins, fresh graves by the road-side and in the fields, many mothers in mourning. The damned enemy does evil things. I must talk differently, or they will pronounce me mad and godless. What can I do? I am not alone. 'Neither punish nor reward me, dear God, more than the others,' as they say; as long as He saves the children I still have, one must go on living."

From then on Jelka controlled her grief and bore it without resent-ment, like her mother. She gave the impression of being resigned to it, but gall had crept into her soul and she could no longer rejoice in anything. It seemed to her that she would not feel even a new sor-row: there was no room, her heart was crammed with pain. She went out little, to the church for communion, on All Saints' Day and on Good Friday, but not on joyful holidays, Easter, Christmas, or the Holy Trinity, when people assembled to celebrate with mirth. She went regularly to the cemetery, and preferred it when she found no one there.

Once she set off from home at twilight. The snow was falling, there was no path, and she stumbled into snowdrifts up to her knees. She stayed some time by Niko's grave, and, although it was getting dark, she did not feel like going home. Suddenly, she felt herself losing consciousness: darkness was falling over her eyes. She leaned her head on the cross and fainted. When she came to, she did not know where she was. It was night, and only the crosses on the headstones were discernible in the whiteness around her. "Why I am here?" With great effort she remembered that it had already been late when she left home. She shuddered, afraid of the darkness, the silence, and the graves, then rose, shook off the snow, which had fallen so deep that the trace of her footsteps was no longer visible, and left. Although visibility was fairly good in the snowy whiteness, she had trouble finding the gate, but once she did, she headed across the monastery pastures toward the Hill. She had to fight her way through the snowdrifts, which in some places reached up to her waist, but finally she struggled home. Thoroughly frozen and exhausted, she took off her clothes and lay down.

The next morning she woke in the grip of a high temperature, and could not get out of bed. When Milena got up and Dzema arrived, they made her a hot drink of raki and burnt sugar, rubbed her down with vinegar and covered her well to get her to perspire. She had to stay in bed several days until the fever subsided, but did not tell anyone the cause of her illness. From then on she did not go alone to the cemetery and took Milena with her.

Milena loved to accompany her mother and felt proud that, in a way, she was looking after her like a grownup. Their graveyard was next to the monastery of the Holy Trinity, on the rocky right bank of the Biserka, clinging to the cliffs. It was as difficult to approach as the monastery was. They would start along the highway leading over Glavica to the village of Rudnica, and when they reached the monastery pastures they would climb over a stile and head up the narrow undulating fields. At the monastery outbuildings, they passed through a small gate and on to the road that led from the town to the monastery and at one point branched off towards the cemetery. From there they made their way over the rough, rocky ground with the roots of leafy trees protruding, to arrive at the entrance.

The cemetery was surrounded by a wooden fence next to which grew aspen, linden, acacia, and willow trees, and was entered through tall wooden gates. At that time it looked impoverished, because there were not many wealthy people left in Plevlje. The new crosses were mainly of wood, many of them cobbled together from planks, and already weathered and decayed. The old crosses made of rough-hewn stone were often neglected and sunk into the earth, while some graves lacked headstones and could hardly be noticed, overgrown by grass, weeds, and thorns. At the top of the cemetery stood two tall tombs of polished granite, as if keeping watch over the dead. A number of marble monuments, strewn here and there amidst the wooden crosses, created more discord than harmony in that ancient ground where, even after death, the poverty survived.

Niko was buried in his grandfather's tomb, which lay on a slight rise in the ground and was surmounted by a tall wooden cross. Beside it stood a bench, shaded by a large rose bush. The entire space was planted with flowers and enclosed by a low fence with a gate in it. Milena would watch her mother as she reverently approached Niko's grave, unlocked the gate, entered slowly and knelt to kiss the head of the tomb. Her lips rested for a long time on the earth, then she would get up, kiss the cross, light the candle, and sit on the bench. Jelka did not cry much, nor did she lament. The pain which at first had torn at her like some angry beast had changed with time into a constant endless sadness to which she had surrendered completely. They would remain silent for long time, each lost in her thoughts, surrounded by a stillness which in winter would descend over the country like a dome, and in summer was overlaid by the rustle of leaves and the song of crickets in the grass. Sometimes they would stay longer and listen to the monastery bells tolling for evening prayers. Their ringing echoed against the sheer cliffs among which the monastery nestled, then faded and died away over the glades and fields. When they decided to leave, they kissed the cross again, locked the padlock on the gate, and returned home with relief in their hearts.

From the front came news of more casualties. Two of Rosa's sons had been killed, as well as the only son of Janko's sister, Stojana. As Stojana had no other children, Jelka often called on her to offer help in her great misfortune and to share her sorrow. She did not go to Rosa, nor did the other come to her—their ancient quarrel lasted forever.

Soon after the death of his sons, Stevo, Janko's brother, also died. Jelka did not attend his funeral, although she had loved Stevo like her own brother, but next morning she went to the monastery with

Milena to say prayers for his soul, and for Rosa too. "May God forgive her everything, and give her strength," she said to Milena. "I know how she feels. It will be hard for her to bear the loss of two such special sons, even though she has another two boys. Stevo could not go on living, his heart simply broke with their deaths. Not long ago their daughter Milica also died, leaving behind two small girls. There, I did not curse her, and look what God has done to her. No, there is nothing, neither curses nor spells nor forebodings, but what is preordained. Some people abandon themselves to their destiny, as my mother did, but I can't. I listened to the priests who read prayers for me in the monastery of High Dechani, and they always referred to me as a sinner because I couldn't obediently accept God's will. They spoke of how God had put Job to the test, and I couldn't help thinking that it would have been better if He had let him die together with his children, than rewarded him after their death. I can't even pray any more, nor do I know how; so I only cross myself when I mention God's name and appeal to Christ, because only he knows what people suffer."

Milena had already noticed that Jelka pretended in front of other people to be more religious than she was, because some had started referring to her as an infidel, seeing that she seldom went to church and observed only Lent and the first and last weeks of the pre-Christmas fast.

Mobilization took further reinforcements to the front, and Jelka's three Montenegrin sons-in-law were called up by the army and sent to the Drina. The newspapers continued to report fierce battles being fought on all fronts, and in Plevlje they followed the news with a blend of admiration and anxiety. Along the Drina, Serbian forces held Gorazde, Cajnice, and other towns that had been captured from the Austrians and advanced all the way to Pal, near Sarajevo. In Serbia the enemy attacks were repeatedly thrown back, despite the arrival of Austrian reinforcements, and the most furious battles were around the Cer and Rudnik mountains. Many had been killed on both sides, tens of thousands of university and school volunteers alone. The paper wrote how highly the Allies regarded Serbia, and how these battles would go down in all the world's histories. The Czechs and Croats, who had been sent to the Russian front, deserted the Austrian army and put themselves under the Russian command. Meanwhile, however, despite all these encouraging newspaper reports, talk of the retreat of Serbian troops began to spread among the people. Soon afterwards came the first refugees from Bosnia and Serbia, whose numbers swelled within a few days so that it was a problem finding accommodations for them in the private houses and empty barracks.

All hopes turned on Montenegro, and its mountain defenses. "The army will fall back on them," it was said, "and then hit out at the Shvabas from those high cliffs. They'd be able to defend themselves if they had nothing but the rocks to fight with, never mind cannons and bombs." The Montenegrin army retreated through Plevlje, and the Serbian in the other direction, through Macedonia. The refugees from Serbia continued over Prijepolje to join their army, while the Bosnians remained to await the Austrian occupation and return to their homes. Jelka's sons-in-law returned with the army, and when their units left for Montenegro, they took their families with them. All the tenants of the Kojic houses also left.

Fear reigned in Plevlje before the arrival of the enemy troops. The last Montenegrin soldiers cut the telephone lines as they withdrew, pulled down pylons, set the barracks on fire, and blew up the ammunition stores. The bombs that they could not take with them were thrown into the lake. Jets of water rose sky-high, higher than the roofs of the tallest houses. The explosions defeaned the ears, glass shook in the windows, and the mountains echoed.

Cannon fire began around the town, from hill to hill. Some Montenegrins were dug in around Ilino Hill to cover the retreat, and the Austrians opened fire from the high ground on the opposite side. The artillery roar shattered the very sky, and the shells flew across the town. The houses that were hit burned, illuminating the whole of Plevlje like giant torches: it was bright as day in the middle of the night. Tongues of flame poured out of the window openings, licked at the walls, and spread to join fires that burned fiercely on the wooden roofs. The air was filled with smoke and the smell of burning.

Jelka could not sleep all night, and kept going to the balcony with Milena to watch the flashes from the cannons when the firing rang out. She feared for the lives of Djana and her children, though she

292

was slightly reassured when she saw no reflection of any buildings burning on the estate.

At long last the shooting stopped. The houses were still smoldering in the deserted streets when the Austrian reconnaissance party appeared at the Barracks, followed by the other troops. The town had not officially surrendered. All the inhabitants shut themselves in their houses and kept out of sight. A deathly silence awaited the enemy. The Austrians were billeted in the barracks, which had not been too damaged, and in private houses. All Jelka's apartments were once more occupied by officers, the bar was turned into a canteen, horses were installed in the cowshed and their cow moved out into the back yard. Jelka had sent it to Ilino Hill at the first opportunity, because the grooms were eyeing it and she was afraid they might kill it by stealth one night. The storage room was also requisitioned, and the batmen housed there.

Jelka had difficulty in keeping possession of the first floor of one house where she and Milena had moved. Had the Serbian-speaking military doctor who was billeted in one of the flats not interfered, she would have been thrown out with Milena into a small house where the kitchen and servants' rooms were. Soldiers were put in there instead, and Jelka moved a stove into one of her rooms. The army also commandeered more and more furniture, mattresses, and bedding, until finally the doctor saw that she would be left with nothing, and told her not to give up anything else, and if anyone tried to take things by force he would protect her. All night there was noise, drinking, and singing in the bar. The piano had been taken from her too, and was played long after midnight, sometimes until dawn, which hurt her most because she had only heard Niko play it and it seemed to her that every note pierced her wounded heart. She went outside only when she had to, to avoid seeing the enemy uniforms, which reminded her of death, sorrow, and devastation.

No news came from her three daughters who had gone with their husbands to Montenegro, no one came to town from Ilino Hill, and Jelka had heard nothing from Djana either since the attack on Plevlje had begun. On the eve of the war Marija had moved to a large two-story house which could be seen from Jelka's, and although she did not visit them, at least she was near. Whenever the upper windows of Marija's house were opened, Jelka looked at them for a long time and could sometimes catch sight of her.

The news spread that King Nikola had abandoned the Allies and concluded a separate treaty with Austria, and that Montenegro had capitulated. All hope that freedom might be regained from that source disappeared, but it was believed that this could alleviate the conditions of the population and that the occupation would proceed more peacefully. It turned out, however, that the Austrians were much more brutal now than in Turkish times. They first collected all eligible males and deported them to prisoner-of-war camps, among others, two of Jelka's sons-in-law from Plevlje. Immediately afterwards, they issued an order that all food reserves must be declared, and half of them surrendered to the authorities. Should anyone be caught disobeying this order, he would lose everything and would also be punished.

In these precarious times, Jelka was worried that famine would set in and she decided not to declare anything, although she had several sacks of wheat grain and some flour hidden away. She worried most about Marija, since Petronije had been taken to a prisoner-of-war camp and she was left alone with six children, besides being pregnant.

Just then, Marija's neighbor came running one night and told Jelka to come straight away because Marija had had a miscarriage and was dying. Terrified, Jelka went to the Austrian doctor, woke him up and begged him in tears to come with her. She told Milena that she would be back soon and locked her room. Milena could not sleep all night. She was anxious to know what was happening with Marija, worried that her mother was not yet back, and afraid of being alone in the house with the Shvabas. Jelka returned just before dawn, pale and exhausted. She told Milena that Marija was very ill, helped her to dress quickly, and left with her.

It was getting light when they came to Mocevac, and the mist was receding from the plains and gradually creeping up the Hill. They walked in silence. Everything was quiet around them; only the murmur of water from the Mocevac fountain could be heard. Jelka stopped by the fountain and said in a whisper, "My darling, don't cry out loud when you hear what I have to say. There are sentries everywhere and they might turn us back. Our Marija is dead."

Milena's whole body convulsed with the sharp pain that pierced her chest. She took her mother's hand and pressed her face to it, overcome by stifled sobs. Jelka cried too, quietly, for fear of being overheard. She held Milena tightly, and led her into the house.

Marija was lying in state as if asleep, beautifully dressed. Her face, fresh and unmarked by a long illness, expressed the relief and calm she had found in sudden death after excruciating pain. Her hair had the color of old gold, plaited like a crown above her high smooth forehead. Her hands were crossed over her breast; their long slender fingers had the pallor of mother-of-pearl. She appeared still taller and slimmer as she lay on the table covered by a white cloth, and looked to Milena more beautiful than ever. Milena could not believe that she was dead, that she could be buried in the earth, beautiful as she was, and rested her lips on the forehead in a long kiss. The thought that this was the last time, that she would never see her again, or hear her voice, was unbearable: she could not part from her. She cried so much that they had to pull her forcibly away from Marija and lead her to another room.

Milena was not allowed to go to the funeral. Jelka sent word to Djana to come, but she arrived only on the following day because the sentries did not allow her across the Cotina and she had to wait until she obtained a pass from the authorities in her village. Immediately after her arrival, she went with Jelka to the cemetery. As they climbed Mount Glavica, Jelka began to talk softly, as if lamenting. "Her Petronije did not look after her properly. He gave her so many children, one after the other, and left her pregnant before they sent him to the prisoner-of-war camp. My poor daughter, in her twenty-seventh year she had borne six children and had conceived the seventh.'

"Did she try to have a miscarriage?"

"She told me she did not, but she carried some heavy sacks of flour to hide them in the store-room, and covered them with firewood. With the strain, she began to bleed—she said that all the blood poured out of her, but not the fetus. She called the midwife, some relative of Petronije, to take it out, but she only damaged her insides and nothing came out. When they saw what this wretch had done, they sent for me. The doctor knew immediately that it was too late. He did not touch her, only said that blood poisoning had set in that he could not help her, then turned and left. He couldn't have reached the footbridge over the Mocevac brook before she died."

Djana cried quietly as Jelka went on in a low voice, without tears, "And if you only knew what awaited me afterwards. Petronije's mother had to look after the children—what else could the poor soul do, six of them and the youngest not even walking?—so I, myself, had to bathe Marija, with the help of a neighbor. What an ordeal for a poor mother. I did not know how beautiful she was, white as if carved out of snow, her skin like silk. She was not ailing, did not lose weight, so one couldn't tell what was more harmonious about her, her breasts or hips, or those long arms like swans' necks. God help my wretched soul, to have to let her be buried, that her body and youth should perish as Niko's did."

When they reached the monastery pasture, they paused for breath by the stile. Djana was weeping, while Jelka just stared in front of her as she continued in a sing-song voice, "And now listen to what happened then. There was nowhere to buy a coffin, nor was there anyone to find one for me. No man anywhere, all taken prisoners of war, and whoever was left was in hiding or had escaped to the villages, so as not to be sent to forced labor. Eventually, one peasant in the monastery, who was doing some work there, made me a makeshift coffin from rough planks. You can imagine what the funeral was like, with no one to carry her but women. They stumbled as they went, and I was afraid they might lose hold of the coffin, so I ran from one to the other to give a hand, I the wretched mother, but they did not let me. There were no grave diggers, and had it not been for the monastery staff, there wouldn't have been anyone to bury her."

Sobbing, Djana reached for Jelka's hand and started kissing it. Jelka went on, "My child, only then did I see that there is worse than the worst, and harder than the hardest. Had Marija been saved, I would never have mentioned Niko again. When he died, I thought, let come what may, but now I see that suffering has no limits."

They climbed over the fence and headed towards the park through the grass until they reached the pebbled road leading to the monastery, then turned left past the rocks and arrived at the cemetery. As they passed Niko's grave, they only crossed themselves and continued towards the fresh mound of Marija's grave, which stood at the far end under the branches of a willow tree.

Djana fell onto the grave, spread her arms around it as if in an embrace and began to lament, "Marija, my tormented sister! How am I to bear the sorrow? How will your children fare without your loving mother, without her motherly care? The agony of your maternal wounds, my poor martyr. In childbearing all your youth has gone, my fair nymph . . ."

Jelka stood listening with lifeless eyes, still and dumb as a stone, until Djana's lament sank into the rustle of willow leaves swayed by the breeze coming from Biserka.

They lit the candles, kissed the cross, and went to Niko's grave. Jelka knelt beside it, still quite silent as tears poured down her haggard cheeks. The monastery bells began to ring for evening prayers and their sounds reverberated over the cemetery. Djana approached to light the candles and, seeing that Jelka did not stir, she tenderly embraced her shoulders. "Don't, Dada, it's no use. We won't bring him back even if we all killed ourselves."

Back at the house they relaxed a little and drank coffee, then Djana rose to leave. Jelka wanted her to stay overnight, but she was anxious not to leave the children alone with the servants and was worried about her youngest son, who had not been well the last few days.

"I'm afraid the sentries may stop you. It's getting late."

"If I hurry, I'll reach the Cotina before dark, and after that they won't ask for a pass."

Jelka saw her off at the gate, said goodbye and stayed for a while longer to watch her walk away down the deserted street and fade into the azure twilight. Her heart was a little lighter now, because she had had to withhold from Milena the days of dammed up grief which had oppressed her. With Djana she could abandon herself to it, and confide in her as in no one else, and that gave her strength to get to grips with life again.

Marija's children stayed with Petronije's mother because this was the wish of his family. Jelka was very upset about it until Petronije returned from the prisoner-of-war camp, but then she had to accept the fact that it was their father's right to bring them up as he thought best and that she could not interfere.

Life under the occupation was becoming more and more difficult. Since Montenegro had capitulated, the Austrians faced no danger on that front, and they used all their military forces from these territories to squeeze as much as possible out of the occupied land. First they began to buy up wool, at compulsory prices determined by themselves. It was delivered to the Krstata Barracks, where women laborers sorted and combed it and put it into bales which were then duly sewn up and stamped. The bales were stacked in the street against the wall of Jelka's house and later loaded on to trucks and transported to Austria.

Milena discovered that it was possible to get on top of the stacks from the window of her room, and together with Pava's Misho and his friends, she climbed on to them, slid down to the sidewalk and ran back into her room to start all over again, until Jelka noticed their perilous game. She gave Milena a hiding, and the others a good telling off, before she threw them out of the house. "What if you fell between the bales and suffocated before anyone saw you? Or fell down, hit your head on the cobblestones and died at once, God forbid?"

When all the wool had been dispatched, wheat grain was confiscated, then copper and timber, and finally livestock. The peasants had to bring the livestock to the Trainer, where it was loaded live into special vehicles and sent to Austria, and for days Plevlje echoed with the mooing of cattle and the bleating of sheep.

Famine spread. It was impossible to buy wheat grain or flour anywhere. Meat and lard could be had at a price, but bread became a rarity. People went out into the fields and bushes around the town to gather wild spinach and nettles which they mixed with a little flour to make a palatable dish. Whoever had pumpkins cooked them with a little cornflour. Everybody struggled as best they could: people stripped the bark off oak trees, ground up the acorns to add to barley or buckwheat, poured the mixture into trays and took it to be baked in the bakery ovens, as it could not be done on the hearth. First the poor from the gypsy quarter began to die. People who had never begged started to beg. Labor was dirt cheap, and people went from door to door to look for work, in return for food alone. Weak and swollen, they walked along swaying from side to side like loose sacks ready to topple. Hunger peered from many eyes, and even those who tried to do so could not conceal their destitution.

As soon as the famine became widespread, Jelka, with the help of the Austrian doctor, emptied the store-room, put a partition across it, and on one side installed the cow she had brought back from Ilino Hill, and on the other the pig. She obtained scraps for the pig from the army cooks, who were Bosnian Serbs, forcibly conscripted into the Austrian army. From them she learned that the doctor was from Sarajevo, a Jew, and that he was friendly to the Serbs. The income from rents was no longer coming in, and she could not change the gold as she had not declared it and was afraid that it would all be confiscated if found. She managed somehow, like the others in her neighborhood, on her garden produce and the livestock. She too prepared wild spinach and pumpkin meals, but in secret, because she still considered scarcity to be shameful. Bread was baked only for Milena and Marija's children, but even to them she gave sparingly. Milena never went hungry, and out of all the usual food, she only missed bread. When at school, which had started again, some child would bring in a bun or a roll, she pretended not to be hungry if she were offered a piece, however difficult it was for her to refuse. Once she told her mother that a friend of hers from a good home had accepted a piece of bread which she had declined, and Jelka was shocked.

"What a disgrace that glutton is, especially as her people are merchants and have more than we do, while you, my blessing, protect the name and honor of our house. Stay as dignified as you are, no matter what life has in store for you, and hold your head high. Honor is more important than life, and I'd rather you were dead than that you should disgrace our name."

However gratified Milena was because her mother was pleased, it hurt her to think about those who were really hungry, and she asked herself how she would have borne it.

The Austrians opened the storehouse and began to sell flour and wheat grain, but only for gold. When they had thus extorted all the gold, jewelry, cigarette boxes, and ornaments, they started selling small quantities for kronen, but at such high prices that only a few could afford it. Famine ravaged the villages too, and the fields went unsown because the villagers had to survive on the seed during the hunger-ridden winter. They peeled the germinating potatoes, planted only the peel with the new shoots, and ate the rest. The livestock was mostly requisitioned, and what was left the villagers had slaughtered for fear that it too would be confiscated. Many herbs that were not bitter were discovered and mixed with nettles and wild spinach to make soups, or were eaten raw.

In spring Spanish influenza swept through the town and surrounding countryside and began to devastate entire villages. The embittered population, which till then had suffered all its hardships without resistance, started to rebel and took up arms. The Austrians retaliated with executions and hangings. They emptied the Krstata Barracks of the stockpiled goods, repaired and painted it, then turned it into a military court. The large house next to it, which belonged to the monastery, was converted into a prison, its tall windows walled up, leaving only narrow gaps at the top, with heavy bars, and the whole building fenced in by two rows of barbed wire. Here they brought the prisoners accused of high treason because arms had been found buried under their houses or in their fields. The majority of those arrested were peasants and Montenegrins from the territories that fell under Plevlje's administration.

Jelka hung thick curtains at all the windows facing the Barracks, as she had during the *asker* occupation—then because of the shameful behavior of the soldiers, and now out of the sorrow she felt for the prisoners who were taken to their deaths. The Austrians carried out the death sentences in broad daylight and with ceremony. Milena was forbidden to go out on to the street on those days, but she would secretly lift the curtain over the window of her room and watch the condemned as they were led from the court and escorted down the street.

A large crowd of Serbs, Turks, and children would assemble in front of the court. They all waited inquisitively for the prisoner to be taken from the prison to the court, where his sentence was read out to him in German, then he was led out under guard. Milena's heart would sink when she saw the condemned man emerge, pale and bewildered, looking with amazement at the people around him and obediently following the orders of his guards. Tears flooded her eyes, but she continued to watch, as if mesmerized by the spectacle, how he was placed at the front, flanked by a squad of armed soldiers.

If the man was condemned to death by hanging, behind him came the hangman, a gypsy; if he was to be shot, instead of the hangman a squad of soldiers with rifles accompanied him. In both cases, a priest walked beside him, talking all the time. The condemned man would either answer and repeat the prayer, or remain silent and remote, as if none of it was happening to him. Milena pitied those who were followed by the hangman more, because it seemed to her that shooting was less horrifying, less degrading. When the procession went away, the street became empty as if there was not a living soul in it. Those who did not go to see the execution locked themselves in their houses. Then Milena would steal away to her uncle's house and wait for Misho to come back, as he watched all the executions and described them to her in detail.

"With a hanging, the hangman takes the condemned man to the gallows, puts the noose around his neck, throws the other end of the rope over a beam and passes it through a ring, then tightens it. Then the Austrian officer reads something in German and signals with his sword to the hangman. The other pulls the bench from under the condemned man's feet . . . and he hangs, trembling at first, then swaying until he dies. One of them, in his agony, put out his tongue and stayed like that after he died. Another one wetted himself."

"Do they do it in Bogishevac, by the Shvabas' cemetery?" Milena could not imagine these cruel scenes in the quiet part of the town where she had often walked before, and had sat reading for hours on end in the shadowy deserted graveyard.

"No, the hangings are on the other side of Bogishevac and the executions by firing squad are next to the Shvabas' cemetery. There are usually several condemned men then. They are brought to the already dug grave, and lined up facing the soldiers, who hold their rifles at the ready. The officer reads the sentence, then one soldier approaches with blindfolds and ties them round each man's eyes. Afterwards, the officer raises his sword and shouts something in German, rifles are fired, and they all fall. You can't see them any more." The shooting seemed too ordinary for him and he paused, trying to remember something that would make it more interesting. "Once one man fell before the rifles were fired, and they had trouble making him stand up again before they killed him."

On such days, Milena could neither learn nor play, and she dreamed horrifying dreams at night from which she woke screaming in tears. Her mother comforted her, gave her sugar and water, and asked her what was tormenting her, but Milena did not dare admit it.

12

The living conditions under the occupation were deteriorating still further and Jelka grew afraid that the famine might also affect her own household, so she decided to go to Sarajevo to change some gold coins for cash. She had intended secretly to exchange a few napoleons in Plevlje, but after the town crier had announced that those who sold gold to anyone except the Austrian authorities would be shot, she feared informers. Jelka did not tell anyone why she was going, not even Djana, but said she wished to see her sister Jula, who had recently become a widow and was living in Sarajevo with her two daughters. Only Milena knew, as Jelka confided everything to her, and consulted her as if she were an adult.

Milena was delighted about the trip, because she would be seeing Sarajevo and her aunt, but also because her mother had prepared a big loaf of wheat flour and had baked it in a deep dish to get it to rise higher. Jelka also prepared a roast chicken, a meat pie, fresh cheese, and eggs, a meal they no longer had on feast days, but there was nothing that Milena looked forward to more than to the bread.

Every now and then she entered the kitchen to touch its warm, rough crust and inhale the irresistible aroma of freshly baked dough, but she did not eat any of it, as her mother had asked her to wait until they reached the village of Rudnica, where they hoped to hire horses. It was impossible to get any means of transport in Plevlje, so they had to go to Rudnica on foot.

Jelka engaged a woman from the neighborhood, Neda, to carry the luggage. On the day of the journey, she got up before first light to prepare a big breakfast for Neda, then woke Milena and they left as soon as she had some food. Neda carried the big suitcase on her back, tied with cord crossed over her chest. Jelka carried the baskets of food and Milena the bag with a change of clothing. It was getting light when they started to climb Glavica. The sun lit all the hills around while the town was still in shadow, wrapped in mist. It was the Sunday before the Easter fast, and as Easter fell on St. George's Day that year, spring was in full bloom.

They soon reached Rudnica, but could not find horses for hire, though they went from house to house in the hope that some peasant would let them have his plough horse. It turned out that these too had all been confiscated, and people were having to harness cattle to the plough. Finally, Neda suggested that they should go on foot all the way to Rudo: she would carry the suitcase and lead the way by short-cuts, however long it might take to get there. Jelka was relieved not to have to call off the trip and decided to start immediately to avoid being benighted in open country.

"God bless you, Neda, you have done me a great service by coming with us. But for you, we would have had to turn back. By myself I wouldn't know the way, nor could I carry such a load."

"Ah, my Jankovica, I have done it for the food's sake as much as for yours. I was starving, sister, and having proper nourishing meals for a day or two will do me a world of good."

"You shall have some money as well, and when we get back, I will give you potatoes and pumpkins. I kept the potatoes in a clamp and still have some, and the pumpkins are in the store-room. The frost did not get them, so they are still sound and fresh, and pop when I cut them. I won't forget your kindness. If you only knew how I feel going through these parts." A sigh escaped her like a suppressed cry, and she stopped to look at the mountains, blue in the distance, merging with the sky. "Along this road I took my ailing soldier, my only son. His mother tried to save him. We went on horseback, through snow and slush, and I feared that in his delirium he would plunge down the cliff, so I dismounted and led his horse. A mountain pony is wise, and when unsure it stops to search with its hoof for a firm footing. When it goes uphill, it lowers its head so as not to let a sick rider slide off its haunches, and when downhill it lifts its head to stop him from slipping over its neck." Her voice began to tremble, she shook her shoulders and looked at Neda with clouded eyes. "God, what a human being can endure. My heart must be made of stone not to have burst from the pain. And I cannot take my own life, I can't do it because of this child. She was small when her father died and has suffered a lot with me. Janko pledged me to have her educated and I must live to see it through."

"Don't, Jankovica, don't talk like that in front of her, she is sensitive and it upsets her."

"You're right, I can see it's not good that I can't hide my sorrow from her. Perhaps that's why she looks so pale and underdeveloped."

They did not stop again until the sun had climbed high in the sky and began to burn, then they found a pleasant spot with a spring of clear water emerging from under a rock, and forming a narrow brook which made its way through the grass, so they sat down to relax and have something to eat. They spread a cloth over the grass and placed a stone on each corner, because in these high mountain glades the wind blew from all sides. Jelka took the food out of the baskets and put a flask of raki into the brook to cool. She and Neda drank a glass of it and made Milena take a sip to warm her and strengthen her for the long walk ahead. Around them spread a carpet of yellow daffodils, the air was filled with a heady fragrance and the brook tinkled softly. Milena ate her fill of bread with some cheese and scallions, and would have preferred to fall asleep in the scented grass, but she knew they would soon have to start walking again, because it was almost noon and they were not yet halfway on their journey. Jelka spread her shawl for Milena to rest a little, while she and Neda lit a fire of dry twigs to make coffee. When they had drunk it, they set off again.

305

They skirted forests, and took short-cuts over fields and through glades and thickets. Neda kept reassuring them that they would not have to climb any more, as the way led downhill from there on and they would be able to reach Rudo before dark. Whenever they saw a brook or spring, they would stop for a drink of cool fresh water and to splash their faces and necks. Jelka saw with what difficulty Milena bore the heat and fatigue, so she took from her the bag she was carrying, undressed her, leaving on only her slip of thin woven cotton buttoned at the shoulders, and tried to comfort her. "Once we get to the mountain pass and across the Sutjeska, we'll be at Rudo in no time. Then we can go all the way by train."

A few times they stopped to rest, and ate a few mouthfuls to keep up their strength, but Milena could not touch the food. She felt unable to get to her feet again, and was in tears from exhaustion, however much she tried to control herself for fear of upsetting her mother.

Neda coaxed her to go further—"Here, as soon as we get past this hill, the going is downhill to the mountain pass"—but behind that hill another one would appear, and Milena felt in the depths of her disappointment that the journey would never end.

Finally, they reached the steep masses of rock through which the Sutjeska cut its way. They clambered down the path to the narrow road that ran alongside the troubled mountain river. The sharp peaks of the cliffs loomed over them and sliced into the sky like blades of slate. Here and there, out of the sheer stone, there sprouted an occasional stunted pine with sparse branches, which stood up to the ceaseless winds that scoured the path. When the road descended to the very edge of the Sutjeska, they entered a narrow passage in which nothing except the path and the river could be seen because the tall cliffs screened the sky. The sun did not reach there at any time of the day and, although they had put on all the clothes they could, they shivered in the cold wind and the icy breath of the river. They could hardly lift their tired feet, yet still they tried to hurry, to escape from this freezing wasteland.

Jelka remembered with anguish how she had journeyed there with Niko, hoping that she would save him if they reached Plevlje alive. Neda noticed that she was sad and, to draw her attention away from her thoughts, she pointed out a cave in the rocks, mysterious, dark, and inaccessible to man. The sides of the rocks were steep and smooth as if cut out of somber gray glass. She knew this region well because she had followed this path several times and had heard many stories about it and its secrets.

"Stop and listen. Can you hear something tapping, tap, tap, then it stops and starts again?"

Milena thought she really could hear a hollow rhythmical echo.

"Well, it comes from that highest cave, where a highland nymph lives and weaves. That soft whirring is the shuttle, which can be heard flying through the golden threads of the warp, and when it taps it is when she is battening the weft. And so the nymph weaves day and night."

"Has anyone ever seen her?"

"Yes, a young man called Stojan. Poor boy, he was passing this way and glanced up at the cliffs just as she looked out of the cave. She was so beautiful that he could find no peace after he saw her. She took up all his thoughts. Day after day he climbed and crawled up the rocks, and tied ropes where the pine trees stuck out. He had to get to her at all costs. Finally, he somehow reached the cave, but when he looked inside and met her blazing eyes, his mind clouded in an instant and he slipped down the cliff. Not even his bones were found."

"When was that?"

"Long, long ago. My grandmother told me about it, and she heard it from her grandmother."

"Can that nymph still be living then?"

"Of course, they never die, nor do they age or grow ugly, but they are eternally young and beautiful. No one can catch them, hold them, or kill them."

"Prince Marko could. I read it in some folk tales."

"Well, I can't read or write, nor do I believe what's written in books. I only know what my grandmother told me."

The sun was setting when they emerged from the path and saw Rudo in the distance, already cloaked in twilight. They reached the town just before dark, and headed towards the first more spacious inn to look for overnight accomodation. It happened that it belonged to the husband of a woman from Plevlje, and when he heard who they were he immediately took them to his home, where his wife welcomed them wholeheartedly and asked them to stay the night as her guests.

Milena was too tired to wait for dinner, and as soon as she had washed she went to bed. The moment her head touched the clean, fragrant pillows, she fell asleep. When she awoke it was already daylight. The sun flooded the spacious, whitewashed room, the sound of a river could be heard through the wide open windows, and the thought that she was in Rudo and would soon be traveling by train, which she had never seen before, filled her with a joy she had not experienced for a long time. She got up, changed into clean clothes, and went downstairs. Restless with excitement, she asked permission to go out and wait for Jelka on the bank of the river, which flowed close to the railway station. Broad and undulating, much bigger than the Cotina or Sutjeska, the river glittered in the opulent morning sunshine, fracturing the green reflections of the trees that overlooked its banks.

Just before the train arrived, Jelka came, accompanied by Neda and their hosts, and they all went to the station. Milena watched the tunnel impatiently, and the train soon came bursting out of it as if from a cave, wreathed in smoke and smaller than she had imagined, then snaked along the bends of the river and drew up at the platform. There were four classes in the train: first for the Austrian dignitaries, second for the officers and very wealthy civilians, third for the middle classes, and fourth for ordinary people. Jelka and Milena entered the third class, and their hosts and Neda fetched in their luggage, said goodbye, and left the train.

Milena stood at the open window, and when the train pulled away she started to wave excitedly until the station disappeared behind the oblique stone wall and everything plunged into darkness and smoke. She could hardly refrain from screaming: the acrid smoke and soot choked her, her eyes burned, and her ears were deafened by the rhythmic thunder of the wheels, until finally they came out of the tunnel and into the light. Before her eyes spread gently rolling fields, meadows, and forests, surrounded by mountains, golden in the morning sun, and glided past to be lost in the distance. Captivated by the beauty of nature and the speed with which they reached the far horizons and flew through space and time, it was ages before she could tear herself away from the window.

At Vishegrad, two *bulas* and their children came into their compartment. They too were traveling to Sarajevo and they fell into conversation with Jelka. While the three of them spoke about the good old days, sighed and complained about the hardships which had now descended upon them, Milena made friends with the girls who were of her own age. They counted the frequent tunnels, waved to the shepherds and laborers in the fields beside the railway track, exchanged tiny mirrors, marbles, and other trifles they carried in their pockets, and pointed out to one another oddly shaped rocks, giant trees which towered above all others, and villages nestling between the hills and the fast-flowing mountain rivers. When they grew tired, they sat down and had something to eat. Then again they went to the window, which continued to draw Milena irresistibly until darkness fell.

It was after nightfall when they arrived at Bistrik, the first station in the city. In front of Milena, Sarajevo glittered as if strewn with precious stones, lit up by electricity. She had never before seen electric lights and it seemed to her that the town stretched into infinity, that if floated in the darkness, wrapped in a dazzling net, magical. She was in a trance as she parted from the girls, who were going on to Marindvor station, and left the train.

Jula and her daughters had come to meet them. Still mesmerized, Milena exchanged kisses with her relatives and went with them into the street, bright in the middle of the night, with tall houses clinging one to another, higher than the rows of trees that grew in front of them. They walked up the hill towards Bembasha, where Jula lived. The air was warm, the night more beautiful and luxurious than the day, and below them shimmered Sarajevo. Jula's was a big house, built in the Turkish style. Since her husband's death, she had to lease a part of it in order to be able to keep it up, and they lived off the small income and the provisions she received from the family estate at Kozja Cuprija. Her daughters were much older than Milena, more her sisters' ages. They had both passed lower matriculation and were working as clerks in a government office, so they also earned some money, enough to dress elegantly. They welcomed them warmly, as close relatives, and treated them as well as was possible in those troubled times.

The following day they rested from the long journey. Jelka and Jula spent all their time together, longing for each other's company, for they had not seen one another for years, separated both by distance and by the difficulties of living under dangerous and unsuitable political conditions. While they were having a comforting cry, and talking to their hearts' content, Milena amused herself by looking at the town through the windows, which gave views of Beledija, the Miljecka River with its promenade, and parts of the outskirts of the city.

The day after that, Jelka went to visit her relatives and friends who had moved to Sarajevo, to enquire whether she could secretly change her gold. She had intended to go to the bank as well, to ask for Janko's money, but when she heard how persecuted the Serbs were here, and that she could only bring trouble on herself, she changed her mind.

Milena knew the reason why her mother could not take her along, and she was not upset at being left at home with her aunt. Her cousins sometimes took her out to show her the Bashcharshija, or the bridge over the Miljecka where Franz Ferdinand had been killed. They taught her how to use the tramcars, which gave her the utmost pleasure and made her feel independent. She would take a month's supply of tickets and, whenever she felt bored at home, would run down to the station below Bembasha and ride all the way to Marindvor, alongside the promenade, and back, several times. She looked at the Miljecka, and the network of streets full of enormous houses with harmonious facades, and she watched the people who got on and off the tram, so much more smartly and fashionably dressed than in Plevlje. Most of all she liked the young Turkish girls who were still not covered by a *zar* and veil. They wore *dimije* trousers and jerkins in bright colors and of unusual design. Their heads were covered by large scarves which fastened under their chins and fell in rich folds, trimmed with thick tassels, down their shoulders to their waists, swaying and shining in time with their graceful movements.

One afternoon, as she sat with Jula waiting for her mother to return, she asked, "Is everyone here rich?"

"No, my child, there is poverty here as well, but it isn't obvious. In this town no one will leave home unwashed, uncombed, or in dirty clothes. If they had to go hungry, they would still buy clothes, if only of cotton, and footwear. It is no shame to be poor, but it is a great shame not to be decently dressed like others, to be dirty or in rags." She sat down beside Milena at the window through which the people in the street could be seen, and went on, "Besides, this part is one of the nicest in Sarajevo and the people are better off here. The Bashcharshija and Beledija are near, and the European part of the town starts there. All the houses there are built to a plan, and the shops are luxurious, with window displays of imported goods from Vienna, all in the latest fashion. Everything is expensive and only the wealthiest can shop there."

"Are there many wealthy people?"

"They are many, though not as many as the poor. The richest are the Jews, and that's why everybody dislikes them. They are merchants and bankers as well as scholars and others. There is poverty among them too, but they help one another. You won't see a Jew who is a beggar or a servant, a porter or a laborer. He may be an artisan or the smallest shopkeeper, but they don't allow their people to become destitute. They are hated too because of their unity, and for not mixing with others. Although they do no one any harm, they are different. They don't like to be called Jews here, or Chivuts, they say they come from Spain and speak that language."

"And the Turks? Do they mix with the Serbs?"

"Here we call them Muslims. In their neighborhood I have several acquaintances with whom I am on good terms, but now in Sarajevo the Serbs are extremely unpopular. We had some freedom before, like the others, but since Franz Ferdinand was killed, everyone has turned against us. The Shvabas growl at us like mad dogs: they would destroy us all if they could. We keep quiet, we've no other choice."

"Did you see the assassination?"

"No, I didn't. From here you can see the spot where Princip killed him—there, that fourth bridge over the river—but I happened to be in the Bashcharshija that day. God, how terrifying it was. I didn't hear the shot, but suddenly there were shouts and running. They began to grasp hold of the men, whoever they spotted nearby, and curse and beat them. The Shvabas ran amok and some Turkish dogs were helping them too. Everybody attacked the Serbs, breaking open Serbian shops, smashing the windows and throwing the merchandise into the streets, grabbing and looting. I was frightened stiff with all that fury. I felt sorry for those who were being beaten, but I was too afraid to say a word. My legs gave way, and I had no strength to reach Bembasha. Then one of my neighbors, a Muslim woman, spotted me and called out from her window, 'Come in, dear, can't you see you're going to faint?' When I went in, she gave me a glass of water and sugar cubes, and made me some coffee, so I recovered, and stayed with her until things calmed down a little in the town."

"Did you see Gavrilo Princip?"

"No, I didn't, the poor soul, God help his mother. They say he was beaten, he was covered in blood when they dragged him to prison. There they tortured him until he finally died under torture."

"But why did he kill Franz and his wife?"

"That I don't know. They say that Franz came to enslave all of us Serbs, that he used to say our people are like beasts and should be kept in chains, so the Bosnian Youth, students, they wanted to prevent it. Those are the rumors. Why else would he sacrifice his life? He knew what to expect."

"But why did he kill Ferdinand's wife? She was not guilty."

"He didn't want to kill her, but one bullet hit her by mistake. I too feel sorry for her, though not for him. They've become really vicious toward us Serbs. Times were better even under the Turks. Life was just about bearable before the annexation, but afterwards, God help us? The Turks have begun to hate them too."

"Then why did the Turks help them to arrest the Serbs and to beat them?"

"Some did. There are boot-lickers everywhere, and they are the worst when they are given their head."

"And the Jews?"

"They never get involved in anything. They look after their own affairs."

That evening, Jelka began to discuss their return home, and Milena knew that she had succeeded in changing the money and would be able to take her along when visiting and shopping, which was still to be done. She was looking forward most to visiting Djana's sister-in-law, Jovanka, because she had three children of about her age, a boy, Rajko, and two girls, Rada and Beba. Milena had heard about Jovanka at the start of the war, when she was sent to Ilino Hill. She was the teacher who, after Ferdinand's assassination, had managed to hide several members of Young Bosnia, her former pupils, and send them to Father Oshtric in Rudo. Later, when she learned that because he had helped them he had been arrested by the Austrians, tortured, and put to a horrifying death, she had made contact with a secret movement for the liberation of Bosnia and she and her husband, a building engineer, were giving it help.

Jovanka and her family welcomed them as if they had known them for years, with spontaneous friendship, and extended the generous hospitality of their home to them for a whole day. For Milena, the stay in their modest but modern house, with its many books and paintings, was a discovery of an entirely new world. The children went around freely and behaved towards their parents without inhibition; they were sure of themselves and kind to her. They all attended high school already, even Beba, who was younger than Milena, because the school in Sarajevo had kept open without interruption. They learned foreign languages—German at school and French privately—took chemistry, physics, and geography lessons, and knew history better than she did. Her sole advantage was that she had read more books than any of them. They showed her on a map countries and towns with strange names, whose history conjured up visions and events which she could see only in her fantasies or in the books she had read, they explained how electricity is conducted, how crystals are formed . . . and she listened with admiration and a certain covert sadness for lagging so far behind them. Realizing how interested she was in everything, and how unhappy because the high school in Plevlje was closed, they suggested that she should ask her mother to leave her with them in Sarajevo, where she could continue her education. Milena agreed, in the flush of her irresistible desire to learn, but she knew that Jelka would not let her.

In the evening, they got up to leave. Milena found it difficult to part from these relatives with whom she had become more friendly in a single day than with any of her school friends. Jovanka made them take with them some food she had prepared for their journey home, because it was difficult to obtain any provisions in Sarajevo, and she saw them off to the tram station, talking to Jelka in whispers all the way.

That night, when they were alone, Jelka sat beside Milena's bed and began to comfort her tenderly. "Hold on a little longer. Freedom will come and the high school will start again in Plevlje. I heard from Jovanka that a new front has been formed in Salonika. When our army retreated across Albania, it endured much and suffered many casualties from hunger and cold. Now it seems that it has recovered in Corfu and in France, and is being sent by the Allies to the Salonika front. They say our soldiers are singing as they charge into battle with the Shvabas and Bulgars. The decisive victory will be won on that front and Jovanka believes it will be ours. She told me to be careful and not to talk about it, but to tell whoever I think fit when we return to Plevlje, so that people may hope and rejoice." She crossed herself, stood up, and continued in a whisper, "If only this war would end and the murderers leave. They are worse than the Turkish *asker*. The *asker* came out of the wilderness, and we had to lock ourselves in because of their rowdy behavior, but they did no harm to anyone, nobody was executed or hanged, and there were no forcible confiscations."

Milena could not sleep for a long time. She felt that she could not wait for the liberation, however soon it came, and in the morning she asked her mother for permission to buy some school books for advanced courses. Jelka gave her the money, and promised she would find someone to teach her the sciences and the French language as soon as they returned to Plevlje, but she would not hear a word about German. "That cursed language will be forbidden in Sarajevo too, as soon as freedom comes to them. We will never forget the hangings and shootings, and we will hate all that is German for ever."

They decided that Milena should go with one of Jula's daughters to buy the books, and Jelka went to visit Pasha Bajrovic's wife, having discovered from Jovanka where she lived.

It took a long time to find her in the lower part of Sarajevo, on the left bank of the Miljecka, in one of the small houses that clung to a hill. While she climbed the steep uneven lanes, she thought, "God help us, where's my Pashinica living now? When I think of her women's quarters, beautiful and spacious as a palace, encircled by two gardens with fountains, flowers, trees, and every other luxury—a real paradise. And inside, a royal splendor, carpets everywhere, everything glowing with opulence and lavishness. She would be seated on a divan among cushions, like some sultan's wife. She only had to clap her hands and her maids instantly materialized beside her, served the guests, and when they withdrew they walked backwards, so as not to turn their backs. And now, see where her fate has brought her."

With these thoughts in her mind, Jelka found a small neglected courtyard, crossed it and opened the door. The pasha's wife was seated on the floor beside a copper brazier, smoking and absently stirring the embers with tongs. Dressed in cotton clothes and wearing a scarf, she nevertheless looked beautiful, though older. Her face lit up when she saw Jelka. "Do come in, Jankovinica, welcome. What brings you to Sarajevo?"

"I came to see my sister, and when I learned that you were here too, I very much wished to see you."

"I, too, am glad you came. There's no one I would be more delighted to see, unless the Pasha could somehow appear. You and I had good times together and were fond of one another; none of my relatives would have brought me so much joy."

They embraced and Jelka gave her a gift of tobacco and coffee, saying apologetically, "Look what I have brought you. I could find nothing better, times being as they are."

"My dear, I prefer these to anything else. I can't be without coffee and tobacco, and I spend all I have on them."

Jelka sat beside her. "How are you, Pashinica? I heard that your husband died."

The Pashinica burst into tears. "Yes, he died, and since then I've nothing to look forward to. Nor do I care about lacking the comforts I used to have, or feel upset for having fallen so low. Since he is no more, I don't need anything. You know how good he was to me. He did not bring another wife into our home, although he could, being a pasha, have had a harem of ten wives. Cursed Shvabas, they persuaded him to come here, and it's my belief that he died from pining for his family and his birthplace. If only it had been God's will that we had stayed in Plevlje, come what may. No one would have harmed him. He was kind to the Turks and to the Serbs alike."

"And how are your children?"

"In Vienna, still studying but not yet graduated: wasting our capital, misbehaving, learning the worst, spending their money on drink and women. God knows how our home is split apart—they couldn't care less about me—but I don't mind, for my husband is gone, and Satan can take everything. I keep my body and soul together on what I get from the *vakuf*, through the muftis, from what the Pasha left, and I don't need more."

"Don't talk like that, Pashinica. At least your sons are alive. Had my Niko lived, even if he had become corrupt, an adventurer, a vagabond, or a drunk, anything would be better for a mother than to see him in his grave."

"I'd heard, Jankovica, about your great sorrow. It is not easy for you to bear it, but as long as your other children are well and alive, they'll give you consolation. Your daughters are around you, you are in your own home and among your own people. Here everything is strange to me and hateful. I don't like going anywhere or having anyone call on me, so that I'm not pitied by strangers."

"Courage, my Pashinica, troubles are everywhere, we are not the only ones. The world is full of grievances, there is hunger and illness back home too, and the cursed Shvabas hang and execute innocent people."

They stayed together for a while longer, drinking coffee and turning the conversation to memories of old times, trying to raise each other's spirits. When they parted, their hearts were heavy with the knowledge and they would never see each other again.

A day later, Jelka and Milena left Sarajevo. Milena burst into tears when she looked out from Bistrik and her eyes lingered on the town she had grown to love more than her own birthplace. The return journey was much easier, because they managed to hire horses in Rudo, thanks to the help of the owner of the inn where they again stayed for the night.

On their return, they found all Plevlje in an uproar. The Austrian authorities had announced that the prior of the monastery of the Holy Trinity, Serofim Djeric, was to be hanged. It was rumored that he had been condemned to death because arms had been found close to the monastery grounds.

On the day of the execution, the whole town gathered around the court to see the condemned man. People cried and protested and began to threaten the Austrians, so they had to bring in more soldiers to keep order. Relatives and friends from Mocevac and Golubinja assembled at Jelka's home. This time she did not draw the curtains at the windows but allowed them to watch and see what happened when Prior Djeric was brought out. In front of the court building, surrounded by a squad of soldiers, the priest and the hangman, who carried the rope, were already waiting. That day the proceedings lasted longer than usual. Suddenly, several officers appeared at the door, waited for a carriage that made its way through the crowd with great difficulty, got in and drove off in the direction of the monastery. Someone spread the news that they had gone to measure the distance between the fence of the monastery grounds and the spot where the arms had been found. People waited in suspense, noisy and defiant. When the carriage returned and its officers went inside, there was a commotion everywhere, the Shvabas grew alarmed and began to shout, the entire crowd stirred, and a tense, dangerous atmosphere developed. Then came the announcement form the court that the sentence had been annulled, and the people were ordered to disperse. The soldiers marched off, the priest and the hangman went away, each in his own direction, and the people waited until the guards escorted Prior Serofim Djeric back to the prison building behind the court, then began to cheer and rejoice. It occurred to Jelka that this had happened because of the new front, and she thought, "They don't dare, the dogs! They know what will happen to them if fighting breaks out here too."

After a while, the Prior was freed. It transpired that the new judge, of Czech origin, had established that the arms had been found at a distance from the monastery grounds for which the law did not prescribe the death penalty.

Several officers moved out of Jelka's houses, and in their place came others who understood the Serbian language and, in some cases, spoke it well. All the same, she was guarded towards them too, although they seemed less loathsome to her once she learned that they were Croats, Bosnians, Czechs, and men from Vojvodina, as were many new members of the court council and the military command. The only one she trusted was the doctor from Sarajevo, whom she had known longer and who had protected her before. By now he was also giving her news from the front. Milena was warned not to say anything to anybody, but she had already heard from other children what was happening on the Salonika front because the tidings were all over the town. Hope revived among the people: they were cheered and encouraged by the news. Secretly they sang about King Petar and his allies, especially about France:

Far, far away, where yellow lemons bloom,
Is our father Petar and his two sons.

or

The French ship is sailing from Salonika harbor,
Serbs are sailing in it, young men with battle wounds.

In time, the Austrians almost completely abolished the death penalty and replaced it with imprisonment. They stopped ransacking the villages to confiscate the meager food that the peasants managed to produce, and although the people still lived in fear and on the verge of starvation, everything was more easily endured because their faith in the approaching liberation had lifted their spirits.

Jelka noticed that Milena was still pining for Sarajevo, and she remembered her promise, which had been driven out of her mind by the pressure of new events and the important changes taking place in Plevlje. So she spoke to Darka, her cousin's daughter, and asked her to give Milena French lessons to cheer her up a little. "The child is sitting idle day after day, the school is closed, our home is miserable, and she's often sad. Why don't you teach her French? I'll pay you for the lessons."

Darka was pleased. Her husband was a prisoner of war and she had no children, so the change was welcome for her too.

"All right, Aunt Jelka, I'll think about it and let you know. I learned French at school and my husband taught me as well before he was sent to camp, but I don't know whether that is enough. I could also teach her other subjects that are introduced in the higher grades if she wishes and if that suits you."

She came again soon after, and they agreed to start with Milena's lessons the next day, not only French but also the subjects from the textbooks Milena had bought in Sarajevo. Darka was young, cheerful, and patient, her lessons were interesting and Milena made effortless progress. The very discovery that knowledge was accessible to her, and that she could find in it the same pleasure she had found in literature, awoke in her the passion that had smoldered in Janko all his life.

One day the doctor arrived, very excited, and said that he wished to speak with Jelka alone, and could Milena leave the room.

"You can talk quite freely, she won't say a word to anyone. We've learned to be silent."

"The Salonika front has been penetrated. The Austrian troops will soon withdraw from here, and you will be free."

"And where will you go?"

"As an officer I must go with the army, but I hope that Bosnia will also soon be free. There won't be any fighting here, and if it comes to a capitulation, all your men will soon be returning from the front and the prisoner-of-war camps."

Tears flooded Jelka's eyes. "God bless you for this news, let all other mothers rejoice in it. But no one is coming back to me. My children lie buried in their graves."

Saddened by her sorrow, he said nothing, only took her hand to show he understood, and left in distress.

Jelka sat down and continued through tears, "It's not right to talk like this. I should be glad that all other mothers are not bereaved and that many will find joy and happiness again, but to tell you the truth, it will be even worse for me to see the young men returning home while my son has gone for ever. May God keep them well for their mothers' sakes, and may they all find happiness on their return, but I have no one to look forward to, my heart is forever locked in sorrow." When she calmed down a little, she told Milena to sit down beside her and gently warned her, "Don't say anything to anyone. If it came out that the doctor has told us about this, it could cost him his life, being still under their command. Pretend you know nothing, but if you hear more from anyone else, come and tell me."

There was no talk of the collapse of the Salonika front in the town, whether because it was kept secret or because it was not yet known. Jelka sent word to Djana to come to her with the children from Ilino Hill. Although the doctor had told her there would be no fighting, she feared that the soldiers might do violence as they retreated, and Djana was alone with a few maids on the entire estate.

Not long after Djana and the children had arrived, rumors spread that the Shvabas were going, and that people had seen them preparing for retreat. When it came to it, they left suddenly, quickly and quietly, as if fleeing. They did not have time to take anything with them and left behind storehouses of foods, barracks full of furniture, army uniforms, blankets, bedding, utensils and other goods, and hospitals with all the instruments and medicines. The hungry population, realizing that they had gone and that no other authority had arrived, rushed in to plunder like a swarm of locusts over fertile fields. Down the lanes rolled tin drums of oil, and wooden ones of marmalade, lard, and butter. Somebody dragged an enormous barrel of raki on to the street and opened the spigot. People surged around it as though to a public fountain, filling their various containers and going off to fetch others. There was sudden pandemonium. Fighting broke out, and one man grabbed the spigot, pulled it out and threw it away. Raki gushed and poured down the street. Whoever tried to block the opening was splashed by the powerful jet and, drenched to the skin, staggered out of the crowd. Jelka watched from the window, astonished to see people from better homes among the rest. When she saw that one group of women contained members of the Zarkovic household, she was flabbergasted. "Since my uncles died, they too have begun to slide downhill," she thought, "but I didn't expect that they would forget themselves so far, and forsake their reputation."

Just then Milena came in to ask whether she could go with her cousins to get something from the Barracks, as they had seen other children in the crowd.

"God forbid. Looting is looting, even if it is from the Shvaba army. You are not to budge. I don't blame the poor, only those who grab and disgrace themselves without real necessity."

Disappointed, Milena returned to her cousins. When they heard what she had been told, Drobrila, who was the boldest of them, although the youngest, said, "Let's go, everyone else is there. Dada doesn't have to know. If you don't have the nerve, then we shall go without you."

Unable to resist the general excitement, Milena also agreed. They sneaked out of the house and bypassed their street, so as not to be seen by Jelka. Not knowing where the storehouses were, they wandered into a stable. Milena had begun to pull out some ropes, this being the first thing she could get hold of, when Dobrila started shouting at her:

"Come here, for God's sake, what do you want rope for? I've found two pigs, help us to get them home."

One of the pigs was small but the other quite big, and they managed to take them across their uncle's field to the shed in their lower courtyard, where they locked them in and then left again before anyone saw them. This time they found the storehouses, but could not push their way through the mass of people fighting to get in and those who were getting out laden with booty. They were all jammed at the doorway to the point of suffocation. The girls were pushed into a corner, and from there they watched helplessly as the cases and sacks were carried out to disappear in the crowd. One young man, covered in sweat, put quite a large case right next to them and went back to get another. Dobrila quickly whispered to her sister, "Let's carry it away."

"How can we, it's not ours," Milena began, but when the two started to pull it away, paying no attention to her, she too joined in to help. Somehow they dragged it to the house, put it in another shed, locked it and headed to the storehouse.

People were hurriedly removing sacks, barrels, and cases similar to the one they had just deposited at home. The three of them stopped by the door to wait, and when they saw someone putting aside a case, they grabbed it as soon as he went back for other things and dragged it home. When they returned for the third time, people were taking mainly furniture, blankets, utensils, and similar objects that came to hand, so they wanted to go home. As they were about to leave, a man brought out a big sack and asked them to look after it until he had fetched another. They lifted it and, because it was not as heavy as the cases, they ran with it all the way home. Once again they went back to the storehouse, more out of curiosity, but when they heard that in the meantime sacks of wheat grain had been discovered, they began to hover again. Next to them lay a huge sack of grain, but they could not move it. Magda found a gypsy and asked him to carry it to their home, and she would pay him ten kronen.

He lifted the sack on to his back and asked, "What's in it?"

"Wheat grain."

"All right, where do you live?"

"Not far from here."

He started off with them, but as soon as he reached the road heading to Jalija, he turned into it and ran away. They began to shout after him, but when they saw that he didn't even bother to look back, they decided not to return to the Barracks and furiously headed for home. Once they had calmed down and cleaned themselves up, they went into the room where Jelka and Djana were, and sat primly by the window. From time to time, they glanced at each other meaningfully, finding it increasingly difficult to control the secret pleasure of their successful plunder and the impatience to see what they had brought home. Soon, Jelka went out to take a look round the houses and lock the gates; when she returned she asked angrily, "Whose are those pigs in my shed?"

Magda and Milena were tongue-tied, but Dobrila answered resolutely, "Ours, we brought them over from the Trainer."

"What a disgrace. Didn't I forbid you to go stealing?"

"Leave it, for heaven's sake," Djana began to appease her. "They're children and like all children, no one will hold it against them. Everybody went. You yourself saw from the window. All the women from the Hill and Mocevac joined in, not to mention the men. There were people from Golubinja too, even your Zarkovic women."

Jelka said nothing more. It was too late to do anything about it, and to punish the children now would serve no purpose. The three girls summoned up the courage to say that they had brought other things as well. Jelka did not want to look at them, but Djana went with the children to the shed. First they opened the sack, to discover that it was crammed with crackers, which delighted them because they were craving for bread. One case contained cans of goulash and the other packets of butter. That same evening Jelka decided to hire a man to slaughter the bigger pig, and left the smaller to be raised. She put some of the meat into the drying shed to be smoked, salted the rest to keep it fresh longer, and rendered the fat. The house was as full of provisions as it had been before the war. She felt ill at ease, but things being what they were, she allowed Djana and the children to enjoy their unexpected riches.

When the food storehouses were empty and the blankets, beddings, beds, instruments, medicines, and all other utensils and furniture had been taken away from the Barracks and the hospital, the people ripped out the bronze stoves, window frames, doors, floorboards, fences, and even the basins from under the fountains. It was autumn, and all the fruit was out, so that basketfuls of nuts, pears, apples, and quinces disappeared from behind the Barracks. The vegetable beds were dug up and loads of potatoes, cabbages, onions, and pumpkins taken away. All that was left were buildings without windows or doors, trees with broken branches, and ravaged gardens without even their fences remaining. Things that neither the *asker* nor any other army had destroyed, the peaceful inhabitants of a sleepy provincial town had obliterated in a few days of lawlessness, caught up in a frenzy of looting and destruction. Finally, a temporary council was organized in the town, to supervise the population until a permanent government brought police or the army to establish law and order, but no one paid much attention to this council.

Armed thieves began to haunt the richer Muslim houses at night, pretending to be freedom fighters. In the name of the "new government," they stole money, gold, silver, and other valuables, even carpets and food. At first the terrified Turks surrendered everything, but when they realized that they were not government representatives, they began to defend themselves, using arms. The thieves now turned to the well-to-do houses, Turkish and Serbian, where there

were no men. Fear possessed the whole of Plevlje, and people hid
everything they valued in their attics and cellars. It did not help locking
the doors; this only enraged the robbers, who would then break in
and cause havoc.

Jelka hid the money and gold under the roof in one of the attics,
but decided not to move everything else. "Let them take all of it.
We've lost so much, let these too go to the devil, as long as we keep
our heads." She knew she was in danger. In the whole street of Kojic
houses there remained only Rosa with her two children, Petko, the
sole man, living at the far end of the street with his second wife and
two daughters, and Jelka with Milena. Djana had returned to Ilino
Hill to look after the estate, and all the other houses in the street
had fallen empty since the Austrians had left.

One night, before dawn, there was a loud banging at the gates.
Jelka rose and woke Milena. They had been sleeping fully dressed,
so as to be ready to escape if anyone attacked them. When the knocking
was repeated, she whispered to Milena not to be afraid, then opened
the window and asked, "Who is it at this hour?"

"Open in the name of the law."

"I'm coming as soon as I get dressed," she answered confidently,
almost cheerfully, took Milena's hand and they descended. She left
Milena on the landing and went to open the gates. In front of her were
three armed men with cartridge belts across their chests, dressed partly
in town and partly in peasant clothes, with fur hats on their heads.

"Open up everything in the name of the law," one of them snapped.
"We must inspect the whole house."

"Come in, come in and welcome. You are our first government,
our liberators and heroes," she said, opening the gates wide, and led
them up the stairs.

They followed her, still frowning, but somewhat unsure. To Milena
they appeared enormous and she began to tremble even more.

"Kiss their hand, dear child, don't be afraid. They freed us from
the enemy, and now they are searching our houses to see that everything is in order, and that no one is mistreating the people. We've
suffered enough from the cursed Shvabas."

Milena kissed the hands of all three men and Jelka took them to
the visitor's room. When they saw that all the floors were carpeted

and everything around them was sumptuously furnished, they became embarrassed because their boots were muddy.

"Do come in, don't bother about the carpets," Jelka urged. "Who can I welcome more than those who brought me freedom? I couldn't wait for this day to come, so how can I worry about the carpets? May you keep well and healthy, you've driven out the cursed Shvabas. Because of them, I lost my only son . . ." and genuine tears flooded her eyes.

They too grew solemn, "That's war, Mother, it did no good to anyone," said one of them hesitantly.

"Yes, please God it never happens again," she whispered, wiping away her tears. "Sit down while I get some raki and coffee, I can welcome you with that at least. This is an important day for us."

She went to the kitchen with Milena. "You put the coffee on while I serve the drinks. I didn't want to leave you alone with them," she said in a whisper, taking out a bottle of raki and some glasses. Milena lit the spirit stove with trembling hands and put the coffee pot on top of it. When Jelka returned, she made the coffee and poured it into cups, and they both returned to the visitors' room. The men stayed a little longer, then exchanged glances and got up.

"Now you can look around if you wish," Jelka said.

"No, we won't bother, everything is quiet and in order, and we ought to go. It'll be light soon, we need to rest a little after being on guard all night."

Jelka and Milena saw them to the gates. Jelka picked some sweet basil on the way and tucked it into the men's cartridge belts. "For luck and happiness in our freedom." When Milena kissed their hands again, each of them gave her ten kronen. As soon as they were gone, Jelka locked the gates and, deathly pale in the twilight, took Milena's hand and drew her into the house. "Thank God they went away," she said, crossing herself. "I wouldn't have minded the loss, but had they run riot and attacked us, you might never have got over your fright. This way, I addressed them as human beings and made it clear that I didn't care about these trifling possessions, so I suppose they felt embarrassed. Thieves too want to appear human, and are ashamed of what they do, I think, but the Devil himself and their laziness drove them to stealing."

They could not fall asleep again. When it was daylight, Jelka went to the visitors' room, and only then did she notice that the candlesticks under the icon of Saint Stevan were gone, together with the silver cigarette boxes which she had left out on purpose to indicate that nothing of value had been hidden away. She said nothing to Milena, so as not to add to her fear.

That same day she went to the town council to demand that measures be taken to prevent people from being robbed, but did not mention what had happened to her because she did not want it talked about. The members of the council had themselves realized that "heaven has no value without thunder," and they decided to organize and arm a body of temporary guards who would patrol the town at night. From then on, the authority of the council increased, thefts stopped, and people began to prepare a festive reception for the liberators.

The Serbian army arrived at Plevlje before sunrise and was billeted in the suburb of Strazica because the barracks were uninhabitable. By the time it was light, the news of their arrival reached the town and all the population rushed to Strazica to greet them. *Kolo* dancing broke out all along the Charshija and the town crier announced that an official reception and festivities would be held that afternoon in front of the monastery of the Holy Trinity.

Jelka was relieved that the army had finally arrived, and with it the new government to put an end to lawlessness, but she could not participate in the general rejoicing and revelry, nor attend the festivities. She felt that she belonged to the world of the past, together with her dead, and that she could find more consolation and solace in her memories than in the future. Unable to stop herself crying, she went outside so that Milena would not see her, and sat on the bench in the neglected garden. "My Janko," she thought, looking at the unkempt flower beds around the fallen branches of the rose bushes, "it is better that you have died without having to endure the sorrow and pain that have befallen me."

From the distance came the sound of singing and the lilt of a harmonica. Someone's footsteps echoed down the cobbled street, there was a breath of autumn chill in the air, and from the chimneys of the neighboring houses the smoke rose towards the high clear sky. She sighed deeply and wiped away her tears, not wanting to upset

Milena on this day. Her whole childhood had been spent in sorrow, and she should at least rejoice in the liberation. Ever since her early days, Milena had been rather neglected because she had been born after the deaths of Chedo and Vaso, and because she was a girl. Later, she had lived through the tide of sorrow and misfortunes that had struck her mother. And yet she had grown up better and cleverer than all the rest of Jelka's children, and she loved her most, although she did not dare admit it to herself because she had only loved Niko as deeply as this, and losing him had caused her to fear her own love. She rose to her feet and went indoors to change into festive clothes before waking Milena.

Around noon, Pava's Misho came to take Milena to the monastery, where a crowd of people had already gathered. *Kolo* dancing had begun, songs that until then had only been sung in secret rang out from all sides, groups of young girls, soldiers, and officers set up a babble of joyful laughter and friendly voices, while at the top of the steps leading to the monastery courtyard, a long table for the speakers and dignitaries was being decorated with flowers and flags.

Milena was shivering with excitement, but she did not feel the same happiness as on that occasion a few years before, when she had first set eyes on the Serbian army, when her father and Niko and Marija were still alive. It seemed to her that among the people too there was not the enthusiasm and joy she had encountered then. Many young men had died in the war, many homes had been bereaved, much suffering and fear endured, and the people were exhausted. She listened to the speeches, full of unfamiliar words: about the national honor, and the new kingdom of Serbs, Croats, and Slovenians that would be bigger and more powerful than Tsar Dushan's, and would spread from Triglav to the Djevdjelija, from the Adriatic Sea to the Djerdap Straits. She could not understand everything, but she longed with all her heart for the new horizons that their words proclaimed, and she knew that the past and the future were parting before her, as the dawn parts night from day.

Glossary

Adzo Respectful term for addressing an older man or relative—father, uncle, grandfather, etc. The similar affectionate term for addressing an older woman is *Nana*.

Ahmedgia Turkish coin.

Aksham The time immediately after sunset; the fourth of the five Muslim daily prayers.

Asker The Turkish army; soldiers.

Azurele Get ready; let's go.

Bujrum Welcome.

Bula Turkish woman.

Burek Turkish savory pastry.

Cepenak Old-fashioned Turkish-style shop front and display space.

Dimije Woman's trousers in the baggy Turkish fashion.

Doksat Enclosed balcony with windows.

Fermen Part of the old-fashioned Serbian national dress, bolero style.

Fistan Dress or skirt.

Grosh Austrian coin.

Gusle Traditional stringed instrument, used to accompany folk songs.

Hamam Turkish bath.

Hanuma Turkish lady; respectful term for a married woman.

Icindija The time between noon and sunset; the third of the five Muslim daily prayers.

GLOSSARY

Jacija The time between sunset and midnight; the last of the five Muslim daily prayers.

Kadaif Sweet Turkish pastry.

Kafana Popular bar and coffee house where food is also served.

Kalkan Woman's headdress, sometimes adorned with gold and pearls.

Kandilo A special type of small ornate oil lamp made of glass and metal, suspended below the icon.

Kolo Folk dance in which all participants hold hands to form a ring or chain. Accompanied by accordions or stringed instruments, or simply by singing, the *kolo* varies in style from one region of Yugoslavia to another and is a vital component of all festive gatherings, celebrations, and spontaneous rejoicing.

Koporan Tunic, part of traditional national dress for men.

Krajcar Austrian coin.

Libade Short jacket with wide sleeves embroidered in gold or silver, part of traditional national dress for women.

Mastika Alcoholic drink, a kind of raki.

Medgedia Turkish gold coin.

Mehana Popular drinking house where food can also be served.

Omaya Water fetched from under the wheel on the eve of St. George's Day, which according to popular belief acquires magical powers from the selected plants and twigs that are soaked in it overnight.

Pashinica The principal wife of a pasha.

Saba The time of dawn; the first of the five Muslim daily prayers.

Secija Ottoman-style long sofa placed against a wall.

Sevdalinka Love songs of melancholy longing, characteristic of Bosnia.

Shalvare Man's trousers in the baggy Turkish fashion.

Shvabar Derogatory term for a German or Austrian national, parallel to "Hun" or "Bosche," and derived from the German region of Swabia.

Slava Serbian holiday celebrating the day of the family's patron saint, probably a reflection of the pagan belief in a household deity adapted into the Christian religion.

Tatlia Turkish sweet pastry.

Tepeluk Woman's formal headdress adorned with gold, pearls, and precious stones.

Urmashica Turkish sweet pastry.

Vakuf A Muslim foundation for religious, cultural, and humanitarian aims; the monetary fund it administers.

Zar Muslim woman's dress worn only out of doors.

Notes

1. The Battle of Kosovo (June 15, 1389) was the last concerted attempt of the fragmented Serbian state to withstand the invading armies of the Ottoman Empire. Despite the defeat, which marks the destruction of medieval Serbia and its Byzantium-inspired culture and the beginning of five hundred years of Turkish rule, the heroic battle remained the most celebrated single event in the nation's history. It could be compared to the Battle of Hastings in English history, and was a key theme in mythology and history.
2. Prince Lazar Hrebeljanivic (*c*. 1329–1389) served at the court of the Serbian Tsar Dusan and his successor Tsar Uros. In 1371 he became the ruler of the biggest region in Serbia, which included Belgrade. Aware of the threat from the expanding Ottoman Empire, he tried to reunite and strengthen the great Serbian state which after the death of Tsar Uros had divided into principalities. Forced into premature confrontation by the rapid Turkish advance, he led his own hurriedly assembled army together with those of neighboring rulers into the Battle of Kosovo, in which he fell.

    Bosko Jugovic was the eldest of the nine sons of a Serbian nobleman, Jug Bogdan, all of whom fought and died in the Battle of Kosovo. The portrayal of Bosko Jugovic in the epic poetry of the Kosovo Cycle remains one of the most impressive images of a brave, fiercely proud medieval warrior and standard-bearer.
3. *As, buki, vjedi* are letters of the oldest Slav alphabet, the Glagolithic, which was introduced by Konstantin Kiril (St. Cyril) in 863. The first translations of Biblical texts from Greek into old Slavonic

were written in this script. Although replaced by the Cyrillic Script in the eleventh to twelfth centuries, it has remained in isolated use for Church texts until the twentieth century, mainly along the Adriatic coast.

4. The treasure of Tsar Radovan is the mythical lost hoard of a demoniac ruler of deep mines producing untold riches.

5. The Kosovo Cycle is the name given to the oldest and most beautiful epic folk poems about the battle of Kosovo. Written records of the sources for these poems go back to the fifteenth century and were expanded in the sixteenth. All the surviving poems of the cycle were first collected in the nineteenth century by Vuk Karazdic, together with other epic and lyrical folk poetry, in a three-volume anthology published in Leipzig in 1823. Their translation into German attracted the attention of Goethe, Grimm, and other major literary figures, who compared them with Homer.

6. A Balkan Alliance of Bulgaria, Greece, Montenegro, and Serbia attacked the Turks in 1912 to liberate European territories that had been under Turkish rule since 1389.

7. The date given for St. George's Day is according to the calendar of the Eastern Orthodox Church, which differs by thirteen days from the Gregorian Calendar.

Other titles in the series

From Chile:
The Secret Holy War of Santiago de Chile
by Marco Antonio de la Parra
trans. by Charles P. Thomas
ISBN 1–56656–123–X   paperback $12.95

From Grenada:
Under the Silk Cotton Tree
by Jean Buffong
ISBN 1–56656–122–1   paperback $9.95

From India:
The End Play
by Indira Mahindra
ISBN 1–56656–166–3   paperback $11.95

From Israel:
The Silencer
by Simon Louvish
ISBN 1–56656–108–6   paperback $10.95

From Jordan:
Prairies of Fever
by Ibrahim Nasrallah
trans. by May Jayyusi and Jeremy Reed
ISBN 1–56656–106–X   paperback $9.95

From Lebanon:
The Stone of Laughter
by Hoda Barakat
trans. by Sophie Bennett
ISBN 1–56656–190–6   paperback $12.95

From Palestine:
A Balcony Over the Fakihani
by Liyana Badr
trans. by Peter Clark with Christopher Tingley
ISBN 1–56656–107–8   paperback $9.95

Wild Thorns
by Sahar Khalifeh
trans. by Trevor LeGassick and Elizabeth Fernea
ISBN 0–940793–25–3   paperback $9.95

A Woman of Nazareth
by Hala Deeb Jabbour
ISBN 0–940793–07–5   paperback $9.95

From South Africa:
Living, Loving and Lying Awake at Night
by Sindiwe Magona
ISBN 1–56656–141–8   paperback $11.95

From Turkey:
Cages on Opposite Shores
by Janset Berkok Shami
ISBN 1–56656–157–4   paperback $11.95

From Yemen:
The Hostage
by Zayd Mutee' Dammaj
trans. by May Jayyusi and Christopher Tingley
ISBN 1–56656–140–X   paperback $10.95

From Zimbabwe:
The Children Who Sleep by the River
by Debbie Taylor
ISBN 0–940793–96–2   paperback $9.95